In this book, Karl G. Heider studies the cultural constructions of emotions, examining how different cultures shape ideas and talk about emotion. The main subjects of the study are the Minangkabau, a matrilineal Moslem culture of three million people in West Sumatra, Indonesia. Comparative data come from the Central Javanese, also of Indonesia, and reference is made to studies of American emotions. The Minangkabau have two different "cultures of emotion," used depending on whether they are speaking their own regional language or the national language. And the Central Javanese have yet another culture of emotion when they are speaking the "same" national language.

Cognitive maps of the emotion terms in each of the languages show lexical proximity of terms, clusters of terms, and relations between the clusters. Conclusions can be drawn about lexical density, about code-switching, and about the use of a national language by peoples with very different first languages.

Antecedents and outcomes for emotion terms provide rich data on the meanings of these terms in Minangkabau and in Minangkabau Indonesian, fleshing out the two different cultures of emotion represented by the two languages.

The innovative methodology allows direct comparisons between cultures of emotion, both precise and richly behavioral. It illuminates the important issues of translation, code-switching, and the relationships between lexicon and behavior.

Landscapes of Emotion will appeal to a range of readers in anthropology, psychology, sociology, and Asian studies who want to understand how different cultures shape emotion.

Studies in Emotion and Social Interaction

Paul Ekman
University of California, San Francisco

Klaus R. Scherer
Université de Genève

General Editors

Landscapes of emotion

Studies in Emotion and Social Interaction

This series is jointly published by the Cambridge University Press and the Editions de la Maison des Sciences de l'Homme, as part of the joint publishing agreement established in 1977 between the Fondation de la Maison des Sciences de l'Homme and the Syndics of the Cambridge University Press.

Cette collection est publiée co-édition par Cambridge University Press et les Editions de la Maison des Sciences de l'Homme. Elle s'intègre dans le programme de co-édition établi en 1977 par la Fondation de la Maison des Sciences de l'Homme et les Syndics de Cambridge University Press.

Landscapes of emotion

Mapping three cultures of emotion in Indonesia

Karl G. Heider

University of South Carolina

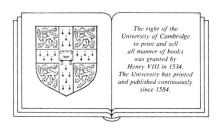

Cambridge University Press

Cambridge
New York   Port Chester   Melbourne   Sydney

Editions de la Maison des Sciences de l'Homme

Paris

Published by the Press Syndicate of the University of Cambridge
The Pitt Building, Trumpington Street, Cambridge CB2 1RP
40 West 20th Street, New York, NY 10011, USA
10 Stamford Road, Oakleigh, Melbourne 3166, Australia
and
Editions de la Maison des Sciences de l'Homme
54 Boulevard Raspail, 75270 Paris Cedex 06, France

First published 1991

Printed in the United States of America

Library of Congress Cataloging-in-Publication Data
Heider, Karl G., 1935–

Landscapes of emotion : mapping three cultures of emotion in
Indonesia / Karl G. Heider.

p.   cm. – (Studies in emotion and social interaction)

ISBN 0-521-40151-8 (hardcover)

1. Ethnopsychology – Indonesia.   2. Emotions – Cross-cultural
studies.   3. Minangkabau (Indonesian people) – Psychology.
I. Title.   II. Series.
GN635.I65H45   1991
155.8'09598 – dc20   91-8960
                                                              CIP

British Library Cataloguing in Publication Data
Heider, Karl G.

Landscapes of emotion : mapping three cultures of emotion
in Indonesia. – (Studies in emotion and social
interaction).

1. Indonesia. Social interactions. Role of emotions
I. Title   II. Seires
302

ISBN 0 521 40151 8 hardback
ISBN 2 7351 0408 7 France only

In joy and gratitude to my parents,
Grace Moore Heider and Fritz Heider

Contents

Acknowledgments

This book explores emotion as it has been constructed by Minangkabau, Indonesian, and Javanese cultures. It introduces a methodology for developing cognitive maps and scenarios of emotions that allows close comparisons among these cultures of emotion and facilitates recognition of the culturally specific part of emotion behavior as opposed to the part that is more pan-cultural. The data discussed here come from two years of fieldwork in West Sumatra and Central Java, Indonesia, but the project as a whole began in 1981 and is far from closure.

During the course of the study I have accumulated many debts, both personal and intellectual. It is a real pleasure to be able to make formal acknowledgment of at least some of these debts.

During my sabbatical year from the University of South Carolina in 1981–2 I was enrolled in the FALCON program at Cornell University, where I received a marvelous introduction to Indonesian from John U. Wolff and his three teaching assistants, Dede Oetomo, Amrih Widodo, and Ismet Fanany. Both the Department of Anthropology and the Southeast Asia Program at Cornell were extremely hospitable, making what could have been a year of drudgery one of great excitement.

The Wenner-Gren Foundation for Anthropological Research supported my quick but essential visit to Jakarta and West Sumatra in 1982, when I located Bukittinggi as a field site. In Indonesia my research was sponsored by the Lembaga Ilmu Pengatahuan Indonesia. Dr. Mochtar Naim not only arranged local research sponsorship for me from Andalas University, but also introduced me to the local scene in Bukittinggi, and invited me to teach Antropologi each semester at Andalas University. To Dr. Naim, Dr. Khaidir Anwar, and the other faculty and students at the Fakultas Sastra of UnAnd I owe much, for our association became an important part of my education in things Indonesian.

During the first year of fieldwork, 1983–4, my research was supported by grants from the National Science Foundation (#BNS 8310805) and the

National Institute of Mental Health (#MH 38221). The NIMH support continued through three more years of fieldwork and writing. I am very grateful to these agencies for their gamble, and hope that this book in some part vindicates their decisions.

During the two years of fieldwork, my three research assistants contributed immeasurably to the project. They are Ibu Djoestina, Ibu Nurbaya, and Ibu Nurlela, all of Bukittinggi. Syamsuddin, technically our chauffeur, helped in countless informal ways. And I am especially indebted to the many Minangkabau and Javanese who thoughtfully and patiently responded to all these queries about emotion.

At Andalas University, the following Anthropology students helped gather data: Fatma Warni, Guswandi, Irza Alen, Yonef, Fiferi Murni, and Yusmarni. In Yogyakarta, the following Gadjah Mada University students were also helpful: Atik Triratnawati, P. F. Hermiandari, Tri Krianto, Soekadi, and Anharudin. Richard Howard and Ruth Berg Patterson helped in the data analysis at the University of South Carolina. And Alma Kinzley and Renie Counts Yeh, of Computer Services at the University of South Carolina, introduced me to Aldus Freehand, in which the figures were done. To them, and the many others who facilitated this research, go my heartfelt thanks.

Malie Bruton Heider and our three children, Mary Winn, John, and Paul, have been participants in this from the beginning, and have taught me much about emotion. Phillip and Anne Hellman gave much support in Bukittinggi, and many others took us into their lives in Bukittinggi, Taluk, Ladang Lawas, Padang, Jakarta, and Yogyakarta.

Since 1968 I have been collaborating with Paul Ekman, and his encouragement and support have been invaluable over the years. In 1986 I had the great pleasure to actually work in the field with Ekman and Robert Levenson when they came to Bukittinggi for an intense month of joint research.

I have tried out various parts of this book with many people countless times, both formally and informally, and have benefited immensely from their provocative reactions. I should mention here especially Paul Heelas and Paul Harris, and of all the different readers of this in manuscript I must single out Phillip Shaver, who made two close and helpful passes through the entire thing.

Minangkabau speak of two sorts of obligations:

Utang ameh bulieh dibaie, utang budi dibao mati

(A debt of money can be repaid, but a debt of spirit is carried to the death.)

To all these people – and to many others – I have incurred *utang budi*. Most of them know more about one or another aspect of this research than I shall ever know, and I apologize to any whom I have offended by errors I have made in my enthusiasm for exploring these landscapes of emotion.

I wrote this book mainly for anthropologists, for Indonesians and Indonesianists, and for psychologists. But again and again in the course of the study I found myself thinking about three people in particular with whom I wanted to share it: John Echols, the great Cornell lexicographer; Ellene Winn of Birmingham, Alabama, my wife's aunt and one of the most literate people either of us has ever known; and my father, Fritz Heider. They all gave great encouragement at the beginning of this study, and it is my great sorrow that none of them lived to see this book.

PART I

Theory, method, and results

1. Theoretical introduction

1.1. The orienting question

How does culture influence emotion? Obviously, different languages have different words for emotions. But beyond that, how much of emotion behavior is culturally variable? How much overlap is there between, say, Americans' "anger" and Indonesians' *marah*? To answer this raises a whole range of questions about how different people talk, think, feel, and show emotions. For example, can we say that the size of the emotion vocabulary varies from culture to culture? Do emotion words cluster differently in different cultures? Are there culturally unique emotions? Are there emotions emphasized by some cultures and neglected by others? How much do causes of emotions vary, and how different are the outcomes of emotions? Are different facial expressions used for the same emotion in different cultures, and why?

Are those cultural differences merely exotic curiosities or can they be systematically related to other aspects of culture? The task of the anthropologist examining emotion is to look for differences: to identify and to account for culturally variable emotion behavior that takes place against the pan-cultural background.

This volume examines three sets of emotion terms, first mapping out each set to depict the landscapes of emotion. Then it explores the meanings of these maps to describe the cultures of emotion. Each is from Indonesia: One is Minangkabau, one is Minangkabau Indonesian, and the third is Javanese Indonesian.

This project on the ethnography of emotion in Indonesia, designed as a comprehensive approach to the entire realm of emotion, grew directly out of research I began twenty-five years ago with the Grand Valley Dani of Irian Jaya (West New Guinea). That work began with stone adzes and arrow types and eventually led to emotion and sexuality. But emotion and sexuality were at first just peripheral afterthoughts, and they emerged as research problems quite late in the game.

3

Now I am attacking emotion head-on in a broad, comprehensive study. For many reasons I have shifted the locus of the research to the Minangkabau of West Sumatra, Indonesia (not the least of these reasons is that Irian Jaya has been closed to ethnographic research).

For the study of emotion, the Minangkabau seemed a good starting point. They are considered more coarse, or emotionally open, than Javanese. Most Minangkabau are comfortably bilingual in their regional language, Minangkabau, and the national language, Indonesian. This, as will soon become apparent, affords an important opportunity to examine emotion in two different languages that are used by the same people.

Here I treat Minangkabau as a single culture. It would have been possible to make comparisons within Minangkabau, for there are well-recognized linguistic and cultural differences among the different areas of the Minangkabau region in West Sumatra (see, for example, Anwar 1980a, b). But this would have been unnecessarily fine-grained for a first study. On the other hand, it would be possible to study "Indonesians" by lumping together people from the different ethnic groups in the country, as Brandt and Boucher (1986) did. But that strategy would limit the study to a consensus Indonesian, and lose the advantage of comparing regional languages and regional versions of the national language. From the beginning there was good reason to suspect that comparisons at the regional ethnic group level would be revealing.

I carried out fieldwork in Indonesia for two years (between 1983 and 1986), separated by one year at home to work over the preliminary data and make midcourse corrections in the research design. The fieldwork is described in Section 1.6.

The project involved a variety of tasks, but the first problem logically, and the one I want to discuss here, concerns the emotion lexicon. We begin with the lexicon because words for emotions are simple and overt data, readily accessible and easily codable. Actual emotion scenes or outbursts are relatively rare in daily life, and they are usually kept relatively private. A people's thinking about emotion may be relatively obscure, complex, and even contradictory. Ultimately, the goals of this research project involve the analysis and understanding of emotion scenarios and emotion thinking, however complex and veiled. But we begin with words: What words are used to talk about emotion, how are they related, and what are the features of the cognitive realm of emotion? Words are not cognition, of course, but words and other overt behavior reflect cognition. The first problem is to transfer something of what is in people's minds onto paper. How many dimensions does thought have? None? Or an infinite number? In order to comprehend Minangkabau understanding of emotions, we could take the Minangkabau path and grow up in West Sumatra. But for most of us it is too late for that. Here we shall use the alternative tactic of gathering data from many Minangkabau and devising a representation of Minangkabau emotion thought as a two-dimensional lexical map that shows clusters of closely related words as well as relationships between the clusters. This book is mainly about three such maps. The basic mapping questions formulate themselves thus: What is the shape of the cognitive map of emotion words? How do the cognitive maps of the two languages, Minangkabau and Indonesian, differ for these bilingual Minangkabau? How do the cognitive maps of Indonesian differ for Minangkabau speakers and for Javanese speakers? Finally, how do these three maps from Indonesia compare to maps in English for the emotion realm?

This is quite a cerebral, quantitative, lexical approach to what is, after all, a most rich and human subject. But there is a method in this method. It is easy to fall into the habit of equating words with behavior, and of thinking about a word as being the same as an emotion. Words are parts of behavior, and my strategy here is to attack first via words. As we develop the three cognitive maps of emotion terms, we shall be led to think of an emotion not in relation to a single word – say, "anger" – but in relation to a set of closely related words we shall call the "Anger" cluster. An effect of this intense scrutiny of emotion words will be to liberate us from the rigid equation of *one word = one emotion*. (Brandt and Boucher 1986, in their work with Indonesian lexical clusters, have also stressed the importance of cluster, rather than single-word consideration of emotions. See also, Ortony, Clore, and Foss 1988:15). The later stages of this project involved analyses of Indonesian emotion, its management, and its culture-boundedness, all of which rest on the understanding of the lexical maps. During the fieldwork itself, I pushed ahead with all the tasks more or less simultaneously. Because the other tasks involved people using emotion words, however, the actual analysis of these other tasks depended on the lexical maps described here.

There have been a number of excellent ethnographies of emotion, including those by Jean Briggs on the Inuit (1970); Robert Levy on the Tahitians (1973); Michelle Z. Rosaldo on the Ilongot (1980); and Catherine Lutz on Ifaluk (1988). Each of these and many more present vibrant human pictures of the emotional life of a people. I myself have attempted that with my writing on the Dani of Irian Jaya (1979; ms.). But as much as I admire what that sort of ethnography can accomplish, I have not tried to do it here. This book does not attempt a full picture of the life and passions of the Minangkabau. It is a dictionary, a grammar – or, better yet, a mapping of the cognitive landscape of emotion. It is a first step toward a systematic ethnography of emotion. If it is successful, it will stand by itself and will also provide a basis on which Indonesian ethnography can build.

Emotion is a difficult subject for rigorous investigation since it is not amenable to convenient precise definition. Partly because of this it has only recently come into prominence as a subject of anthropological investigation. Because emotion is so fuzzy, it forces reconsideration of some basic problems in anthropology. More than most cross-cultural work, the study of emotion stirs up problems of translation. Emotions are central to much human behavior but are extremely difficult to pin down. Emotions are inner states with external manifestations. Both inner states and external manifestations are shaped, managed, and defined by cultural norms. Often these norms prescribe ways to conceal reality from fellow actors in a culture, not to mention from the outsider trying to understand emotion behavior. And emotions, unlike earlier topics on the anthropological agenda such as kinship terms or color words, are not constructed on an obvious, concrete biological or physical base such as age and gender, or hue and brightness.

In Part I of this book the first five chapters are concerned with the method and underlying theory of lexical mapping. They are followed by a discussion in Chapter 6 of the cultural features, cluster by cluster, of the three lexical maps of emotion terms: in Minangkabau, in Indonesian as spoken by Minangkabau, and in Indonesian as spoken by Central Javanese. Chapter 7 summarizes and draws conclusions. Part II provides the data and detailed analysis of the 44 clusters.

1.2. Conceptualizing emotions

This is not the place for an extended essay on the theory of emotion, but it is necessary to describe briefly two formulations of emotion that are used in this study.

The flow of emotion

Although at times it is convenient to speak as if "an emotion" were a unitary thing, with a name such as "anger," there are often advantages

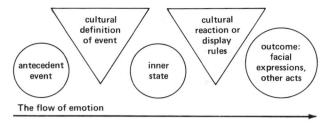

Figure 1. The flow of emotion

in treating emotion as a slice of the continuum of human behavior, a sort of scenario with antecedents and outcomes, where the culture-specific and the pan-cultural play different but complementary roles. Paul Ekman, in his resolution of the debate between the pan-culturalists, who thought that all emotions everywhere were the same, and the culture-specific proponents, who thought that everything was always different, introduced the concept of *display rules* (Ekman and Friesen 1969:75) to refer to the cultural patterning of the flow of emotion. We can develop this a step further and recognize two cultural interventions in the emotion process. The *flow of emotion* scenario runs from left to right across Figure 1. *Antecedent events* can be described neutrally: for example, "the death of a child." The event is given emotional coloring by, first, the *cultural definition* through culture-specific rules that produce simple or complex emotional *inner states.* A second culture-specific intervention, the reaction rules, or display rules, of that culture for that emotion determine whether the emotion of the inner state is altered in its public performance through intensification, diminution, neutralization, or masking by the behavior (usually the facial expression) of another emotion. Ekman, speaking specifically about facial expressions and emotions, used the term "display rules," emphasizing the communicative property of the face. An Indonesian display rule, for example, is reported by the musicologist Mantle Hood: "Among the many refinements of Javanese society is the ideal of concealing the emotions – it is sometimes said that there is a Javanese smile for every emotion" (1963:455). In other words, in Java every emotion is to be masked with a smile. However, one suspects that the real meaning of the saying is that the Javanese have a different smile for each emotion. But, of course, this present study focuses on the Minangkabau, who are not nearly so refined as the Javanese, and who conceal emotions much less (a contrast that runs through the two cultures – in their dance performances, Javanese use wooden masks, Minangkabau dance without masks, and so forth). Ekman has described many different American smiles and how they are used for masking (1985:150; Ekman, Friesen, and O'Sullivan 1988), and a systematic study of Indonesian smiles would surely show as rich a repertoire.

Here we are talking about outcomes of emotion in a broader behavioral sense than just facial expressions. We want to include many other sorts of behavior, and so we can use the term "reaction rules" for those culture-specific norms for behavioral outcomes or reactions to an inner emotion state.

On the whole, this flow of emotion follows a cross-culturally recognizable path with relatively little culturally unique behavior. Probably in most cultures the death of a child is defined as sad, and that sadness is expressed directly with the pan-cultural "sad" face and weeping. However, it may be altered according to some culturally specific reaction rule. Let us return to the flow diagram in Figure 1, where the two cultural interventions are pictured as refracting prismatic wedges. Most emotion scenarios flow in a culturally neutral, and pan-cultural, path across the bottom of the diagram. But a few cultures have strong culture-specific rules that do refract the flow. We can say in such cases that antecedent events are defined culturally: The death of a child may be an occasion for anger (if it is believed to be the result of witchcraft) or happiness (if the child is taken directly to heaven). The second type of cultural intervention is more common: Reaction rules direct the outcome of a scenario. For example, anger is masked by a smile, or happiness is neutralized.

The logical variations in scenarios, or flows, are diagrammed in Figure 2:

Emotion words, then, can be taken as labels for particular scenarios. And as we shall see, the antecedents and outcomes for most Indonesian emotion words give us the very scenarios for emotions we anticipated on the basis of the English-language dictionary translations of words. For example, Indonesian *sedih* is translated by dictionaries as "sad." Its antecedents do in fact concern losing or parting from another, usually a relative or a lover, and its main outcome is in fact weeping. We are thus on firm ground in concluding that *sedih* and Sad share a pan-cultural scenario – the flow of emotion in both instances is unrefracted by special rules of the cultures.

On the other hand, we shall see many instances where the outcomes for a particular emotion are rather unexpected, indicating that a display

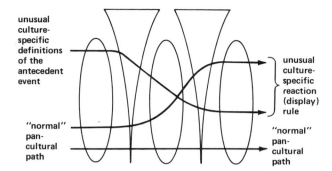

unusual culture-specific definitions of the antecedent event

unusual culture-specific reaction (display) rule

"normal" pan-cultural path

"normal" pan-cultural path

Figure 2. Cultural refractions of the flow of emotion

rule is in effect. For example, the outcomes for Happiness in Indonesian are, expectably, smiling and such, but the outcomes for Happiness in Minangkabau are masking and withdrawal, suggesting a display rule of neutering happiness in Minangkabau.

Inner state versus interaction

Anthropologists, historians, and others have long been aware that a cru-cial dimension on which cultures vary is the relative emphasis placed on the person as an interactive part of the social network versus the person as an autonomous individual. This was formulated in terms of absolute dichotomy when Ruth Benedict wrote of "guilt cultures" versus "shame cultures" (1946). Recently it has been presented in more nuanced terms (see, for example, Heelas and Lock 1981). It has been recognized as rel-evant to recent cross-cultural work on emotion (Lutz 1982) and also at-tacked as simplistic (Shaver et al. 1987). Although we recognize the basic utility of the concept, and indeed shall present much supporting data, still we must avoid absolute dichotomies and emphasize the nuances. Indonesian cultures on the whole place more emphasis on social inter-action, Western cultures on the whole place more emphasis on inner states of autonomous individuals. A diagnostic trait is marriage form: In Indonesia marriages are commonly arranged by family groups; in Eu-rope and America, by the two principal individuals. Yet even this is not an absolute rule, for there are marriages in Indonesia not usually ar-ranged by families (lower-class marriages, or second marriages) and in some circumstances Western families do play crucial roles in deciding who will marry whom.

Certainly, Indonesians have inner state emotions – this study would be impossible otherwise. Indonesians know guilt, although we shall not find a good cluster of "Guilt" words. And Indonesian emotions do involve inner states, although they are more usually about social interactions, especially in traditional Minangkabau when compared with the national language, Indonesian.

But thinking in terms of this inner state – interaction continuum helps to explain much: Why Indonesian behavior is on the whole more interactionally oriented than is Western behavior; and why there is more interaction in Minangkabau emotion behavior when they talk about it in Minangkabau than when they talk about it in Indonesian.

1.3. A theory of culture

A basic definition of culture holds that it is (1) learned, (2) shared, (3) ideas about behavior. But these days we have trouble with the attribute of sharedness, for it is clear that there is considerable variation in thought and behavior among people whom we want to consider belonging to the same culture, or, in Swartz's phrase, there is "incomplete cultural sharing" (1988:22). There are several possible solutions to this dilemma, short of discarding the concept of culture itself:

1. Rely on a single person's understanding of the world at a single moment. This is the strategy of the life-history approach in anthropology, and of the self-introspective approach in linguistics (see Lakoff's study of anger [1987], where he used introspection plus *Roget's Thesaurus*). But this approach is not as elegant as it seems, for there is evidence that people are not even consistent with themselves over a period of time (see Heider's ax stone and sweet potato naming tasks with the Dani [1969]).

2. Achieve cultural group consensus. This solution is represented by the familiar formula "the X people believe that . . ." or "they have only one word for. . . ." The actual methodology that produces such statements is rarely specified, and the statements depend on the (untestable) authority of the ethnographer. However, Eleanor Rosch has shown, in her early color term work, just how such unexamined factors as the ethnographer's own preconceptions and expectations can bias the outcome (1972).

3. Quantitative breakdown of the variation. The statement that "the X people are polygynous" gives us some information but leaves us guessing about ideology versus behavior. An alternative is a table that gives:

% of unmarried adult males
% of males with one wife
% of males with two wives,
etc.

This tells us more about behavior, less about ideology.

Each of the above treatments has its uses and its strengths and weaknesses, depending on the sorts of problems and the particular realms being investigated. Here, however, a fourth approach is used:

4.   The *composite map* solution produces a two-dimensional map of emotion terms that looks rather like a star chart. Each map is based on pieces of data from fifty Indonesian informants. Obviously such a map does not represent what is in a single person's head, nor is it a cultural consensus. Rather, it is a *composite map*. Each map aggregates the notions of fifty Indonesians, and so represents not so much that which is shared but the middle ground on which they all meet, and by means of which they communicate with each other. For communication does take place, after all. We are sometimes surprised at how much, say, people who have communicated with each other for much of their lives may yet disagree about the meanings of their world. They have, indisputably, somehow, been communicating even if the agreements are mostly tacit. Nida speaks to the same point: "No communication, whether intralingual, interlingual, or intersemiotic, can occur without some loss of information. Even among experts discussing a subject within their own fields of specialization, it is unlikely that comprehension rises above the 80% level" (1978:63).

The composite map, then, attempts to represent not some clear, firmly-shared idea present in the minds of all the people but rather the actual, operational common ground on which people in fact interact.

When understood as such, these maps will allow us to compare emotion terms in different languages, to compare the different forms of the same language as used by people of different linguistic backgrounds, and to analyze the emotion words used by people in their naturally occurring behavior, in their fictions (novels and films), and in their responses to such experimental stimuli as photographs of facial expressions and short sequences of emotion behavior taken from scripted commercial films.

To anticipate: We find this same problem of partial sharing writ large when we compare the two versions of "the Indonesian language." Emotion terms in the version of Indonesian used by Minangkabau are not identical to the same emotion terms in the version of Indonesian spoken and thought by Central Javanese. With the methodology of this study we are able to be specific about some of these differences. The implications for national media events in Indonesia are obvious: If movies, magazines, presidential speeches, and standardized school texts are all written in the same "Indonesian," how are they understood by people of different language backgrounds across the Indonesian archipelago? Theoretically this is a fascinating problem and only further research along the present lines can tell us whether it is significant or trivial in actual practice. Elsewhere I have emphasized the construction of a single Indonesian culture through the national cinema (1991). Here I want to focus on how that national culture is locally construed.

1.4. Method and theory of lexical mapping of emotion terms: assumptions

Before considering the mapping itself, it will be useful to lay out some underlying assumptions:

> *Assumption 1. Emotion has both a mental, or cognitive, aspect and a sensory, physiological, aspect. Thus, emotion is manifested as observable, measurable behavior:*
> emotion words
> other talk about emotion
> facial expressions
> other nonverbal communication such as hand gestures
> physiological reactions
> other overt behavioral acts
> *Emotion is also contained in mental concepts which may be constructed by the researcher through elicitation, such as:*
> relations among words
> meaning structures of broadly defined sorts of emotions
> antecedent and outcome scenarios for emotions

> These are some of the customary categories that emerge as targets of research. Arbitrary as they are, they provide an overview of the various elements of the complex interdependent whole that we call emotion behavior.

> *Assumption 2. The words used for emotions are significant data.* Although there are important differences between speech and other behavior, and although talk about emotion may not necessarily use

words for emotions, nevertheless the vocabulary of emotion is a logical access route to the subject of emotion.

Assumption 3. Emotion behavior is a mix of pan-cultural and culture-specific behavior. It is shaped by both pan-cultural influences (perhaps species-common biology) and culture-specific norms.

Assumption 4. Since the culture-specific patterns exist in a context with the pan-cultural, both must be considered concurrently. A noncomparative ethnography of emotion runs the risk of not recognizing much that is in fact pan-human behavior, while an approach that ignores cultural contributions may count as experimental errors some behavior that is in fact normative culture-specific.

Assumption 5. The prime task of anthropology is to work out the role of culture-specific influences on emotion.

Assumption 6. The influence of cultural norms may result in quite different sorts of behavioral reactions to the same basic situation. (In other words, the death of a child may be culturally defined as a source of sadness, or anger, or happiness.)

However, in other contexts:

Assumption 7. Despite the influence of cultural norms, there are behaviors that differ only in nuance (i.e., a word in English, "love," and its nearest Indonesian equivalent, *cinta,* are similar but not identical in denotation, for "love" is closer to "happiness," *cinta* closer to "sadness" – see Section 6.6).

Assumption 8. What is in English understood as the realm of emotion, and what is understood by particular English emotion words, have general correspondences in other languages and cultures.

But, more importantly for this approach:

Assumption 9. Neither the realm of emotion nor the particular words for emotions in one language and culture can a priori be presumed to have exact correspondences in other languages and cultures.

This is hardly novel. In 1816, Wilhelm von Humboldt could write, "It has often been said, and confirmed by both experience and research, that, if one excepts those expressions which designate purely physical objects, no word in one language is completely equivalent to a word in another" (1816, in 1977:40).

Herbert Phillips did not even agree about "purely physical objects." He took this argument one step further when he showed that in translating between Thai and English, even in the apparently simple statement "he has tables and chairs," every word except "and" raises problems of equivalence (1959:185).

And George Steiner, looking at lexical changes over time within a single tradition, pushed the limits when he insisted that "any thorough reading of a text out of the past of one's own language and literature is a manifold act of interpretation" (1975:17).

It follows from Assumptions 8 and 9 that an anthropological task is to determine both correspondences and differences between two cultures in their emotion realms and their emotion words.

The research reported here looks at some Indonesian data, but one could (with considerably more difficulty) compare the emotion lexicons of Navajo and Russian, or of twentieth-century South Carolina and eighteenth-century South Carolina.

A working assumption is that dictionary translations are only somewhat accurate. That is, the best Indonesian equivalents for "love" are *cinta, kasih,* and *sayang.* But, in fact, English "love" is closer to happiness, and, as we shall see, Indonesian *cinta* is close to *sedih* (sadness). True, a handy working translation of "love" is *cinta.* It does capture the general idea, at, let us say, an 80% level of accuracy. But for this present research we need to refine our understanding to determine that other, nuanced, 20% of nonoverlapping meanings.

It will be evident by now that a major concern of this project is translation. And the problem is not merely that faced by most translation theorists, who debate literal versus comparable positions. The demands of this sort of cross-cultural study push the boundaries of translation far beyond the simple choice of the appropriate word or metaphor. As Casagrande, writing as an anthropologist, said: "In effect one does not translate LANGUAGES, one translates CULTURES. Ethnography may, in fact, be thought of as a form of translation" (1954:338).

Assumption 10. *There are no underlying objective ("etic") parameters that allow us to locate all emotion words with precision.*

This is what is meant by the indeterminate nature of emotion. In other realms of cross-cultural concern, we are on firmer ground: kinship terms can be located and defined in terms of Kroeber's 1909 factors (so that Father = male, lineal, one generation older); color words can be located in terms of brightness and hue (so that Red = Munsell hue red 5, brightness 4). Even social exchange can be specified in terms of countable goods and measurable services convertable to a dollar amount. The most ambitious attempt to create a comparably specific measure for emotion terms was the Semantic Differential, with its axes of Evaluation, Potency, and Activity (Osgood, May, and Miron 1975). But these are generalizing rather than specifying, and they have resulted in mappings that have been ends in themselves but have not proven their utility in making comparisons between cultures. Recent psychobiological research has produced evidence that there is different autonomic nervous system (ANS) activity for such emotions as anger, fear, and sadness (Ekman, Levenson, and Friesen 1983), but there is as yet no evidence for such discrimination between emotions as close as surprise, astonishment, and awe. At this point it seems unlikely that the face or the ANS system has the performance precision to specify hundreds of different emotions. "Surprise" and "astonishment" are clearly different words (in lexical performance terms) even if we do not always totally agree with each other on precisely what they mean. Language, with its few dozen phonemes, can "perform" hundreds of emotion words precisely. It seems difficult to imagine that facial muscles or ANS functions can match that number.

There have been various promising attempts to work out on logical theoretical grounds the principles of a cognitive structure of emotion (e.g., Wierzbicka 1986; Ortony et al. 1988). This is a more promising direction than the search for "brightness and hue" sorts of components to emotion. But the cross-cultural implications of the essential indeterminacy of emotion are considerable. For making comparisons across cultures or languages at present, we cannot depend on objective specifications. Instead, we must rely on intuitive judgments of bilingual speakers, on rich ethnographic stories of antecedents and outcomes of emotions, and on responses to standardized stimuli (such as facial expressions.)

The mapping task

Several important assumptions underlie the mapping task:

> **Assumption 11.** *Fluent speakers of a language have mental maps of the words of the language.*

> **Assumption 12.** *In these maps the words are not regularly arranged like lists but are clustered irregularly in groups of similar meanings.*

And

Assumption 13. *These maps can be represented by two-dimensional diagrams.* However complex and multidimensional these mental maps are in fact, reduction to the two dimensions of the printed page retains an acceptable degree of cognitive validity and also allows the maps to be readily understood and used in further research. There is an obvious trade-off: information for accessibility.

1.5. A cultural sketch of Minangkabau

The Minangkabau have long fascinated the world with their apparently contradictory juxtaposition of patriarchal Islam and matrilineal social organization. This has evolved only in the last two centuries. The kingdom of Minangkabau, lying in the rich volcanic highlands of what is now West Sumatra, was a successor state to the great Hindu kingdom of Srivijaya. The Minangkabau heartland provided the world with gold and then, by the eighteenth century, increasingly spices and coffee and tea. By the 1790s several American ships a year came to the port of Padang for the coffee trade. Although the rulers were Hindu, and originally from Java, the population as a whole was more likely to have been basic Southeast Asian animistic (sometimes called "Dongson"), and in the seventeenth and eighteenth centuries, as a result of visits from Moslem traders from the Gujerat of India, the people must have been turning more and more toward Islam.

In the first three decades of the nineteenth century a great set of inter-related changes reshaped Minangkabau: The gold was giving out, and spices and coffee and tea were becoming more important; a radical militant reform Moslem movement slowly swept the heartland in a series of local conflicts now called the "Padri Wars," purifying Islam and killing the Hindu rulers; in 1818, during the brief British rule over that part of Sumatra, Sir Stamford Raffles paid the first recorded European visit to the heartland; he was followed by the returning Dutch, who took advantage of the Padri unrest to extend their influence inland. By the late 1830s the Dutch military had broken the last Minangkabau resistance and had grabbed control of the spice and coffee trade at its source.

By the 1850s, Fort de Kock (now Bukittinggi) in the heartland had become a major center for Dutch schools. The Minangkabau, perhaps more than any other people of the Dutch East Indies, were buying into the Dutch educational system.

By the early twentieth century, Minangkabau – especially Minangkabau men – were positioned to take important leadership roles in the developing nationalistic and literary movements. A new common language was being developed to unite the entire archipelago. Called "Indonesian," it was consciously not based on Javanese, which, although the regional language with the most speakers, was considered too culture-bound, with its courtly status distinctions, to serve as a unifying language. Instead, "Indonesian" was based on the Malay of the Sumatran area, thus very close to Minangkabau. This gave the Minangkabau yet another advantage, for with their privileged linguistic access to Indonesian they were able to participate especially effectively in the early stages of the emerging national sphere.

By the time of the revolution and independence in the late 1940s, Minangkabau had established influence far greater than their numbers would suggest. Much of the literature in Indonesian had been written by Minangkabau men, many of the pioneers of the Indonesian film industry from 1950 on were Minangkabau, and much political power was carefully balanced between Minangkabau and Javanese. The prime example of this balance was the Proclamation of Independence of August 17, 1945, which was announced by Sukarno (a Javanese) and Hatta (a Minangkabau). And this form of Javanese–Minangkabau balance shows up also in the important Indonesian Moslem movement Muhammadijah, which was organized by a Javanese and a Minangkabau (Peacock 1979), and even in the Indonesian communist movement (Naim 1983:66). Even today the basic Indonesian coin, the 100 rupiah piece, has a Javanese motif on one face and a Minangkabau long house on the reverse. Minangkabau predominance on the national scene lessened after their defeat in a brief war of secession in the late 1950s, at the same time that Javanese, Balinese, Batak, and other ethnic groups in Indonesia were becoming more active.

In the late 1980s, there were some 5 million Minangkabau, 3 million of them living in the province of West Sumatra. It is a relatively prosperous area of rich agricultural lands and some industry, little population pressure, and a standard of living enhanced by the remittances from the 2 million Minangkabau living elsewhere in the archipelago. The Minangkabau have long been noted for an especially high rate of nonpermanent out-migration. Usually men, now increasingly accompanied by their wives and children, leave home to study or to work.

Before beginning this study I had been led to believe that the responses of Minangkabau men to the tension between matrilineality and Islam were (1) extreme stress and an exceptionally high rate of mental illness (Mitchell 1969), and (2) the exceptionally high rate of out-migration (Naim 1979). This now seems to be a much more complex problem than anticipated, and I have fewer answers to it than I did before beginning fieldwork.

Certainly migration has been one way for Minangkabau men to manage between the demands of their patrilineal religion and their matrilineal society. Minangkabau do not practice textbook matriliny, whatever that might be. In the Agam region around Bukittinggi, where I did most of this research, there seems to be more gender equality or balance than in other parts of the heartland. Women own the land and the houses and the major traditional wealth, and clan membership is reckoned through the female line. Although men are in some ways peripheral to these matters, they do play important roles. They are not the owners, but they do manage their clan property; they hold the major titles, which are usually inherited matrilineally, and they are the leaders of the clans. Women certainly have strong voices in social and political affairs, but the major ceremonies are run by men alone and women listen in through open windows or from behind screens. Despite the importance of the matrilineal clans, the father's clan does play a ritual role in people's lives.

Minangkabau ideology is strongly egalitarian, but there is a system of ranks and titles with political and religious functions at least up to the level of the *negara*, hamlet cluster, level. Traditionally, Minangkabau was organized in these *negara*, small, fiercely independent neighborhood hamlet clusters that were maximal social and political units. Under the Dutch and now the republic, the central government has taken over most of the educational, political, and judicial functions of the *negara*, and the powers of the men who lead these traditional units have been drastically reduced.

Islam, too, has less power under the republic. The Dutch had reached a modus vivendi in which Christian missionaries would not proselytize among Minangkabau. There were Dutch schools, but much of the education was left in the hands of the village mosques. At about six or eight years of age a boy would leave his home and move into the mosque dormitories where he studied the Koran. Then, at marriage, he would move back to his mother's house, spending the nights with his wife but working his matri-clan rice fields and bringing up his sisters' children. After the revolution, state-run Indonesian-language coeducational schools were compulsory from the first grade. Boys no longer spend important years apart from women in the mosque dormitories, and girls now have full access to formal education through the university level.

The Minangkabau language remains the first language for most Minangkabau. It is the language of domestic life and of traditional rituals and theater. But Minangkabau have made a remarkable commitment to the national language. I never heard Minangkabau used in schools, even at the first-grade level. Virtually nothing is published in Minangkabau except reprints of a few classic epics and some columns on traditional custom and literature in the Sunday editions of the provincial newspapers. The West Sumatran urban scene is a mass of signs of all sorts. There are advertising billboards, hortatory government messages, and T-shirt graffiti, but they are all in Indonesian, or English. Minangkabau and Arabic are virtually absent from the public view.

In the 1980s there were some hints of renewed interest in Minangkabau traditions, especially the folk theater (*randai*) and dance, but for the most part such traditions were submerged in a flood of national and international entertainment and consumer goods.

Yet, despite the lack of support from other facets of culture, Minangkabau language remains strong in its domestic and traditional spheres.

Much has been written about Minangkabau culture and society beginning at least with Raffles's letters concerning his 1818 trek in from the coast to the thrice-burned site of the royal palace. A Dutch expedition produced three volumes about Minangkabau in the 1880s, and more recently there have been dissertations, books, and articles by scholars from at least ten different countries as well as by Minangkabau scholars themselves. We have splendid accounts of Minangkabau history, political and social organization, religion, dance, literature, crafts, migration, and culture in general. However, little of this has any direct bearing on emotion.

There were several reasons to base this study on Minangkabau: The amount already written about Minangkabau meant it was possible to move directly to the psychological issues and not have to work out the basic ethnography of the culture; the two languages used by Minangkabau (Indonesian and Minangkabau) are far enough apart to make significant contrast, yet similar enough to make the learning of both a less forbidding task than it would be elsewhere in Indonesia; the novels written by Minangkabau in Indonesian since the 1920s afford a valuable source of data on the culture; the fact that all Minangkabau speak basically a single version of the language expands the potential pool of subjects; and the pleasant mountain location of Bukittinggi, a small city in the heart of West Sumatra, made it easier to move my family there for two years of fieldwork.

Enough was known about Indonesian cultures of emotion to be confident that Minangkabau was one of the more direct and expressive Indonesian cultures in emotion terms. A few cultures, perhaps, such as Batak or Madura, are more open but would not offer as many research advantages as Minangkabau.

Having chosen to focus on an emotionally open culture, it made sense to use one at the opposite extreme for contrast. For this, the Central Javanese of Yogyakarta were an obvious choice. Many people have noted the sorts of Minangkabau–Javanese contrasts described above. Mochtar Naim (1983) has pushed this line of analysis farthest, using Minangkabau and Javanese as the extremes of an egalitarian/stratified dichotomy that is found writ small within Minangkabau itself but writ large across the Indonesian archipelago. The appropriateness of a Minangkabau–Javanese opposition or contrast is almost inescapable. Javanese generally, and particularly those around the old court cities of Yogyakarta and Solo, are popularly known as the most *halus* of all Indonesians. And *halus*, in emotion terms, means maintaining composure and not revealing emotions.

Central Javanese are nominally Moslem, like Minangkabau, but in fact the earlier Hinduism shows through in Java in a way it rarely does in Sumatra. Javanese theater and dance and art are primarily concerned with the great Hindu epics, the Mahabharata and the Ramayana. In addition, a syncretic mysticism rivals the importance of Islam in Java.

Javanese are as nonegalitarian as Minangkabau are egalitarian. This is reflected in the complex levels of the Javanese language, which must be mastered if one is to speak properly. Certainly Minangkabau can be formal and formulaic, but it is all at the service of ostensible equality. Javanese, on the other hand, expresses class status in every utterance. Javanese is so specialized and so different from Indonesian that in Java the national language must be taught in primary school as a foreign language.

So this, very briefly, is the background of the Minangkabau and the Javanese, whose cultures of emotion we are building here. I have barely footnoted this ethnographic sketch, but for those interested in going deeper into the two cultures, good starting points would be, for Minangkabau: Kahn 1981; Kato 1982; Dobbin 1983; F. Errington 1984; Navis 1984; and Thomas and Benda-Beckman 1985; for Javanese: C. Geertz 1960; H. Geertz 1961; Wolff and Soepomo 1982; J. Errington 1985; and Siegel 1986.

1.6. Doing fieldwork in Indonesia

The specific methodology for the research reported here is covered in Chapter 2. Now it may be useful to describe very briefly the overall research project, since the mapping tasks were carried out simultaneously with several other tasks and each to some extent interacted with the others. Also, because this project involved relocation of researcher and family half a world away for two periods of a year, it imposed special constraints on the research itself – the term "fieldwork" indicates just how displacing such an enterprise really is.

The intellectual problem began to emerge in 1968 and 1970 during my fieldwork on psychological issues with the Dani of the Grand Valley of the Balim in Irian Jaya, Indonesia (Heider 1976, 1979).

In studying sexuality and cognition of the Dani, I strayed into problems of emotion. For a next research step it seemed to make sense to work more directly on emotion. Also, I wanted to work with a different sort of culture. The Dani are preliterate and quite nonintellectual and I wanted to try an intellectual, literate culture. A series of events directed my thinking toward highland Sumatra: I wanted to continue research within Indonesia; during 1957–8 I had studied at the University of Vienna with Professor Robert Heine-Geldern, who spoke often and enthusiastically of Bronze Age survivals in highland Sumatra; I had studied Indonesian in the summer of 1969 at Yale with two extraordinarily stimulating Batak (Ibu Tobing and Tunggul Siagian), and on the advice of a mutual friend I wrote James Siegel, who suggested that I look at Batak, and particularly the Pak Pak Batak. I visited Batak country in Sumatra for a few days in 1970, coming home from Irian Jaya, to get some sense of the place – and the euphony of the name Pak Pak Batak held my imagination during the years I was finishing up my Dani writing and otherwise living my professional and personal life.

By 1981 I was ready to start on this project in earnest. I spent 1981–2 at Cornell University enrolled in the intensive Indonesian FALCON course – the smattering of Indonesian that had sufficed for work with the Dani (who in the 1960s were still effectively monolingual) needed serious improvement before I could begin this project; and as I started to read seriously in the Indonesian literature, it became clear that the Minangkabau would be a better choice for this research – they were still in the Sumatran highlands, but one province south. In June 1982, I made a three-week reconnaissance trip to Indonesia to look at West Sumatra and make arrangements for living, research, and official sponsorship. I decided to base in the mountain city of Bukittinggi, but agreed to teach anthropology one day a week at Universitas Andalas in Padang, the provincial capital.

During the next year I wrote grant proposals and otherwise prepared for the fieldwork. In July 1983 we moved to Bukittinggi (from South Carolina it took "nine airplanes and one tough little minibus," as our children, then one, three, and five, have described that trip ever since). We soon found a large European-style house in the center of the city. If my research design had been different, and my family smaller or older, I would have wanted to live in a village, but this house was such a satisfactory solution that we lived in it both our years in Bukittinggi.

We had a car and a driver (I was reluctant to try my own luck on Sumatran roads), and once a week I drove down to the coast, where I taught anthropology in the Faculty of Letters in Andalas University. This new provincial university was temporarily situated in the center of Padang, a city of 250,000 and the capital of the province of West Sumatra. Anthropology had not been taught there before. It was exciting trying to translate my American version of anthropology into Indonesian. At first it took hours to prepare each lecture, but gradually it came easier and the exercise of translation itself gave valuable insights to my study. I taught introductory cultural anthropology three semesters and the fourth a course in "System Religi." I assigned many short fieldwork projects, which resulted in collections of fascinating data on Minangkabau, and toward the end I asked the class to act as subjects for some of the facial expression identification tasks.

Four days of the week I worked directly on the research in and around Bukittinggi. The data reported in this volume – on the cognitive mapping, on prototypes, and on antecedents and outcomes of emotion words – were all gathered through questionnaires. But as I was developing these, I had begun a longitudinal study of children. Through the good offices of Dr. Mochtar Naim, a sociologist at Andalas University, I found three research assistants who quickly became invaluable members of this project: Ibu (Mrs.) Djoestina, Ibu Nurbaya, and Ibu Nurlela. They located 16 children, each Minangkabau and firstborn; 8 boys and 8 girls, 8 one-year-olds and 8 four-year-olds. The three women accompanied me as guides and chaperones on my visits to the children's homes, and then sat with me at the video playback machine to help transcribe the Minangkabau and translate it into Indonesian. Over the period of three years I made many visits to each of the children, observing, querying their parents, and shooting videotapes (more than four hours each) of their natural, ongoing behavior. (This project was modeled on Gregory Bateson and Margaret Mead's Balinese study of 1936–8, a research design that, inexplicably, had not been emulated since.) The data on children's natural acquisition of emotion behavior will be the subject of another book, now that the present one provides a background against which to understand Minangkabau emotion.

In addition to the cognitive study and the longitudinal study I undertook to collect hand gestures (emblems) of emotions in both Minangkabau and in Indonesian and to compare emotion scenarios in 1930s Minangkabau novels with those from the postwar period. I also made studies of facial expressions of emotion, some of which have already been reported (Ekman et al. 1987; Ekman and Heider 1988); psychophysiological studies of emotion behavior, done in collaboration with Paul Ekman and Robert Levenson during their visit to Bukittinggi in March 1986; and studies of emotion scenarios found in Indonesian feature films, using short excerpts from these films as eliciting devices. I even made a study of cheap quartzite ring stones, which both Minangkabau and Javanese use to regulate their emotions. Like the longitudinal studies, these other tasks can now be analyzed and reported using the maps in this volume as bases.

In the middle of the first year we traveled by ship and train to the Central Javanese city of Yogyakarta, where we spent the break between semesters. This had begun as simply a vacation and change of pace from the supercharged Minangkabau atmosphere of Bukittinggi, but the research possibilities soon became apparent. During the second year we repeated the trip, spending January 1986 again in Yogyakarta, and there, with the help of some students from the Department of Anthropology at Gadjah Mada University, it was possible to collect comparable Javanese data for a few of the tasks. I even visited and videotaped four Javanese children for very rough comparisons with the Minangkabau children. Some of the Javanese data in Indonesian are incorporated in the mapping analysis in Chapter 2.

2. Mapping the realm of emotion

2.1. Procedure

Each of the three maps to be described here represents the way emotion terms in one language are interrelated. For those who want to know just how the maps were constructed, the following pages afford a somewhat detailed account of how I developed the procedure. Other readers might want to proceed directly to Chapter 6, where the analysis of the maps begins.

My first step was to develop a master list of emotion words in Indonesian. (I started with Indonesian, rather than with Minangkabau, because it was easier to approach. At the beginning of the fieldwork I knew fair Indonesian but no Minangkabau, and there are better dictionaries for Indonesian than for Minangkabau.)

Between my own knowledge of Indonesian, various dictionaries, and some Indonesian novels written by Minangkabau, I developed a list of thirty-eight words that were the most obvious emotion words. For each of these Indonesian starter words, bilingual Minangkabau were asked to give synonyms in Indonesian and translation equivalents in Minangkabau. I worked over the results, making preliminary maps of clusterings and expanding the lists. I also began a master list of Minangkabau words.

At the beginning of the second year of fieldwork I reworked the master lists, expanding them to 189 words in Indonesian and 197 words in Minangkabau. At this point another research task became an important source of emotion words. In the first version of this task (already been reported in part in Ekman et al. 1987, and in Ekman and Heider 1988) subjects were asked to describe photographs of emotions using seven basic Indonesian emotion words. This first version was used for cross-cultural comparisons. Then, to explore the Indonesian attributions more exhaustively, I repeated the task in both Indonesian and Minangkabau in an open-ended format, asking for emotion attributions for each photograph but this time not limiting the responses to a specified set of words. This produced many new words, some of which could be added to the master lists.

The next step was to work through these master lists with my three Minangkabau research assistants, culling words that were definitely not emotion words but yet were not cutting too close to the boundary, since the nature of that boundary was to be one subject of the research. Some words that had crept into the lists, only to be discarded later, were ones like *berani* (brave, bold) and *cerdik* (clever) – which describe attributes or characteristics. There is a clearly understood distinction between *perasaan hati* (Minangkabau: *raso ati*), the emotion realm, and *sifat*, the characteristics realm. These are labels for closely related but distinguishable realms or categories of concepts that describe the self in Indonesia. The case has been well made that for some sorts of studies, the inclusion of suspect words distorts the results (Close, Ortony and Foss 1987), but that was not a danger here.

As a result of this culling, in Indonesian 36 words were rejected as *sifat* (characteristics), 149 were retained as *perasaan hati* (emotions); in Minangkabau, 45 words were rejected as *sifat*, 139 were retained as *raso ati*.

Six bilingual Minangkabau provided synonyms and translation equivalents for each word on the Indonesian list, another six Minangkabau did the Minangkabau list, and new maps were made for the clusterings of words. About 100 new words claimed as synonyms emerged. Once more we culled the lists for obvious strays, and finally, at the end of eighteen months, I had two master lists: one of 209 Minangkabau words, and the other of 229 Indonesian words. I had reason to believe that each of these words was supposed somewhere, by someone, to be an emotion word.

The intent was not to produce master lists of words that narrowly define the realm of emotion, but rather to choose enough words to go to the limits and even spill beyond the limits of the realm of emotion. Therefore, words were included that seemed to be to some degree emotion words, and that later (see Chapter 3) would be tested for prototypicality, the strength of their membership in the realm.

I then farmed out the lists to research assistants in West Sumatra and in Central Java and got fifty responses (twenty-five men, twenty-five women) for each of the three tasks: Minangkabau doing the Minangka-

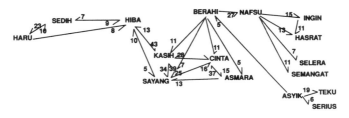

Figure 3. The "Love" cluster BI(M)

bau list; Minangkabau doing the Indonesian list; and Javanese doing the Indonesian list. (Although this last batch furnishes the beginnings of a Javanese list, I have not yet developed the research in that direction.)

For all the tasks, naturalistic observation as well as questionnaires, I kept a matched sample of male and female. Since there are gender differences in linguistic usages in American English, it seemed probable they would be even more evident in a culture like Minangkabau, which has more gender segregation and which, in the childhood of the elder people now living, had quite extreme gender segregation of children and youths. As it turned out, gender differences were much less apparent than anticipated, and would not be a major focus of this study.

For each starter word, then, there are about fifty synonyms and fifty translation equivalents (usually more than fifty, since those who gave extra synonyms overbalance those who gave none). In order to make the analysis manageable and to screen out the idiosyncratic responses, I arbitrarily made the cutoff point at 10%, considering only those response words given by five or more subjects.

Then, through a series of tries with increasingly greater portions of the data, I made up diagrams showing the relationships of these terms to each other.

What emerges is a model like that in Figure 3, which shows the *kasih* (love, pity) cluster in Indonesian. Each arrow points from the starter word to the synonym it elicited; the number at the head of the arrow shows the number of times (out of a maximum possible fifty) that the response word was named. In forcing all these complex interrelationships onto a two-dimensional sheet of paper, it is not always possible to have the lengths of the arrows precisely reflect the strengths of the associations, because the apparent triangles formed by some of the sets of three associated terms are non-Euclidian. That is, it often happens that

A is close to *B*, *B* close to *C*, but *C* very far from *A*. (Griffith et al. 1974:356 discuss this same problem but doesn't come up with a better solution.) Cognition goes where plane geometry cannot follow.

This was a time-consuming task, since the solutions for the mapping had to be worked out by hand and eye. Because of the open-ended nature of the question ("What are the synonyms of *X*?") the results were not amenable to ordinary multivariate analysis. An alternative approach, used by many, is to have informants sort a predetermined set of words into piles of like words. But in the present study, a primary research question concerned the boundaries of the realm: How far do they extend, and what is their nature? It could be assumed that the emotion realm would fade out gradually rather than have a definite sharp boundary. But these questions could not be addressed with a predetermined set of words. Instead, the sets of master words were used to explore the boundaries of the realms. The results retain the expected fuzziness of the boundaries, but at the expense of clean analysis.

It should be emphasized that the errors of mapping lie only in the values of some lines, and not in the connections between words that are shown by the lines. That is, in two dimensions it is possible to show all reported connections, but it is not possible to draw all lines to scale. Errors of scale are indicated by numbers along the lines: A positive number (e.g., 17) means that the line as shown is that many units too long; a negative number (e.g., − 17) means that the line as shown is that many units too short. The scale is a negative scale: the stronger the association between two words, the shorter the connecting line. The highest possible score for any relationship is 100 (if, for the two starter words, the fifty people each volunteered the other word as synonym). In fact, few connections got more than 80. The lowest score plotted was 5. The decision was made to set the minimum cutoff point for each starter word at 5. Then, in adding the scores for the relationship between the two starter words, the lowest possible minimum sum was $5 + 0 = 5$.

This approach does in fact produce clear clusterings of terms. To put it another way, each word is associated with other words within the cluster, but rarely with words outside the cluster. Or, in systematic terms, a cluster is defined as a set of words with multiple associations among themselves and minimal associations with other words. These clusters, although identified in this almost mechanical manner, are in fact theoretically quite important, for it is the cluster of similar words that corresponds best to what we mean by "an emotion" despite our tendency to equate one word with one emotion (see also Ortony et al. 1988:15).

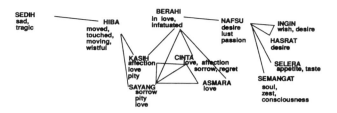

Figure 4. English glosses for the "Love" cluster BI(M)

In Figure 4, I have given English definitions of these words, taken primarily from the Echols–Shadily dictionary. (Here I should admit to a keen sense of compromise, for the whole intention of this cognitive mapping enterprise is to go beyond dictionary definitions. Dictionaries have their uses and, as is evident throughout this study, we cannot get along without them, but finally they are rather blunt instruments for communicating meaning across languages and cultures.)

To return to Figure 3, we see the *kasih* (love, pity) cluster, which is quite typical: There are six words closely associated with each other; one word, *berahi*, has a minimal association with *asyik*, but this is a dead end. *Hiba* is a hinge word, a member of two clusters that have no other associations with each other; and there is an attenuated chain from *berahi* to *nafsu* that leads on to *ingin* and then to the *senang* cluster.

In Minangkabau (Fig. 5) we see a *kasiah* (love, pity) cluster that is very similar to the *kasih* cluster in Indonesian. There are some minor differences: *Ibo* is more strongly associated with the *sadiah* cluster than *hiba* is with the *sedih* cluster; *asmara* has no equivalent in the Minangkabau cluster; and *birahi*, in Minangkabau, is more complexly associated with the *senang* groups than is *berahi*, in Indonesian.

Now let us zoom out to take a quick look at the shape of the entire structure of the emotion space in each language (see Maps 1–3 between Parts I and II). Map 2, for instance, indicates that in Minangkabau Indonesian there are some forty clusters. The structure is branching, and each cluster has ties to only one or two other clusters.

2.2. Map terminology

We can describe the features of these maps in the following terms:

Clusters – defined as three or more words with mutual relationships, plus their dependent branches and twigs. The simplest cluster is a triangle.

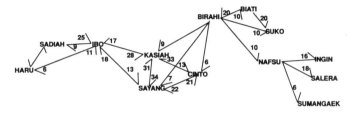

Figure 5. The "Love" cluster in Minangkabau

Area – a complex of interrelated clusters, branches, and twigs whose
    connections are with each other, the whole being relatively un-
    connected to other features.
Branch – several terms on bifurcating lines, one of which leads to
    another, but lacking relationship lines back to form a cluster.
Twig – a term related to only one other term; a dead end.
Chain – a series of terms, each related only to the two terms on
    either side.
Clusters, branches, and twigs may be *linked* to other features or they
may be *isolates*, without links to other features.
    Clusters may be tied to each other by a *hinge word*, which is a member
of two tangential clusters, or clusters may be linked by a *chain*, which
forms a *bridge* that *links* two *clusters*.
    Let us now zoom back in on the *kasih* cluster to explore its structure.

2.3. Key words (Fig. 6)

Not all words are chosen with equal frequency. In most clusters one
word is chosen much more frequently than the others. Here *kasih* and
kasiah clearly dominate their respective clusters, and I am calling them
the "key members" of their clusters. The key words are those with the
most associations: the most general, or multivalent. As we shall see,
they may not be what have been called "focal," or "prototype," terms.
    For each language I treat the entire corpus of words – the master list
plus the other words produced by the synonym-eliciting task – as a category or realm. This realm is called by superordinate terms in each language (Indonesian: *perasaan hati*; Minangkabau: *raso ati*). The realm in
each language corresponds more or less to the English category *emotion*,
and my goal of investigating emotion in Indonesia has led me to identify
and explore this realm. At this level, it makes sense to use the concept
of prototype to determine the strength of membership of each word in

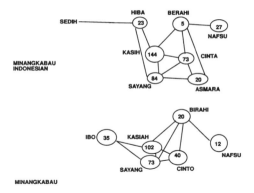

Figure 6. Key words

the realm of emotion (Rosch and Lloyd 1978; Lakoff 1987; Neisser 1987).

However, in exploring the internal structure of these semantic realms, looking at the relationships and clusterings of various emotion words, it does not appear we are dealing with comparable categories. I find myself slipping into category thinking when I speak of the "Surprise" cluster or the "Sad" cluster, but this must be approached with great care. It seems more accurate to think of the internal structure of the emotion category as a map or schema, in which the various concepts are unevenly related to some other concepts, frequently forming those *relationship clusters* that will be the major organizing units of this analysis.

One might well suggest that the very presence of these discrete, identifiable clusters in the maps is itself evidence of native category formation. As we shall see, there is some direct evidence for this, but it remains a matter for future researchers to investigate.

Having determined early in the research that *perasaan hati/raso ati* are categories, I could then ask about the membership of each word in that category. But this was only at the level of the inclusive, superordinate category. Unless one has first established the existence of a category called " 'Sad' cluster," one cannot ask the comparable question of the Sad words.

2.4. Alternative ways of mapping

Before proceeding to the cluster-by-cluster analysis of the three lexical maps, located between Parts I and II, we should review just what these maps represent, and how they compare with other representations of emotion-word realms.

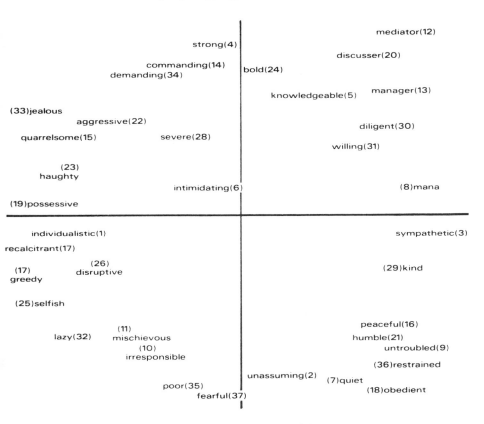

Figure 7. Two-dimensional representation of thirty-seven A'ara person-ality descriptors. Stress = .346. From White (1980:763), reproduced by permission of the American Anthropological Association.

There are several ways to investigate and represent relationships be-tween sets of emotion words.

1. *Multidimensional scaling* solutions are best known from the semantic differential work of Osgood and his associates (1975). In this approach, values for several dimensions are determined for each of the words in-volved by sorting or rating tasks, and then the word is plotted as a point on a two- or three-dimensional grid (for example, Figs. 7, 8, and 10 from White 1980; Lutz 1982; and Russell 1983). Koentjaraningrat (1985) has presented a similar diagram (see Fig. 9) for some Javanese emotion terms, but this diagram is presumably based on his intuition as a Javanese, not on a multidimensional scaling study.

A major strength of multidimensional scaling is the way it can reveal

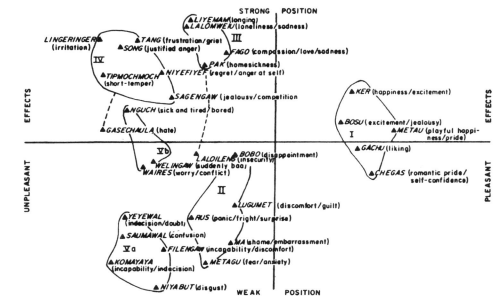

Figure 8. Two-dimensional picture of thirty-one Ifalukian emotion words (stress = .0882). Circles indicate groups found in cluster analysis. Dashes connect outlying members of cluster. From Lutz (1982:121), reproduced by permission of the American Anthropological Association.

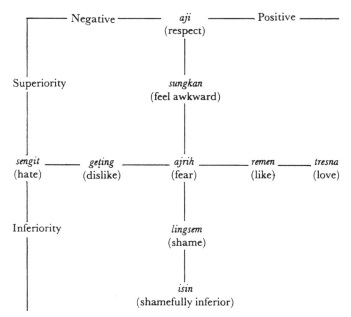

Figure 9. Javanese attitudes toward fellowmen. From Koentjaraningrat (1983:251), reproduced by permission.

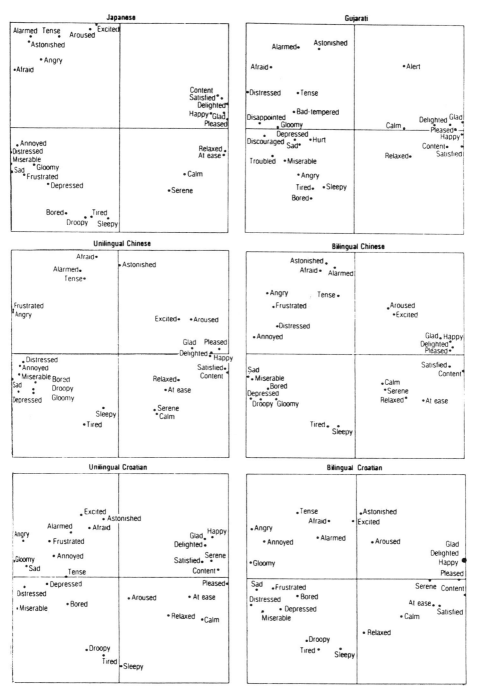

Figure 10. Two-dimensional scaling solutions for emotion-related words in Gujarati, Croatian, Japanese, and Chinese. From Russell (1983:12.85), reproduced by permission.

the dimensions, the essential culture-specific bases for a set of emotion terms. Although these dimensions are not named features in the native system, the analyst does attempt to attribute meaning to them. Osgood, even in his broad cross-cultural work, concluded that the three dimensions of Evaluation (positive–negative), Potency (weak–strong), and Activity (low–high) were cross-cultural constants. However, when Lutz brought her ethnographic perspective to the investigation of the emotion vocabulary of Ifaluk, a small Micronesian society, she concluded that, of the two major dimensions for Ifaluk emotion terms, one was "Pleasant–Unpleasant" (which did correspond to Osgood's "Evaluation") but the other was more culture-specific, reflecting Ifaluk concern with status hierarchy (she calls this "Strong Position vs. Weak Position"). It is significant that Koentjaraningrat uses similar dimensions (Negative–Positive and Superiority–Inferiority) for the Javanese, who are certainly as concerned with hierarchy as the Ifaluk.

2. *Hierarchical cluster* analysis produces a branching tree representation of the relationships between words. It has been used for emotion words in Ifaluk (Lutz 1982), in Samoan (Gerber 1985) and in English (e.g., Shaver et al. 1987). (Figs. 11–14.) Subjects are asked to sort words into similarity groups. The more frequently that words are put into the same group, the closer the branching that separates them. The different levels of branching bear some resemblance to increasingly more inclusive superordinate categories in a hierarchical taxonomy. There is, however, no claim that the higher-level clusterings are actually named categories in the native system, although the investigators analyze them as such and give them category names.

The study of Indonesian emotion words carried out by Jerry Boucher and his colleagues (Brandt and Boucher 1986) used this sorting technique to produce nonhierarchical clusters similar to those depicted in the maps of this study.

3. *Network maps*, because they retain the most information and despite their inelegance, have been used in the present volume. (Similar maps have been used in information processing and memory work – see Fig. 15, from the Collins and Loftus "Spreading-Activation Theory of Semantic Processing," 1975; they have also been used in author and article co-citation studies such as Griffith et al., 1974; Small 1980; White and Griffith 1981, 1982; and White 1983. Although these maps look rather similar to each other, their formal content is quite different. Instead of synonyms for words, they indicate both structure of and transmission of ideas in a scholarly realm by analyzing bibliographic citations in scien-

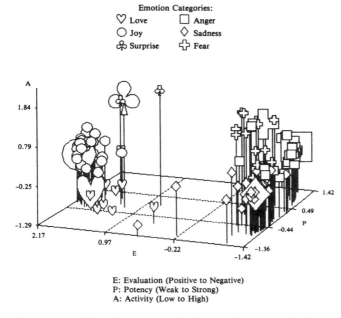

Figure 11. Three-dimensional solution from a multidimensional scaling analysis of the emotion co-occurrence matrix. From Shaver et al. (1987:1071), reproduced by permission.

tific publications.) These network maps used here are only generally similar to social behavior and role networks (see Knoke and Kuklinski 1982).

Network maps have several desirable features for representing relationships between words in the emotion realm.

1. They depict the complexity of interrelationships between words. Multidimensional scaling indicates only similarities on the abstracted dimensions but not the actual relationships. Hierarchical clustering diagrams depict the primary relationships between words but not other relationships. Lutz (1982) addressed this problem by a separate verbal discussion of the importance of secondary relationships, but nevertheless the graphics of a spreading tree diagram omit much information.

2. The elicitation of data bearing on the relationships does not demand a predetermined, closed universe. Both the scaling tasks and the sorting tasks are performed with predetermined sets of words, which form closed universes of items. Often in the emotion studies already mentioned, a subsample of only a couple of dozen words was used.

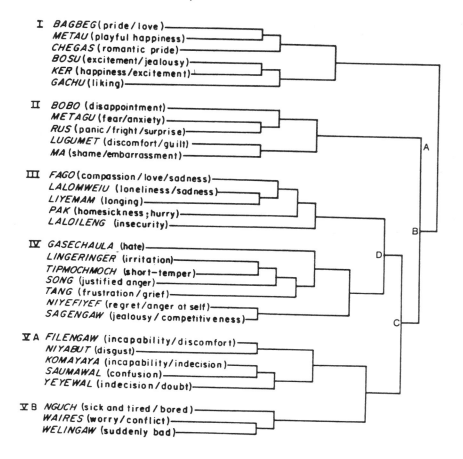

Defining Situations Underlying Major Branchings:

A – Pleasant vs. unpleasant rewards of the situation
B – Dangerous vs. non-dangerous situation
C – Certain vs. uncertain situation
D – Misfortune vs. human error and conflict at base of situation

Figure 12. Hierarchical clustering diagrams of thirty-one Ifalukian emotion words (not to scale; index of structure = .94). From Lutz (1982:116), reproduced by permission of the American Anthropological Association.

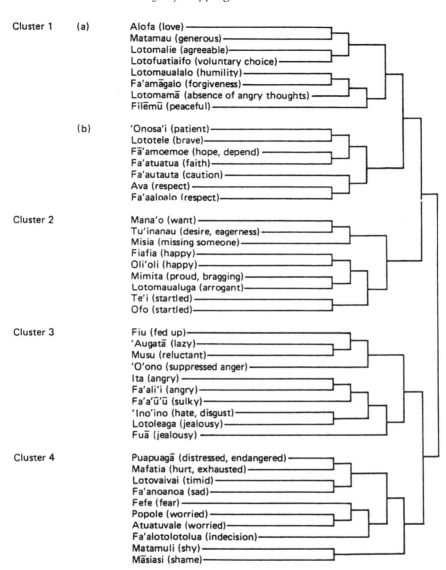

Figure 13. Cluster diagram of Samoan emotion terms. From Gerber (1985:140), reproduced by permission.

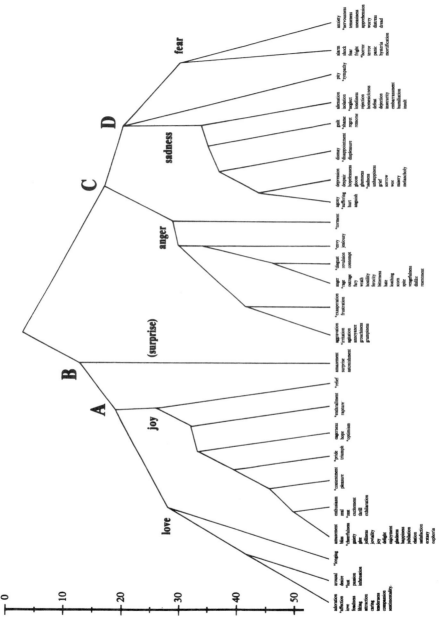

Figure 14. Results of a hierarchical cluster analysis of 135 emotion names. Cluster strength can be determined by referring to numerical scale at left. Asterisks indicate empirically selected subcluster names. From Shaver et al. (1987:1067), reproduced by permis-

Figure 15. A schematic representation of concept relatedness in a stereotypical fragment of human memory (where a shorter line represents greater relatedness). From Collins and Loftus (1975:412), reproduced by permission.

(Lutz used 31; Gerber used 44; Russell used 28; but Shaver et al. used 135.) A stripped-down set does facilitate the task for the subjects and allows more elegant statistical analysis.

However, one goal of this study was to explore the limits of the emotion realms, and I was unwilling to draw boundaries beforehand. My master lists of some 200 words resulted in maps that contain some 300 words.

It might well be that for later studies of these emotion words and realms in Minangkabau and Indonesian, other, more traditional and controlled, approaches would serve better. But for this first study, it is important not to reach premature closure.

3. The network maps can be used to interpret responses to other tasks. Thus, they are "maps" in two senses: They allow one to lay out the internal structure of the emotion realm; they allow one to make sense of the emotion words given as responses in other tasks. In this second sense the network maps serve as a sort of super dictionary, indicating meaning and also pointing out when two words are simply close synonyms or are referring to two quite different clusters. Both the multidimensional scaling and the hierarchical clustering solutions have been treated primarily as ends in themselves, and have not been used for other sorts of intra- or intercultural investigations.

For example: (a) One task in this study used short film clips of emotion scenarios from commercial Indonesian movies (Heider 1987). Subjects were asked to describe the emotions of the several actors in the scene. Usually, each subject gave several emotion words for a single actor. In order to interpret the responses, one had to be able to say that terms A and B were closely linked in the same cluster, whereas C was in quite a different cluster.

(b) In comparing, say, "anger" across languages, it is more defensible to use these network maps produced by a single methodology that is exhaustive rather than some representation based on a stripped-down set of words. An important consideration is that the maps give authority for statements about lexical elaboration or sparseness in the different languages.

In summary: The multidimensional scaling and the hierarchical cluster techniques have advantages for some sorts of studies. But for this book, which is at once exploratory and multifaceted, the network representation of synonym data provides the most advantages.

2.5. Schemata, maps, or what? A terminological note

In this general area of the cognitive sciences, many different subjects have been approached in many different ways, based on many different theoretical positions. But such stimulating diversity has been somewhat hampered by a paucity of terms used to refer to a wide range of disparate activities. Here, I refer to visual representations of relationships between emotion words in a language as "cognitive maps," or "lexical maps."

"Schema" is a possible alternative for either the ideas about emotions or the diagrams used to depict them. Indeed, Casson classifies Lutz's emotion work with "object schemata" on the grounds that it was a study of "categories of concrete entities" (1983:441), and he reserves the term "cognitive maps" for representations of "knowledge about spacial orientations" (444). But emotions are hardly objects, and these clusterings of emotion terms are the structuring of the realm but not necessarily "categories." In any case, in anthropology the term "schema" has been used for more complex notions such as story-line plots (Rice 1980) or ideas about marriage in America (Quinn 1987). I do not intend here to sort out the terminologies (an exercise in metaclassification?). This is a study of the realm, or category, of emotion in different languages and cultures, an exploration of the internal structure of that realm, and I call the graphic representations of relationships between emotion lexemes *cognitive maps of emotion words*.

3. Membership in the realm of emotion: prototypicality

My master lists contained only words claimed by some chain of presumably fluent authority to be emotion words, and the final check in this chain of authority was usually agreement among my three research assistants – three very intelligent middle-aged Minangkabau women.

To be precise, we should recognize that I am not describing emotion in Indonesia, but rather the realm labeled *perasaan hati* in Indonesian, or, in Minangkabau, *raso ati*. These realms are equivalents to the English realm "emotion" but, we must assume, are not identical. These realms are overt categories for Indonesians, familiar and easily recognizable, with a label, *perasaan hati* (the root is *rasa*, an important Sanskrit term for emotions; but pressing the investigation back to India probably does not help us understand the Indonesian usages [Deutsch 1975; Bagchi 1983; Stange 1984]). Although *perasaan hati* corresponds to the English term "emotion," the borrowed term *emosi* is used in Indonesian most commonly for only a subset of strong negative emotions. (However, in other contexts, such as modern Indonesian movies, *emosi* can mean "emotion" in general.)

It is clear, however, that many of the Indonesian and Minangkabau clusters spill out beyond words that have strong prototypicality as emotions. To investigate this, I asked fifty respondents in each language to judge the words on the master list:

Is the word certainly an emotion word?

Is the word certainly not an emotion word?

Is the word sometimes an emotion word?

Figure 16 shows the results for the words of the *kasih/kasiah* clusters, showing the strongest case: the percentage of the respondents who said that the word was definitely an emotion word. I was surprised that only two of these words got 100% agreement. I expected that a word like *asyik* (Echols and Shadily: passionate, infatuated, busy, occupied) would be low, but the low rating of *berahi/birahi* and of *asmara* is surprising.

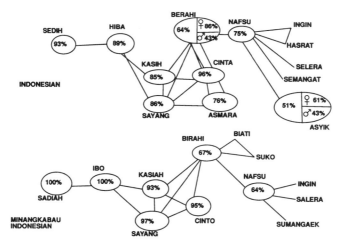

Figure 16. Prototypicality

Prototype theory of categories has been developed in response to just such categories as these: categories that lack absolute boundaries, and whose constituent elements are better or worse members of the category (Rosch 1978). Here, we can identify some words as being strongly prototypical (those in the 90%–100% range), others as being less prototypical (i.e., those in the lower ranges).

Two apparent anomalies should be mentioned. When Poerwadarminta (1982), who prepared the most exhaustive general Indonesian dictionary, defines *rasa*, which corresponds to "emotion" in English, he lists ten words, all of which are on the Indonesian master list in Table 3:

> *rasa* . . . keadaan hati atau batin (terhadap sesuatu); mis.:
> 93%   75%   96%   93%   89%
> *sedih* (susah, kecewa, pilu, senang dsb);
> 19%   86%   100%   86%   89%
> *hormat* (*takut, cinta, sayang, iba* dsb);

Eight of these words have high membership (prototypicality) scores, between 86% and 100%. The low ranking of *susah* (at 75%) is easily explainable on the grounds that although it is in the "Sad" cluster, its primary, most salient meaning, is the nonemotional "difficulty." But what of *hormat*, at 19%? Its meanings have to do with honor and respect. On the one hand, I was surprised to see it included in Poerwadarminta's list of ten, although I felt vindicated when this study showed it with a low prototypicality rating of 19%.

A second surprise is *marah*, the most salient Indonesian word for "anger." *Marah* is listed first in bilingual dictionaries, and it is central in the Indonesian lexical maps of emotion words. Yet Poerwadarminta does not include it in his list of ten, and my informants give it a low prototypical rating of 65%.

I assume here that the realm of emotion in American English as well as in Minangkabau and Indonesian is not a firmly bounded one, but one with fuzzy edges (see also Fehr and Russell 1984). Some research has assumed the opposite, and has tried to establish criteria by which a word or a feeling could be determined to be emotion or nonemotion (Clore, Ortony, and Foss 1987; Ortony et al. 1987). It is possible to work out a componential analysis, as Ortony and his colleagues have done, which logically places "angry" in the emotion realm and excludes, say, "startled." But even when they devise a very precise tool to encourage subjects to distinguish between emotion and nonemotion feelings, the results look very much like these (or, as Table 6 shows, those of Shaver et al. 1987): there was still disagreement and the scores for words were relative, not absolutely emotion or nonemotion. The Ortony study does not provide evidence for strongly bounded realms of emotion, and the prototypicality measures of Minangkabau and Indonesian words as presented here do seem to reflect cognitive reality (in contrast to logic-driven theory), which is consistent with the notion that these realms of emotion dissolve into neighboring realms, especially the realm of *sifat* ("characteristics").

3.1. Gender differences in attribution to the realm

Interestingly, in Indonesian, women admitted *berahi* and *asyik* as emotion words more strongly than did men (in the case of *berahi*, twice as many women as men admitted it as an emotion).

This gender difference showed up across the boards – women made stronger claims for Indonesian words as emotion words (or, women admitted more words more strongly into the emotion realm), but in Minangkabau it was the opposite: There, men made stronger claims for words as emotion words (or, men admitted more words more strongly into the emotion realm). So, in Minangkabau, women were stricter gatekeepers; in Indonesian, men were stricter gatekeepers (Table 1).

I hypothesize that women have a better knowledge of Minangkabau, the domestic language, and so are more precise about which words are and which are not actually emotion words in that language; and that

Table 1. *Words claimed as emotion words by one gender*
at least twice as strongly as by the other gender

	By women	By men
Minangkabau (of 209)	6	20
Indonesian (of 229)	28	6[a]

[a]Of these, 2 Arabic; $\times 2 = 15.83$, $p < .001$

men, who are more involved with Indonesian, the national and official language, are less likely to admit nonemotion words into the emotion category in Indonesian. This assumes that errors are all in the direction of overly generous attribution of emotion status (or that the more generous inclusions are errors); but we also have to consider that most of the respondents were college students whose lives probably do not reflect a traditional split of domestic women and official men.

3.2. Analysis: comparisons of the emotion realms in Minangkabau and Indonesian

Because this task produced a measure of strength of membership in the emotion (*perasaan hati*) realms for each word, one can use these measures to rank the words and then compare the strongest words in each language with their cognates in the other language. Tables 2 and 3 show the words in Minangkabau (BM) and in Indonesian as spoken by Minangkabau (BI[M]) with the strongest and the weakest prototypicality ratings (85% and above, 15% and below).

As Tables 4 and 5 show, there are more, stronger, emotion words in Minangkabau Indonesian for the 93% level and above: There are nineteen words in Minangkabau Indonesian but only thirteen in Minangkabau. Six of the strongest Minangkabau Indonesian words do not have a Minangkabau cognate, while none of the strongest Minangkabau words lack a Minangkabau Indonesian cognate. (This measure includes cognates not in the top group.)

Interpretation: On the whole, Minangkabau Indonesian is stronger and richer in emotion words than Minangkabau. This accords with the general expectations that although Minangkabau is fairly rich in emotion words (at least compared with Javanese), the national language, Indonesian, is richer in emotion words – that is, a stronger arena for the play

Table 2. *Minangkabau Indonesian words. Membership in the emotion realm: level of confidence. For strongest (85%<) and weakest (15%>)*

Percentages	
100	CINTA (love), RINDU (longing), KANGEN (longing)
96	GELISAH (nervous), KECEWA (disappointed), LEGA (relieved), RISAU (restless), TERGUGAH (aroused), TEKAN PERASAAN (strong feeling)
93	BELAS KASIHAN (pity), BERBESAR HATI (pride), CEMBURU (jealous), HARU (moved), MAKAN HATI (sadden), PILU (moved), SAKIT HATI (annoyed), GUNDAH (depressed), WAS-WAS (suspicion), SEHIH (sad)
89	DUKA (grief), HIBA (moved), INSAF (aware), PUAS (satisfied), RUSUH (restless), SENANG (happy), BERDEBAR (to throb), KELUH-KESAH (sigh)
86	DENDAM (revenge), GEMBIRA (glad), RENDAH HATI (modest), SAYANG (sorrow), SYAK WASANGKO (suspicion), TAKUT (fear), PALAK (angry), PANAS HATI (angry) BERAT HATI (suspicion), BAHAGIA (happiness), YAKIN (sure)
85	BENCI (hate), GIRANG (glad), KASIH (affection)
	• • •
15	MEMBUJUK (flatter), MELUS-ELUS (caress)
14	GAWAT (serious), PIKIRAN (thought)
11	HANGUS (jealous), CEMEEH (scorn), EJEK (mock), HENING (calm), AIB (shame), AJAIB (astonishingly), CAMPUR ADUK (confused), CERCA (scorn), MENGIAS (goad), MENGGANGGU (tease),
8	CIBIR (scorn), KOTOR (dirty)
7	DATAR (flat), MENCACI (scorn), SIKSA (torture), MENGUSIK (annoy)
4	TAJAM (sharp), BANDING (equal), BERANTAKAN (chaos), LALIM (cruel)
0	LISUT (exhausted), MEMPEROLOK-OLOK (mock)

of emotions – than are any of the regional languages. Wolff and Soepomo (1982:64) certainly suggest that this is true for Javanese and Indonesian. These present data confirm it in general for Minangkabau and Indonesian. As we shall see, however, the situation is complicated. In one emotion area there is good evidence that in fact Minangkabau is

Table 3. *Minangkabau words. Membership in the emotion realm: level of confidence. For strongest (85%<) and weakest (15%>)*

Percentages	
100	IBO, RISAU, RUSUAH, SADIAH
98	PILU, SAYANG
95	CINTO, GUMBIRA, HARU, RIANG
93	GIRANG, KASIAH, TATAKAN PERASAAN
90	CAMEH, GALISAH, PUTUIH ASO, SANANG, PADIAH ATI, SUSAH
88	ANGEK ATI, BANGIH, BADATAK, GADANG ATI, MANY-ASA, RASAH, SAKIK ATI
85	BANCI, BERANG, BIMBANG, CEMBURU, PUEH, TASING-GUANG, TAKUIK, KUATIR
15	MANCACI-MAKI, JARIAH, MANCACEK, GADUAK
13	ANIANG, BATUA, LANGANG
10	BANDIANG, LURUIH, MARUIH, TALANJUA
8	MANGGADUAH, JALEH, PIKEK, KIEH
5	MANDAPEK, MANUMPALEK, PIRADEN, MANYARIN-GAI, IRUAK, BAKALIBUIK
3	PIGANTA, TAJAM
0	CADIAK CANDAKIA, TAPEK, JAREK

stronger, not weaker, than Indonesian (see Section 5.1). (It looks as if the landscapes of emotion are quite uneven terrains and that what is true for one sector may not be for another sector. It would be interesting in the future to test this relationship between national and regional languages in even more "open" or "coarse" cultures, such as Madura or Batak.)

To the question "Apakah kata-kata berikut ini artinya perasaan hati betul, atau sifat saja?" (Do the following words really signify emotions, or just attributes?), twenty-eight Minangkabau speakers of Indonesian rated 229 words, choosing yes, no, maybe. Table 2 gives the percentages of yes ratings for each word.

Forty Minangkabau speakers rated the 209 words on the Minangkabau master list. They were asked if the word was really an emotion word, and were to answer yes, no, or maybe. The percentages of the yes ratings given words at the strong and weak ends of the scale are shown in Table 3.

Table 4. *Comparing the realms. The words in Minangkabau (BM) with 90% and stronger inclusion in the realm, and their Indonesian (BI[M]) cognates*

Minangkabau word	BM%	BI(M)%	Difference
IBO	100	89	11
RISAU	100	96	4
RUSUAH	100	89	11
SADIAH	100	93	7
PILU	98	93	5
SAYANG	98	86	12
CINTO	95	100	−5
GUMBIRA	95	86	9
HARU	95	93	2
RIANG	95	79	16
GIRANG	93	85	8
KASIAH	93	85	8
TATAKAN PERASAAN	93	96	−3
CAMEH	90	82	8
GALISAH	90	96	−6
PUTUIH ASO	90	75	15
SANANG	90	89	1
PADIAH ATI	90	68	22
SUSAH	90	75	15

Table 5. *Comparing the realms. The words in Indonesian (BI[M]) with 90% and stronger inclusion in the realm and their Minangkabau (BM) cognates*

Indonesian word	BI(M)%	BM%	Difference
CINTA	100	95	5
RINDU	100		
KANGEN	100		
GELISAH	96	90	6
KECEWA	96		
LEGA	96		
RISAU	96	100	−4
TERGUGAH	96		
TEKAN PERASAAN	96	93	3
BELAS KASIHAN	93		
BERBESAR HATI	93	88	5
CEMBURU	93	85	8
HARU	93	95	−2
MAKAN HATI	93	83	10
PILU	93	98	−5
SAKIT HATI	93	88	5
GUNDAH	93	68	25
WAS-WAS	93	62	31
SEDIH	93	100	−7

Table 6. Mean prototypicality ratings (M) and unfamiliarity proportions (UP) for 213 emotion words

Emotion word	M	UP	Emotion word	M	UP	Emotion word	M	UP	Emotion word	M	UP
love[a]	3.94	.00	agitation[a]	3.29	.01	triumph[a]	2.95	.00	calmness	2.63	.00
anger[a]	3.90	.00	outrage[a]	3.28	.00	joviality[a]	2.94	.05	respect	2.62	.00
hate[a]	3.84	.00	resentment[a]	3.28	.00	wrath[a]	2.93	.07	somberness	2.62	.02
depression[a]	3.83	.00	dislike[a]	3.27	.00	arousal[a]	2.92	.03	vehemence	2.62	.34
fear[a]	3.83	.00	glee[a]	3.24	.02	attraction[a]	2.92	.00	sulkiness	2.59	.03
jealousy[a]	3.81	.00	alienation[a]	3.23	.01	contentment[a]	2.92	.04	encouragment	2.58	.01
happiness[a]	3.77	.00	distress[a]	3.23	.01	grumpiness[a]	2.92	.00	frenzy	2.58	.01
passion[a]	3.75	.00	enjoyment[a]	3.23	.00	irritation[a]	2.92	.00	obsession	2.58	.00
affection[a]	3.72	.01	relief[a]	3.23	.00	malevolence	2.92	.32	success	2.56	.00
sadness[a]	3.68	.00	gloom[a]	3.21	.00	ferocity[a]	2.91	.00	forgiveness	2.55	.00
grief[a]	3.65	.01	misery[a]	3.20	.02	enthrallment[a]	2.90	.13	indignation	2.55	.17
rage[a]	3.64	.00	euphoria[a]	3.19	.16	revulsion[a]	2.88	.10	discomfort	2.54	.00
aggravation[a]	3.63	.03	bliss[a]	3.18	.07	alarm[a]	2.87	.00	vindictiveness	2.54	.13
ecstasy[a]	3.63	.00	gladness[a]	3.17	.00	eagerness[a]	2.87	.00	aversion	2.52	.25
sorrow[a]	3.62	.00	regret[a]	3.16	.00	hysteria[a]	2.87	.00	power	2.52	.00
joy[a]	3.61	.00	rejection[a]	3.16	.00	liking[a]	2.87	.00	vibrance	2.52	.13
compassion[a]	3.62	.00	pride[a]	3.14	.00	neglect[a]	2.87	.00	sheepishness	2.50	.14
envy[a]	3.58	.00	gaiety[a]	3.13	.04	insult[a]	2.86	.00	jitteriness	2.49	.01
fright[a]	3.58	.00	homesickness[a]	3.13	.00	mortification[a]	2.85	.04	virtue	2.48	.01
terror[a]	3.57	.00	jolliness[a]	3.12	.00	tenseness[a]	2.85	.00	mirth	2.47	.36
elation[a]	3.55	.10	nervousness[a]	3.12	.00	contempt[a]	2.84	.03	demoralization	2.46	.05
guilt[a]	3.53	.00	woe[a]	3.12	.05	amazement[a]	2.83	.00	fierceness	2.46	.01
excitement[a]	3.51	.00	longing[a]	3.11	.00	amusement[a]	2.83	.00	effervescence	2.44	.43
anguish[a]	3.49	.01	loathing[a]	3.10	.05	zeal[a]	2.83	.15	fervor	2.44	.23
embarrassment[a]	3.49	.00	satisfaction[a]	3.10	.01	scorn[a]	2.82	.02	complacency	2.42	.27
worry[a]	3.49	.00	hope[a]	3.08	.00	zest[a]	2.82	.03	nostalgia	2.42	.03
panic[a]	3.48	.00	abhorrence[a]	3.06	.30	astonishment[a]	2.80	.00	modesty	2.40	.00
unhappiness[a]	3.48	.00	insecurity[a]	3.06	.00	titillation	2.80	.27	disgruntlement	2.37	.20
anxiety[a]	3.46	.00	defeat[a]	3.05	.01	torment[a]	2.80	.02	inconsolableness	2.37	.34
desire[a]	3.45	.00	dread[a]	3.05	.00	optimism[a]	2.78	.01	belligerence	2.33	.20

Word	Rating		Word	Rating		Word	Rating		Word	Rating	
horror[a]	3.45	.00	fondness[a]	3.05	.00	vengefulness[a]	2.78	.03	disconsolateness	2.33	.41
sympathy[a]	3.45	.00	enthusiasm[a]	3.05	.00	impatience	2.75	.00	determination	2.30	.00
shame[a]	3.44	.00	sentimentality[a]	3.05	.00	persecution	2.75	.01	doubt	2.30	.00
lust[a]	3.43	.00	hopelessness[a]	3.04	.01	viciousness	2.75	.01	superiority	2.29	.00
disgust[a]	3.42	.00	annoyance[a]	3.03	.00	edginess	2.74	.05	vanity	2.28	.05
hostility[a]	3.41	.00	cheerfulness[a]	3.03	.00	awe	2.73	.03	acceptance	2.26	.00
jubilation[a]	3.41	.01	displeasure[a]	3.03	.00	despondency	2.73	.30	abandonment	2.23	.01
loneliness[a]	3.41	.01	melancholy[a]	3.02	.02	gratitude	2.73	.00	carefreeness	2.22	.00
delight[a]	3.40	.00	glumness[a]	3.01	.02	mellowness	2.71	.00	exhaustion	2.19	.00
pleasure[a]	3.40	.00	shock[a]	3.01	.00	vexation	2.71	.32	craving	2.16	.00
tenderness[a]	3.40	.00	spite[a]	3.01	.01	enchantment	2.70	.01	inclination	2.16	.00
pity[a]	3.39	.00	suffering[a]	3.01	.00	exultation	2.70	.15	approval	2.14	.01
bitterness[a]	3.38	.00	dismay[a]	3.00	.01	sullenness	2.69	.06	distraction	2.14	.01
disappointment[a]	3.38	.00	exasperation[a]	3.00	.02	surprise[a]	2.69	.00	freedom	2.13	.00
humiliation[a]	3.38	.00	infatuation[a]	3.00	.04	discontentment	2.67	.01	startle	2.11	.01
dejection[a]	3.37	.04	apprehension[a]	2.99	.03	discouragement	2.66	.00	indecision	2.02	.01
despair[a]	3.37	.01	caring[a]	2.98	.01	boredom	2.65	.01	interest	1.96	.00
frustration[a]	3.37	.00	isolation[a]	2.98	.00	exuberance	2.65	.05	self-control	1.95	.00
hurt[a]	3.37	.00	exhilaration[a]	2.96	.00	forlornness	2.65	.25	alertness	1.94	.00
adoration[a]	3.36	.07	rapture[a]	2.96	.11	lividness	2.65	.20	carefulness	1.84	.00
agony[a]	3.35	.01	uneasiness[a]	2.96	.00	moroseness	2.65	.25	practicality	1.75	.00
thrill[a]	3.34	.00	grouchiness[a]	2.95	.00	dolefulness	2.64	.40	deliberateness	1.73	.05
fury[a]	3.33	.01	ire	2.95	.57	wonderment	2.64	.01	intelligence	1.57	.00
remorse[a]	3.30	.03									

Note: Ratings were made by 112 subjects on a 4-point scale ranging from 1 (*I definitely would not call this an emotion*) to 4 (*I definitely would call this an emotion*). The words *abhorrence, ire, malevolence,* and *titillation* were excluded from the sorting study because many subjects were unfamiliar with them.

[a] Words used in the emotion-sorting study.

Source: Shaver et al. 1987.

3.3. The nature of the realm of *perasaan hati*

These data help us to approach the basic question of translation: What is included in the *perasaan hati* realms in Indonesia, and how do these realms correspond to the realm of emotion in English?

There is now substantial comparative data from experiments done with English-speaking subjects. Fehr and Russell (1984) elicited prototypicality ratings for twenty English emotion words from 55 Canadian subjects at two different times, five months apart, using a rating scale of 1 to 6. Shaver et al. (1987) performed a comparable task with 213 English emotion words (compared to 209 in Minangkabau and 229 in the Indonesian list). They asked 112 subjects (considerably more than the 40 for Minangkabau or the 28 for Minangkabau Indonesian) to rate the emotion-ness of each word on a four-point scale, producing a "mean prototypicality rating" (Table 6). (In the Indonesian study there were the three choices – yes, no, maybe – and the measure of the emotion-ness of each word is the percentage of Yes answers.) Thus, the measures used in the two studies are not strictly comparable, but the rank orders of the words can be compared. Shaver et al. report that the correlations between their results, the Fehr and Russell results, and other prototype ratings experiments in English are uniformly high (1987:1064).

As is usual in such experiments performed in the West we are told little about the linguistic or general cultural background of the subjects: The Shaver et al. subjects were "students in introductory psychology courses" in Colorado and the Fehr and Russell subjects were "all undergraduates of the University of British Columbia." One can by no means claim with certainty that culture (including first language experience) has no effect on emotion thinking. It seems likely that the subject groups included people of different subcultures. Without controlling for culture, the results may aggregate important differences and smooth over the culture differences. Then, when the results show little or no evidence of cultural effect, there is a legitimate suspicion that the experimental protocol itself obliterated any possible cultural effects. If an experiment is to make a claim about culture in its conclusions, it cannot ignore culture in its subject selection process. This is not merely the complaint on principle of an ethnologist. As we shall see in the process of this analysis, the results for the *Indonesian* language are very different from the two different subject pools, those who learned Minangkabau first, and those who learned Javanese first. The influence of local cultures in Indonesia, (as to some degree in North America) is not trivial.

The most obvious difference between the Shaver et al. American English rankings and the two Indonesian rankings is the great strength or salience of anger/hate in English, compared with its later, lower appearance in the Indonesian lists. Conversely, sad and confusion words are stronger in the Indonesian lists than they are in the English list.

What does this say about the differences between English "emotion" and Indonesian *perasaan hati?* Certainly anger falls within the Indonesian realm, but the focal strength of the Indonesian realm is elsewhere. Conversely, sadness and to a lesser degree confusion are indeed emotions in English, but they are not as central as they are in Indonesia. The implications of this will emerge as we inspect each cluster in turn.

This particular task, however, discusses differences only in the few strongest focal words of the "emotion"/*perasaan hati* realms. Evidence for the spread or extension of the category will emerge later.

3.4. Semantic differential

Another useful tool in revealing the structure of clusters is the semantic differential approach, in which different terms are judged independently on the same set of attributes. At this point, it looks as if such an approach will be of minor significance within a language but very useful in comparing languages.

The standard semantic differential, as developed by Charles Osgood, rates words on the basis of several seven-point scales and then by factor analysis isolates the major principles that have turned out to be what Osgood calls Evaluation, Potency, and Activity. Starting with Osgood's scales for Malay (virtually the same language as Indonesian), I chose six variables that seemed most likely to get responses. Forty subjects ranked twenty-four key words in each language. The results are not particularly helpful in working out the structure of clusters, but, as will be seen, are useful in comparing languages (see Section 5.1).

4. Emotion scenarios: antecedents and outcomes

> The first and most obvious way in which culture may affect the emotions is by determining what situations will give rise to them. Depending upon its cultural context, the same external occurrence may arouse diametrically opposite responses in two different societies.
>
> Otto Klineberg 1935:278

Eventually we circle back to the problem of translation: How are we to understand these Minangkabau and Indonesian words through English? We have already stated the assumption that single-word translations are, a priori, suspect. In fact, there are some translation equivalents that may turn out to be quite satisfactory: "anger" and *marah*, for example, match very well. In other parts of the emotion realm the correspondence is less good: *cinta* is close to "love," but it implies more of pity and sadness, less of happiness, than does the English word.

The most economical solution would be to compare unabridged dictionary definitions for closest-fit words in two languages. This move would be based on the (ironic) assumption that although a one-word translation is likely to be off, lots of these inaccurate words will describe a lexical concept better.

Here we can draw on several rich sources. For English, we have the definitive *Oxford English Dictionary* and the study by Joel R. Davitz, "The Language of Emotion" (1969). (Davitz used a checklist of 556 possible statements about emotions. Fifty American subjects selected the appropriate items on the checklist for each of fifty common emotion words. The "definition," then, of each word, consists of those checklist items used by more than one-third of the subjects. These items were grouped in similarity groups and order by frequency. The result is a profile of characteristics of emotion words that in fact corresponds more closely to this present study than does the ordinary dictionary definition.) For Indonesian, there are the 1963 Echols and Shadily Indonesian-English dictionary and its supplement, the 1981 Schmidgall-Tellings and Stevens

dictionary, together with the most comprehensive Indonesian dictionary (Poerwadarminta 1982). (This study was completed before the appearance of the 1989 third edition of the Echols and Shadily dictionary.)
Minangkabau sources are the van der Toorn (1891) and the Pamoentjak
(1935) dictionaries.

However, even this lexicographical overkill depends mainly on dictionaries whose methodology is quite implicit. At best, these sorts of data
can serve as supplements to more systematically collected data on the
antecedents and outcomes of particular emotions.

To get richer cultural data on various emotion terms, I gathered responses from fifty Minangkabau on a sentence completion task. The task
asked for antecedent conditions and outcomes of different emotion words.
Each word was coupled with one or two other closely associated words.
For the within-language sets, these were the words with the strongest
associations in each major cluster. There were also between-language
sets contrasting the closest non-cognate translation equivalents. I chose
only non-cognate word pairs for the between-language task in order to
get the clearest possible differences. In fact, apparent close cognates between two languages often constitute an especially interesting phenomenon of nonequivalence. They fascinate and repel language teachers,
who call them "deceptive cognates" (Seward 1947), "*mots perfides*" and
"*faux amis*" (Derocquigny 1931), or "*falschen Freunde*" (Wandruszka 1978).
But because of their apparent identity, I feared that most respondents
would simply merge the ideas of the two languages and not make meaningful distinctions even when such might exist. This is a problem and
an opportunity for future research, with different methods. The task
went like this:

> X and Y are almost the same. Please clarify the differences by com-
> pleting the following sentences:
> He/she is X because . . .
> He/she is Y because . . .
>
> When he/she is X, he/she . . .
> When he/she is Y, he/she . . .
> (The third person singular word, *dia*, is gender-neutral.)

Or, for the between-language sets:

> A, in Indonesian and X, in Minangkabau, are very similar. Please
> clarify the differences by completing the following sentences:

(In Indonesian) He/she is *A* because . . .
(In Minangkabau) He/she is *X* because . . .

The results of this task clarify the clusters and also provide data on the flow of emotion, that is, provide ideal statements on the cause of anger, the outcome of sorrow, and so on. When the task is put in terms of closely related sets of words, people are encouraged to attend to nuances of difference – for example, in English the difference between "anger" and "fury."

The trap of inadvertent simplification is a danger here as elsewhere. That is, people may respond to only one aspect of a complex stimulus, thus giving a deceptively simple picture. This certainly happened with the emotion words of the Indonesian master list when Javanese were asked for the Javanese language equivalents. Although for many of the Indonesian words there are two or more Javanese possibilities, invariably the subjects produced the Low, or *ngoko*, word. On the basis of this evidence alone one would have no hint that there is also a High, or *kromo*, vocabulary in Javanese. I suspect that this absence of *kromo* is an artifact of the study: asking for vocabulary through an Indonesian language questionnaire in a university setting puts a rather modern, non-hierarchical cast on the situation.

When asking for antecedents and outcomes, the eliciting questions were intentionally neutral. In fact, both Indonesian and Minangkabau allow even more neutrality than does English, since one does not even specify gender. But it seems very likely that emotion scenarios are to some extent context-specific (this includes such variables as gender). Abu-Lughod has demonstrated this dramatically in her work on Bedouin expression. For the antecedent condition of "loss" (e.g., a man's bride runs away) a man may express anger and outrage in public discourse but despondency through lyric poems that are recited in domestic settings. Abu-Lughod suggests that even the "coexistence of two sets of contradictory sentiments expressed in different media and social arenas, a phenomenon which may be far more common cross-culturally than anthropologists have suspected, can better be interpreted with reference to cultural ideals than to psychodynamic processes" (1985:258).

It is precisely such subtle complexity that is not likely to be revealed by this sort of questionnaire approach. It is a first step, to be sure, but in the end it is no substitute for ethnographic fieldwork that sees larger and alternative contexts.

4.1. Other antecedent studies

Jerry Boucher and his associates have carried out somewhat similar investigations of antecedents for six emotion words in English and their closest equivalents in Malay, the language of Malaysia, very closely related to Indonesian and Minangkabau. They elicited two stories for each emotion in Malay from fifty Malays, in English from fifty Americans. Then through a series of seven steps they reduced each story to one of twelve basic acts. It turned out that the stories for each emotion were concentrated in one or two of the twelve acts, but that there was little difference between Malay and American distributions (Boucher 1981).

In a reverse experiment, a sample of ninety-six of these stories, half originally from Americans, half translated from Malay to English, were given to Americans, who were asked to identify which emotion the story corresponded to. Actually, the Americans judged the Malay stories slightly more accurately (68.9%) than they did the American stories (65.8%).

Boucher casts his results in terms of deciding the issue of whether emotions and their antecedents are culture-specific or pan-cultural. He feels that his evidence supports the pan-cultural position. In fact, this may be the wrong issue. It now seems evident that emotion behavior is partly pan-cultural, partly culture-specific. Put another way: Emotion behavior is culturally constructed on a pan-cultural base, and so it follows that an ultimate goal of research is to tease apart the two. Here Boucher's results are very provocative, and we shall return to them later.

The important differences between this study and those of Boucher are that here we are looking at both antecedents and outcomes; we are using several words in a cluster (e.g., six "surprise" words in Minangkabau, four in Indonesian); we are maintaining the specific detail of the antecedents and outcomes to a greater degree; and we shall be able to make several kinds of analytical cuts of the same data set (at his Level 7, for example, Boucher had to put a story into either the "Ego may be injured" category or the "Ego experiences something unexpected" category, even though the story might contain both elements).

In another study referred to in passing (Boucher and Carlson 1980:272) they defined twelve clusters, or categories, or emotions in Malaysian. Six of these include the six words Boucher used to elicit the antecedents; and the labels for the categories, one or two Malaysian emotion words, are even more similar to my Indonesian choices.

Specifically, four of the Indonesian choices were the same. The two disagreements are worth looking at. I had seen Boucher's 1981 paper and was interested in what differences, if any, would emerge between Malaysian and Indonesian. The two languages are closely related members of the Austronesian language family. Both were developed from a widely used trade language whose main roots were in the area of Sumatra and the Malay Peninsula. Both languages emerged as full languages during this century, but in somewhat different linguistic environments. Malaysian was influenced by English, whereas Indonesian was influenced by Dutch and by the languages of other islands of the archipelago, especially Javanese.

Thus, comparisons between the two studies can only be suggestive – although the languages are close, they are not identical and we have already noted that many differences appear between the nominally identical Minangkabau Indonesian and Javanese Indonesian. So there is strong reason to assume that the Malaysian examined in Boucher's study is different from the Indonesian examined here. And, of course, the two research methods are different. Despite these differences, it is worth comparing the results.

Boucher worked with only six words, one to represent each of six key emotions. The implicit assumption is that each of these words is the prototypical word for its cluster, and so represents that cluster. Whatever position one takes on the validity of a single word to represent a cluster, there are times when the research design forces one to choose a single word. In a study of facial expressions of emotions (Ekman et al. 1987) I had to choose a single word for the same clusters. The comparison with Boucher's list is interesting.

We see from Table 7 how even the four words on which we agree raise problems. For "anger," *marah* does seem like the appropriate word, but it is not the key word for all the anger clusters in Minangkabau Indonesian, and it has a relatively low prototypicality rating (see Fig. 22.2 in Part II).

For "happiness," *gembira* is the key word, but *senang* has a higher prototypicality rating.

For "sadness," *sedih* is the key word, but *sedih* and *pilu* have equally high prototypicality ratings.

Only *takut*, for "fear," is the choice by all criteria, but ironically, as we shall see, there is a strong element of guilt in *takut* that potentially skews the experimental results if one uses *takut* to stand for the simple English language idea of "fear."

For "surprise," the Indonesian *terkejut* seemed the better choice, although the Malaysian choice, *hairan*, has an equivalent in Indonesian,

Table 7

Boucher's Malaysian choices	Heider's Indonesian choices	Present results		Echols & Shadily dictionary
		Key word	Prototypicality rating	
MARAH (anger)	MARAH	MARAH	PALAK 86% PANAS HATI 86% MARAH 65%	MARAH
BOSAN (disgust)	JIJIK	JEMU	JEMU 71%	JIJIK
TAKUT (fear)	TAKUT	TAKUT	TAKUT 86%	TAKUT
GEMBIRA (happy)	GEMBIRA	GEMBIRA	SENANG 89% GEMBIRA 86%	GEMBIRA
SEDEH (sad)	SEDIH	SEDIH	SEDIH 93% PILU 93%	SEDIH
HAIRAN (surprise)	TERKEJUT	TERKEJUT	TERKEJUT 63%	HERAN

heran, which is close to *terkejut* in the map. In fact, the Echols-Shadily dictionary gives *heran* as the first choice for "surprise."

For "disgust," the Malaysian choice was *bosan,* although Boucher noted that it seemed to be more "boredom" than "disgust." The Indonesian choice was *jijik,* but the map and other data do not make any word the obvious easy choice.

This only emphasizes and illustrates the problems one runs into when forced (1) to choose a single word and (2) to correspond with an emotion determined on the basis of data from another culture.

Shaver et al. (1987) carried out a more extensive study to determine not just the antecedents but the entire emotion experience for five basic emotion words ("fear," "sadness," "anger," "joy," "love"). In their coding, they reduced the different stories to sets of between twenty-three and twenty-nine "prototypical features" for each of the five emotion words. Because this study retains much of the specific richness of the original responses, the prototypes, or cultural models, they describe for these five emotions will be useful as a comparative base in the subsequent sections of this book, when describing the Minangkabau and Indonesian antecedent and outcome results.

The most ambitious and systematic cross-cultural study of emotion scenarios to date was carried out by Klaus Scherer and his collaborators (1986) using subject groups from eight European countries (including

Israel) in six languages. Subsequently they expanded their study to include U.S. and Japanese subjects (Scherer et al. 1988). They elicited recent emotion experiences for four basic emotions, joy, sadness, fear, and anger, asking for "the antecedents, the reactions, and the potential regulation or control attempts." (1986:23). Their results are provocative and because of their methodological caution and self-consciousness they open the door and provide direction for further cross-cultural work of this sort.

All of the previous studies, as well as this one, have approached the question of antecedents by beginning with an emotion and asking for its cause. One example of another approach is the study of Ortony, Clore, and Foss (1988) in which all possible antecedent events are ordered in a single structure. Although they do not deal with actual data in the same way these other studies do, their results are suggestive for cross-cultural work. For example, their scheme produces descriptions of two emotions that have no single-word English labels (1988:174):

> Displeased About the Confirmation of the Prospect of an Undesirable Event
> Pleased About an Event Presumed to be Desirable for Someone Else

Another formulation is:

> Pleased About an Event Presumed to be Undesirable for Someone Else

Here there is an American English term, "gloating," but it is not included in most researchers' lists (e.g., the Shaver et al. 1987:1066 list omits it).

The potential of this approach for cross-cultural study is intriguing: to direct attention to emotions that might be overlooked because they are not at all salient in the researcher's home language. (It is hard to imagine that a German, with *Schadenfreude* in mind, would neglect the third emotion just described.)

5. Comparisons between languages

This chapter anticipates briefly some of the comparisons these cognitive maps now allow us to make between the languages. Again, thinking about the *kasih/kasiah* (love, pity) cluster, we can talk about lexical elaboration. Ever since Franz Boas discussed the many words Inuit have for snow (1911:26), we have worried about the relation between an elaborated lexicon and cultural salience. It seems obvious that cultures should have more words available in those areas of greatest cultural concern, but in fact this is more often only a slight difference in quantity.

Taking the *kasih/kasiah* cluster as an example, the single major difference between Indonesian and Minangkabau is that Indonesian has *asmara* in the Love area, while Minangkabau lacks an equivalent (compare Figs. 3 and 5). This does not seem to be a very great difference. Indonesian has six words where Minangkabau has only five. But *asmara* is Sanskrit, and it seems to be marginal as an emotion term. My sense is that it is a bit more exotic and formal than the other members of its cluster.

At this point we can note some important differences between Minangkabau and Indonesian elsewhere in the cognitive maps. For example, *marah* (anger) and *malu* (shame) are certainly two of the most culturally salient emotions for Indonesians. Anger, especially, is noteworthy for the ways in which it is supressed, managed, controlled, diverted, and masked. There is quite a luxuriant elaboration of the Anger cluster, leading us to say that although the expression of anger in other respects is minimized in Indonesia, there is a huge vocabulary available in the national language to discuss anger. But then we turn to *malu* (shame), surely no less important to Indonesians than *marah*, and there we find the opposite. In both Indonesian and Minangkabau we find that *malu* is relatively isolated. It has no cluster but is linked to only two other words, and these are not associated with each other.

5.1. Intensity

The sociolinguistic literature on Indonesian and local languages like Minangkabau or Central Javanese is ambiguous about the status of the national language vis-à-vis the local languages. On the one hand, Minangkabau and Javanese are the languages of the home and of personal relationships, including emotions, whereas Indonesian is the more formal language of national politics, business, and higher education (Anwar 1980a). Yet there are also claims that people may shift to Indonesian to say things too emotionally intense for the local language (Wolff and Soepomo 1982); and the most intense behavior of all is that depicted in the Indonesian cinema, which is all in Indonesian (Heider 1987).

Analysis of the semantic differential data for the main terms of the *kasih/kasiah* clusters suggests that for Minangkabau, their home language is indeed more intense than is Indonesian (Table 8). For this analysis the two most useful dimensions are *good–bad* and *strong–weak*. All the words in these two clusters tend to the *good* and to the *strong* ends of the scales, but we can differentiate them on the basis of how extreme they are rated – and here we see that the Minangkabau words are consistently rated more intensely (but see evidence for the opposite position in Section 7.7).

Table 8 shows, first, a sample of the semantic differential answer sheet – here for *cinta* (love) rated for *kuat* (strong) – *lemah* (weak). The second part of the table shows the percentage of ratings for each word that are one of the two strongest possibilities. The third part shows the percentage of total ratings for all six dimensions that are neutral, or dead center. In aggregate and in particular the Indonesian words are good but less good, strong but less strong, than are the Minangkabau words.

It is also evident in a translation phenomenon in emotion and other words. For example, in Minangkabau, *jae* – "naughty" – is casually used for the minor misbehaviors of children, but its Indonesian cognate, *jahat*, is reserved for quite serious adult transgressions, and when speaking Indonesian, children are called *nakal*, never *jahat*. Here we have a pattern in which there is an obvious cognate pair between the two languages, but the Indonesian word is reserved for a more intense situation. It suggests that in this area, at least, Indonesian manages to modulate the intensity of Minangkabau. Moving from Indonesian to Minangkabau, there is a kind of heating up, a linguistic red shift (and, from Minangkabau to Indonesian, a cooling down, a blue shift [See Section 7.7]). One reason for adding the Javanese data to this study is to investigate the hypothesis that the Indonesian language conveys an emotion cul-

Table 8. *Semantic differential: KASIH/KASIAH clusters*

a. Sample scoring form for the strong–weak dimension for cinta (love) (English added).

CINTA (love)

	ter/paling (-est/ most)	*lebih* (more)	*agak* (somewhat)	*lebih* (more)	*ter/paling* (-est/ most)	
KUAT (strong)	O	O	O	O	O	LEMAH (weak)

b. Percentage of choices that fall into the two extreme position (ter-/paling, lebih)

For BAGUS (good) in Indonesian

Sayang	30/34	70%
Kasih	26/41	63%
Hiba	26/41	63%
Cinta	19/41	46%
Asmara	6/36	17%

For KUAT (strong) in Indonesian

Sayang	27/44	61%
Hiba	21/46	46%
Cinta	20/45	44%
Kasih	18/44	41%
Asmara	8/43	19%

For BAGUS (good) in Minangkabau

Sayang	26/32	81%
Ibo	21/30	70%
Kasiah	20/28	71%
Cinto	19/29	66%

For KUAT (strong) in Minangkabau

Cinto	23/37	62%
Sayang	19/34	56%
Kasiah	17/34	50%
Ibo	16/35	46%

c. Between-language comparison of intensity for KUAT and BAGUS

	KUAT		BAGUS	
	BI	BM	BI	BM
Sayang	61%	56%	70%	81%
Kasih	41%	50%	63%	71%
Cinto	44%	62%	46%	66%
Hiba	46%	46%	63%	70%

d. Percentage choosing SEDANG (neutral)

	Indonesian		Minangkabau	
Sayang	27/267	10%	12/191	6.3%
Kasih	45/266	17%	34/202	17%
Cinto	63/259	24%	20/185	11%
Hiba	32/261	12%	22/193	11%
Asmara	75/260	29%		

ture that is intermediate between the relatively coarse, open Minangkabau emotion language and the relatively refined, controlled Javanese
emotion language.

5.2. Comparisons between Minangkabau Indonesian and Javanese Indonesian

Of course, both Javanese and Minangkabau speak Indonesian. But because each group comes to Indonesian as a second language, and starts
with its own language, it is reasonable to hypothesize that the Indonesian spoken by Minangkabau will be in some sense different, more Minangkabau, than the Indonesian spoken by Javanese. It happens that Indonesians readily recognize regional accents in Indonesian, and there is
a genre of jokes that hinge on mistakes that one or another group falls
into because of false cognates between languages. But here we can compare the cognitive maps of the two versions of Indonesian. Figure 5 shows
the Javanese Indonesian *kasih* cluster, derived in the same way as the
Minangkabau Indonesian cluster, on the basis of fifty responses to the
same Indonesian master list. Although in other clusters there is quite a
striking difference between the two Indonesians, here the only obvious
difference seems to be the lesser importance of *asmara* to the Javanese.
This is surprising, since *asmara* does not occur in Minangkabau but apparently does in Javanese (see Horne 1974).

5.3. Minangkabau and Indonesian versus English

An obvious difference between the two Indonesian languages and English is in the positioning of the *kasih/kasiah* clusters in relation to their
neighboring clusters. "Love," in English, if unmarked, is clearly close
to "happy." (For a reasonably similar description of emotion terms in
English, see Davitz 1969.) But in Minangkabau and Indonesian the "love"
words *cinta, berahi*, and *asmara* are more closely associated with "sad"
than with "happy" (D'Andrade [1987:141] has noted that similar associations appear in Lutz's Ifaluk work and Gerber's Samoan work). The
kasih/kasiah clusters could be glossed as the Love/Pity/Nurturance/Ten-
derness cluster. The data from the sentence completion tasks on antecedents and outcomes show clearly that this cluster is most appropriate
to parent–child feelings of tenderness. *Cinta* is used for love in a Western sense, just as *cium* (which really means "sniff") is used for Western-

style kissing, but the associations of *cinta* are not those of happy romantic love but rather those of parental nurturance and pity.

5.4. Summary: characterizing this approach

In summary, the basic differences between this approach and other comparable approaches to emotion revolve around two basic themes:

1. In this approach the data are more inclusive and more comparable. More terms are included in the three directly comparable maps that have been made of the different languages; explicit connections are drawn between the maps; more passes are made at the internal structure of the realms, utilizing different techniques; outcomes as well as antecedents for emotions are elicited; more words are used for eliciting; in eliciting antecedents and outcomes, both within and between language words are paired to encourage more precise stories and to contrast the languages.

2. The analysis of the lexicon, as well as of antecedents and outcomes, remains at a more concrete level. The mapping represents actual synonym relationships reported by informants rather than the dimensions or hierarchies of analysis; the antecedent and outcome stories are analyzed at a more concrete, intact stage rather than at the seventh level of essence.

These are the strategic choices made by an ethnographer, and they reflect to some extent ethnography's predeliction for data that are

complex rather than simple
inclusive rather than exclusive
concrete rather than abstracted.

I do not claim that one style is always preferable. However, for this project I made these choices, and it is important to be explicit about them.

6. The composite maps of emotion terms, cluster by cluster

This chapter discusses in turn each of the 44 clusters of emotion terms across the three cognitive maps that appear between Parts I and II: Minangkabau, Minangkabau Indonesian, and Javanese Indonesian. Those who wish to dig deeper will find data, analysis, and maps for each cluster in Part II, under the number of the cluster. Here I give a more general comparative idea of the characteristics of the three maps, the prototypicality measures, and the scenarios.

In these descriptions the Indonesian and Minangkabau words are italicized and the best English translations are in quotations. When close cognates are referred to, the Minangkabau word is always given first, the Indonesian word second (e.g., *gumbira/gembira*). Clusters and areas are labeled with an appropriate Indonesian word, usually the key word, and are given an English title that best approximates the meaning of the entire set. Occasionally the following abbreviations are used for languages (the Indonesian word for "language" is *bahasa*):

BM   Minangkabau
BI(M)   Indonesian as spoken by Minangkabau
BI(J)   Indonesian as spoken by Javanese

1. "Surprise" clusters (*terkejut*) (for detailed treatment of each cluster, see Part II, under the cluster number)

In each map (Figs. 1.1, 1.2, 1.3) there are about a dozen words, the same or close cognates. We see a pattern occurring in most clusters: The words that are all linked in a single cluster in Minangkabau Indonesian are less closely linked, forming several clusters, in Minangkabau (three clusters) and Javanese Indonesian (four clusters).

This is not one of the stronger "emotion" clusters according to the prototypicality measures. The key words have prototypicality of only

63% to 75%. Actually, the word with the strongest prototypicality, at 89%, is the Minangkabau Indonesian *berdebar* ("excitement"), which is peripheral to this cluster, lying off on a branch, and which seems more related to physiological manifestations like "throbbing" (*berdentut*) and "trembling" (*bergetar*) than to the real emotion words.

The scenarios show little difference between Minangkabau and Minangkabau Indonesian but considerable difference between various cognate pairs. One can distinguish two meaning areas here, better shown by the two independent clusters of Minangkabau than by the single large cluster of Minangkabau Indonesian:

1.   A negative physiological reaction to a sudden unpleasant audible antecedent (*takajuik/terkejut, taparanjat/terperanjek*). In English this would be like "shock," "startle," "surprise."
2.   A more neutral cerebral reaction to an unusual non-sudden visual antecedent (*tacangang/tercengang, heran*). In English this would be like "puzzled interest."

Then we have scenarios for a Minangkabau pair, *badabok–tasirok*: a negative physiological reaction to a sudden, usually negative antecedent (although with a substantial 35% minority of positive antecedents). The most striking difference is that the antecedents for this pair involve much social interaction, while explicit interaction did not figure in the antecedents for the other scenarios in this area.

The three Minangkabau and Indonesian clusters compared with the English "Surprise" area

For *tercengang/heran* (which we have found is unusual, not surprising, neutral, with cerebral outcomes), the Indonesian–English dictionaries give us "amazed, flabbergasted, puzzled, surprised, astonished."

For *terperanjat/terkejut* (which we have found had sudden negative antecedents with unpleasant physiological outcomes), the Indonesian–English dictionaries give us "startled, surprised," with the root *kejut* meaning "frightened, scared."

Coming at it from the English side, we can look for the comparable description of "surprise," which is the most salient term in the comparable cluster.

Davitz (1969:84) presents one picture of "surprise" in terms of outcomes. His informants choose descriptions that indicate pleasurable arousal, with no hint of the dominant negative tone of the Indonesian responses.

The *OED* definitions of "surprise" emphasize the sudden, the unexpected, and as an obsolete meaning (4.1) *OED* gives "alarm, terror, or perplexity, caused by a sudden attack, calamity or the like."

It appears, then, that whereas the "surprise' area in modern English is generally positive, its closest correspondence in Indonesian and Minangkabau is negative – more like the English "shock" or "startle." One could phrase this in either of two ways:

1.   Surprise is positive in English, negative in Indonesian; or
2.   Surprise, in English, has no exact equivalent in Indonesian but is closest to Indonesian "shock" or "startle."

The ethnography of surprise

It is not enough to be able to specify the differences in meaning between these Indonesian emotion clusters and English "surprise." We need to take a further step, to relate the Indonesian clusters to broader Indonesian, and specifically Minangkabau, cultural patterns.

Here, the Indonesian concern with order and the concomitant fear of disorder, appears strongly. Probably every culture has some concern with order and resists manifestations of disorder, but in Indonesia the focus on this dichotomy is especially strong. It has often been noted, and it pervades Indonesian life. As we shall see, it is especially evident in the emotion realm and we shall be tempted to characterize the entire central area of these lexical maps as "the emotions of disorder" (see Section 7.11).

In the "Surprise" area, we find high unpleasantness in both antecedents and outcomes, and this negative tone is strongly associated with the sudden, unexpected antecedent events. To be sure, in English there are unpleasant surprises, startles, and shocks, but the dominant tone of the surprise area is positive except, according to the *OED*, in obsolete usage.

Conversely, those few emotions in the Indonesian clusters that are not the result of sudden unexpected antecedents are not negative in tone (they are neutral).

This interpretation of unpleasant disorder is not acknowledged explicitly in either antecedent or outcome statements. The actual words for disorder do not appear. However, although disorder is not named, it is unmistakably described. What Keeler has written about the Javanese would as well describe the Minangkabau: "They fear the eruption of the unusual or conflictual in any encounter" (1983:153).

James Siegel, also speaking of Javanese patterns, says "to be surprised means always to be thrown off-base or upset in some way" (1986:211).

Further, it is worth observing that for this cluster at least, the emphasis is very much on internal states and physiological reactions. Both Lutz, for Ifaluk (1982), and Gerber, for Samoa (1985), have reported a strong emphasis on emotions as external, social, and interactive: "Samoans were primarily concerned with social interactions and important relationships in which emotion played a role. My informants almost never mentioned proprioception of bodily sensations spontaneously" (Gerber 1985:137).

This is surprising – one would have expected the Minangkabau antecedents and outcomes to be strongly interactive as well. Minangkabau and perhaps Indonesian cultures in general are strongly interactional on a scale running from inner state to interaction. But it turns out that only one, or possibly two, of the ten words examined could be characterized as having interactional antecedents and outcomes. Gerber herself notes that one of the two Samoan "startle" words, *te'i*, "is often associated with noninteractional events" (1985:141).

2. "Happy" clusters (*gembira*)

Each map (Figs. 2.1, 2.2, 2.3) has a major cluster including two key "happy" words and their cognates (*gumbira/gembira, sanang/senang*). The words that form interconnected clusters and branches in the two Minangkabau languages are scattered in three unconnected units in Javanese Indonesian. There is some cultural implication in the Javanese Indonesian isolation of the two "proud" words (*bangga, berbesar hati*). In English we lump the two prouds, "arrogant" and "happy," but Indonesians make no connection between them – the "arrogant pride" (*sombong*) cluster is discussed in Part II. Although Minangkabau incorporate the two other "pride" words in the "Happy" cluster, Javanese do not make any such positive connection. This is consistent with the much stronger Javanese tendency toward modesty, even self-effacement.

These are relatively strong emotion clusters. In both Minangkabau maps there are several words with prototypicality percentage ratings in the high 80s and low 90s.

The scenarios for the words in these clusters reveal strong differences between languages:

> when Minangkabau are speaking Minangkabau, "happiness" tends to be the result of gifts or luck more than of personal achievements and "happiness" is rarely displayed overtly;

but when Minangkabau are speaking Indonesian, "happiness" is more the result of personal achievement, and overt displays such as jumping, or smiling, are common.

We are talking here about linguistic code-switching on the part of these bilingual Minagkabau. We can go further and think of the two *cultures of emotion* available to the Minangkabau: the first, the traditional mode, when people are functioning in the regional language at home or in village life, and are in the context of traditional communal values that downplay individual achievement; the second, when the same people move into the national arena in government, business, or school contexts where individual achievement is stressed. In the schools I knew around Bukittinggi, Indonesian was used exclusively even in the first grade, and much emphasis was placed on individual competitive recitation.

An important methodological note: This strong cultural effect occurred only when a direct comparison between the two languages was forced on the informants, that is, when the pair of words used on the question sheet included one word from each language. When people responded to two words, both of which were in the same language, the scenarios all turned out like the cosmopolitan–modern pattern already described for Minangkabau Indonesian.

3. "Desire" areas (*ingin*)

This extensive, sprawling area lies between the large clusters of "Love" and "Happy," and its meanings range from "lust" to "like." Only in the Minangkabau map is there a single clear cluster.

Prototypicality ratings of these words are in the moderate range, and clearly Minangkabau do not consider them strongly "emotion" words.

Antecedent and outcome scenarios were not elicited for these words. This is especially unfortunate in the case of *nafsu*, because it is such an important word elsewhere. James Siegel (1966) has examined the meaning of *nafsu* for the Acehnese, a culture at the northwestern tip of Sumatra, not far from the Minangkabau. The word itself comes from the Arabic and refers to the animal lust of man, which is in opposition to his rationality (*akal*). *Nafsu* pulls man away from God, and a central concern of Acehnese culture is dramatizing man's struggle against *nafsu*. However, the Aceh, the most devout Moslems of Indonesia, are a people who were and are strongly and directly influenced by Arabs and Arabic Moslem theology to a degree that Minangkabau are not. True, Minangkabau consider themselves *"Islam Fanatik,"* but that is only in comparison with other peoples of Indonesia, such as the Christian Batak and the mystical or Moslem Javanese.

Single-phrase characterizations of cultures have been getting anthropologists in trouble ever since Ruth Benedict followed Nietzsche down that particular road (1934). But they can also contain important truths. Thus, looking at Indonesian cultures as variations on a common theme, we could characterize Aceh as being concerned with lust versus reason; and the Javanese as being concerned with harmonious compatability (see C. Geertz 1960:31). For the Minangkabau, however, what seems most important is order versus disorder, and for them *nafsu*, although a well-known word, has none of the theological terror Siegel describes for the Aceh. Rather, *nafsu* for Minangkabau is curiously denatured. It is used widely, the way Americans use the word "love" – one can *nafsu* ice cream, one can *nafsu* clothes, and it is all quite permissible.

4. "Honest" clusters (*ikhlas*)

In both of the Minangkabau maps these words are tied to the "Desire" clusters; but in the Javanese Indonesian map they form an isolate, for which there is no obvious cultural explanation.

This is a prime example of a set of Indonesian words whose English translations sound more like attributes than like emotions: "Honest," "willing," and "sincere," the best English translations of some of these words, are hardly emotion words. In fact, they do not even appear in the Shaver et al. list of 213 English emotion words (1987:1066). Yet the Minangkabau subjects gave them fairly high prototypicality ratings – seven of ten are 70% or higher.

This seems to be a case in which the boundaries of the realms – "emotion" in English, *perasaan hati* in Indonesian – are markedly different. Unfortunately, we do not yet have enough data to be able to explain just how this difference shows up in behavior.

The comparisons between the two Minangkabau languages and Javanese Indonesian offer a good instance of false cognation. There is an *ikhlas* in Javanese, and it is the apparent cognate to the Indonesian *ikhlas*, but it has a sense of "not caring," or "indifference" in social situations when the person gives something away or loses out (H. Geertz 1959). However this meaning does not appear in the Minangkabau scenarios of *ikhlas*. For the Javanese subjects, there seems to be some confusion between the two kinds of *ikhlas*. Even when these Javanese subjects were supposed to be thinking in Indonesian, they did not map *ikhlas* the way the Minangkabau did. Yet, when they were asked for translation equivalents of Indonesian *ikhlas* in Javanese, they did not give the Javanese *ikhlas*.

In short, it seems that the strong meaning of *ikhlas* in Javanese has seeped into the Javanese understanding of Indonesian, and has given a sense of *ikhlas* for Javanese when speaking Indonesian that is not shared by Minangkabau when they are speaking Indonesian.

5. "Tired" clusters (*letih*)

These are marginal clusters, tenuously linked to the "Sad" clusters in Minangkabau and Minangkabau Indonesian, with an additional link to the "Surprise" cluster in Minangkabau.

These "Tired" clusters make an interesting contrast to the preceding set, the "Honest" clusters. On the basis of the English translations alone, neither set seems to fall within the emotion realm. For the Indonesian languages, the prototypicality ratings suggest that although neither cluster is strongly emotional, the "Honest" clusters are much more strongly within the emotion realm than are the "Tired" clusters.

6. "Love" clusters (*kasih*)

In all three maps the "Love" cluster is situated between "Sadness" and "Happy." Indeed, the cluster itself could be glossed as something broader than "love," including "pity" and "sadness." In American English, "love" seems much closer to "happiness" than to "sadness." The Shaver et al. data support this (1987:1067): Love and joy are closely related but neither has any strong obvious links to sadness, except that a few words like "caring," "tenderness," and "compassion," which are in the American English "Love" area, do hint at such links. The cognates *cinto/cinta* and *asmara* resemble in their scenarios the American English "love," but in each language they are firm members of the clusters dominated by the "pity"/"compassion" words (*kasiah/kasih, sayang, ibo/iba*). A superficial glance at the Indonesian and the American English diagrams gives an exaggerated sense of this difference. Yet it does exist, and one can confidently point to this as an important difference between these cultures of emotion: American English "love" is closer to "happiness," whereas the Indonesian equivalents are closer to "sadness."

These words are strong members of the emotion realm. Their prototypicality ratings, especially in Minangkabau, are very high.

Table 9

	Antecedents	Outcomes
Minangkabau		
CINTO	desirable other	Help, sacrifice, emotion
KASIAH	suffering other	helps
SAYANG	suffering other, admirable child	helps
Indonesian		
CINTA	desirable other	sacrifice,
KASIH	suffering other	helps, interaction
SAYANG	admirable child	protects, helps interaction
ASMARA	desirable other	emotion, interaction

The scenarios for these words show the range of meanings in the clusters, from "pity"/"nurturance" to romantic love. (Biblical scholarship has long noted the difficulties of having to use the single English word "love" for the several Greek words *phileo, stergo, eros,* and *agape* [see, e.g., Brown 1966:538]). Here, too, we are frustrated by the poverty of English.

The dictionary translations, although more elegant, are considerably less revealing than the scenarios in Table 9. Two words, *kasiah/kasih* and *sayang,* are closest diagrammatically to the "Sad" cluster and have much of the sense of pity and nurturance. *Asmara,* a Sanskrit word that does not exist in Minangkabau, sounds more like contemporary romantic love, whereas the *cinto* "desire for another" characteristically results in sacrifice, not consummation. *Asmara* seems anomalous here, and raises interesting historical questions. Why is it found in the modern language Indonesian, as well as in Javanese, but not in Minangkabau, which until the early nineteenth century was Hindu? In fact, surprisingly little Hindu survives in present-day Minangkabau, especially in comparison with Java, and it may well be that the Hinduism of the Minangkabau royalty did not penetrate very deeply among the people. It may be that as Indonesians find more need for a word meaning "romantic love," they resurrect the Sanskrit *asmara.* In fact, the English word "love" appears in Indonesian popular songs. It, like *asmara,* does not have the strong "sad" cast that *kasih, sayang,* and even *cinta* retain. It looks as if the lexical situation here reflects broader cultural changes associated with the emotions of this cluster.

7. "Offended" clusters (*tersinggung*)

These are small clusters peripherally related to the "Sad" clusters, which are particularly difficult to match with English emotions. They are curiously misrepresented by the dictionary definitions, but they are important for Indonesians: Emotion prototypicality ratings were high in Minangkabau (83%–85%) and ranged widely in Indonesian (21%–96%).

Although the dictionary definitions offered little help, the scenarios give a fairly consistent picture: The most frequent antecedent is belittling talk, often shaming talk or even actions, often by a friend, and the result is commonly negative feelings (more sad than angry) and, rarely, retaliation. There is a hint that in Javanese (not examined directly here, of course) these words refer to an uncomfortable feeling on having one's personal space invaded.

These clusters seem to have a strong "shame" element, although it is not even hinted at in the dictionary translations. We shall deal with this ephemeral "shame problem" (Section 7.11).

8. "Longing" clusters (*rindu*)

On the maps these words are insignificant – one cluster, two twigs – but the prototypicality ratings reveal how important they are: *Rindu* and *kangen* are two of only three words in the Indonesian list with 100% prototypicality as emotions.

The scenarios show that both *rindu* and *kangen* are: the result of absence, nonpresence, or distance from another person. The *kangen* antecedents often include places rather than people, but in popular usage *rindu* certainly refers to nostalgia for places as well as people. The outcomes rarely involve another emotion, but rather some sort of action to end the separation (e.g., return home) or to ameliorate it (e.g., by writing a letter).

Rindu especially is a common word in popular songs, and the nostalgic longing for parents and the home village is a strong element in Minangkabau as well as Indonesian literature. (See, for example, Aveling's discussion of Indonesian poetry, and especially that of Amir Hamzah: "Like other Indonesian poets in the prewar period, he was concerned with melancholy recollection" [1974:27]. This was, of course, *rindu*. And Hamzah was from eastern Sumatra, near Minangkabau country.)

There is a bit of doggerel in Indonesian but written in Arabic script on a batik shawl, sold in Bukittinggi and intended to be sent to an older woman living abroad to induce her to return (I have used a copy of it for the jacket illustration):

> *Pesan dan seruan dari kampung*
> *dagang di rantau lakehlah pulang*
> *sudah tinggi rumput di halaman*
> (A message and an appeal from the home village:
> That the merchant abroad comes home soon.
> The weeds are high in the yard.)

This is the essence of *rindu*. But note that neither the word *rindu* nor any other emotion word is used, and Minangkabau indirectness is nicely shown by not talking about any person as the subject of nostalgia, but instead using the cliché image of the overgrown yard of the deserted or neglected house.

It would not be too much of an exaggeration to call *rindu* the Minangkabau emotion par excellence. This is not really a surprise – although I had not anticipated these results – for Minangkabau are famous among all the peoples of Indonesia for their pattern of temporary out-migration called *merantau*. Most Minangkabau men, and now, increasingly, Minangkabau women, have spent some years away from West Sumatra studying or earning money. The many functions of this pattern have been widely discussed (see Naim 1979 and Kato 1982). From an emotional standpoint, it is worth noting that, on the one hand, *merantau* is strongly valued and encouraged, yet is accompanied by this feeling of *rindu* for people and places far away. Interestingly enough, *rindu* is as salient for those Minangkabau who stay at home as for those who are living far away. Incidentally, there is a Polish word, *tesknota*, with a similar meaning, which Wierzbicka has suggested is "a reflection of Poland's history and the predominant national preoccupations" (1986:588).

9. "Sincere" clusters (*benar*)

These words form small clusters eventually linked to the "Desire" clusters.

The prototypicality ratings range from the moderate 55% to the quite strong 86%, indicating we are dealing with words that Indonesians confidently situate in the realm of emotion (or, actually, the realm of *perasaan hati*). But scenarios were not elicited for any of these words, and such dictionary translations as "sincere," "serious," and "sure" do not explain just how these words are to be understood as emotion words.

"SAD" AREA

The "Sad" area is both large and important. It includes fifty words in Minangkabau Indonesian and twenty words in Minangkabau, but in Maps 1 and 2, despite the internal complexity, the area itself has clearly defined boundaries with few external links. In Part II we dissect this area in detail for all three maps, but here we can present the meat of the findings by focusing on three clusters that in Minangkabau Indonesian overlap and converge on the two core "sad" words, *sedih* and *susah*. These three clusters, "Difficult," "Sad," and "Gloomy," are shown disentangled from one another in Figure 10.3 in Part II. (A fourth, extremely peripheral, cluster, "Torture" [*siksa*], will also be mentioned.)

10. "Difficult" clusters (*sulit*)

This is a triangle cluster in both versions of Indonesian, with *susah* ("worry, difficult") as the hinge word to other clusters in the larger "Sad" area. The ambivalence of these words parallels that of their English translation, "difficult." Although the primary meanings are not emotional, there is a secondary emotion meaning with "sad" connotations.

The very modest prototypicality ratings of these two distal words (32%, 46%) also reflect the ambivalent meanings.

This set is an excellent example of how a cluster can be firmly located in a peripheral position in the emotion realm.

11. "Sad" clusters (*sedih*)

This core of the "Sad" area is well represented in each of Maps 1, 2, and 3.

Prototypicality ratings are extremely high for the words of these clusters, and most of the highest words on both Minangkabau and Minangkabau Indonesian lists are in this "Sad" cluster (only the two "nostalgia" words in Minangkabau Indonesian, discussed under the "Longing" cluster [#8] can compete for saliency).

In the scenarios, suffering dominates the antecedents. But whereas in the "Love/Pity" cluster it was usually another person who suffered, here in the "Sad" cluster it is more usually the self who is suffering. The outcomes are turbulent and not masked, and compared with the outcomes of the "Longing" cluster, are much more final.

The degree of expressiveness in the scenario outcomes is unexpected. More masking or muting of sadness would have been predicted. In a rare statement about Minangkabau reaction rules, A. A. Navis, a Minangkabau writer, discusses sadness:

> Minangkabau are forbidden to moan, weep, or complain about their "sadness/difficulties" [kesulitannya] in front of others. To overcome their personal "sadness/difficulties" [kesulitan] they would rather sing or go abroad taking their "sadness" [hati yang iba] along. Moreover they don't even like to share their "sadness/difficulties" [kesulitan] with their nearest and dearest. (My translation, with Indonesian words retained in brackets) (1984:65n9)

The scenarios that emerge in this present study certainly do not reflect the reaction rules as described by Navis.

This area – and the "Sad" cluster in particular – seems to be the focus of Indonesian and, to an even greater degree, Minangkabau emotion. And the antecedent/outcome scenarios involve interpersonal relationships, specifically the severing of those relationships. Again, this is even stronger in Minangkabau than in Indonesian. Other emotions, such as love or happiness, are less central and their scenarios show less interpersonal interactions. "Happy," for example, might logically be considered the opposite of "sad," but it has a prototypicality rating much lower and its antecedents are centered on personal achievement, not on the behavioral opposite of the "sad" scenarios, namely, being with, or joining, another person. What we label the "Love" cluster, and where we might expect to find interpersonal closeness, turns out to be, in its scenarios, strongly "pity" and secondarily involves much attraction from a distance.

Thus, starting with the hypothesis of Indonesian emphasis on interaction over inner states, with the corollary that in such a culture even emotions are oriented toward interaction, then it makes sense that the prototypically strongest emotion area should also be one that emphasizes interaction most. What is unexpected is that these factors should converge on "sadness."

These Indonesian scenarios for "sad" look very much like the American English scenarios for sadness described by Shaver et al. (1987:1077), although the typical antecedent event, "disruption of an interpersonal relationship," is even stronger in the American than in the Indonesian scenarios, and the outcome of "withdrawal" is more common in the American scenarios. This is unexpected. The prediction would have been that the Indonesian scenarios would be more, not less, concerned with interaction. But in both, "weeping" is the most common outcome. (Perhaps one should specify that in the Indonesian scenarios, that is the most salient outcome. In my methodology the subjects were encouraged less to elaborate on outcome scenarios, whereas the Shaver study pushed them further.)

Although in some emotion areas there is considerable difference between the Indonesian and American cultures, in this "Sad" area there seems to be little cultural difference. If, then, "sadness" and *sedih* are virtually identical, certainly in comparison with other translation pairs, it is not surprising to find cross-cultural facial expression recognition tasks showing exceptionally high agreement scores in this area.

Such is the case in a ten-culture study on the recognition of Caucasian facial expressions (Ekman et al. 1987). Members of different cultures, European and Asian, were asked to identify the emotion expressed. Each representation was of a good example of the pan-cultural facial expression for one of six basic emotions. The Minangkabau subjects were lowest or near lowest in percent that chose the "correct" emotion attribution for five of the six emotions, but for "Sadness" they were tied for second highest. This is suggestive evidence for the hypothesis that when the scenarios of comparable emotions match in two different cultures, facial expressions will match also.

However, when we talk about exceptionally high agreement between "sad" and *sedih*, we mean only the prototypical "Sad" words. If we consider the entire "Sad" area, then important differences do appear. For example, the position of the "Love" cluster in the Indonesian maps is tangential to the "Sad" cluster, but in American English it is far away – or, at least, one has to say that the links between "love" and "sad" are not evident in the cluster analysis approach (e.g., Shaver et al. 1987:1067).

So this is an example where the focal emotion is very close cross-culturally, whereas the broader areas themselves differ.

12. "Gloomy" clusters (*murung*)

This is another set of small, multivalent peripheral clusters that, like the "Difficult" clusters, have a secondary emotion meaning. (They were identified in the two Indonesian maps but not in the Minangkabau map.) Again, there happens to be an English word ("gloomy") that captures both senses of the cluster: the physical darkness and the emotional sad-like tone. The three "gloomy" words are in the moderate prototypicality range of 54% to 71%.

13. "Torture" clusters (*siksa*)

This is a triangle cluster linked by three bridges to the "Sad" cluster, and shows up only in Minangkabau Indonesian. Its prototypicality ratings are a low 7% to 44%. It is worth mentioning only as an example of the extremely ambiguous nature of the periphery of the emotion realm. The cluster has just enough sense of "emotion" as measured by both the mapping procedure and the prototypicality ratings to warrant inclusion here.

"INDECISION" AREA

14. "Fear" clusters (*takut*)

In the two Minangkabau maps, "Fear" is a small cluster hinged to the "Indecision" cluster, whereas in Javanese Indonesian it is only a branch in the "Confusion" area, but there are obvious cultural reasons for the difference in placement. In any case, both placements emphasize the disorder aspect of fear.

"Fear" turns out to be much more complex than it would at first appear. The key and obvious "fear" word is *takuik/takut*, which is the hinge word between this cluster and the larger "Indecision" clusters. These words of the "Indecision" cluster adjacent to the hinge also seem to mean "fear," although they are clearly tied to the other "indecision" words, not to the other words of the "Fear" cluster.

The scenarios show that the antecedents for the "Fear" cluster words involve direct threats to oneself (a "fear–terror"), whereas the words of the "Indecision" cluster are more general anticipatory of misfortune (a "fear–anxiety").

But nearly a third of the scenarios for *takut*, the key "fear" word, look very much like "guilt" or "shame." They are the feelings that result from having done wrong and, usually, not being caught or exposed. This secondary scenario embedded in "fear" is quite unanticipated, and certainly not suggested in the dictionaries. It raises several methodological questions (see Part II) and also contributes another piece to the "shame problem" (see Section 7.11).

15. "Jealousy" clusters (*dengki*)

This set of strongly emotional words (with prototypicality ratings in the 70s and 80s) includes "jealousy" and "envy," a combination also found in American English data (see Shaver et al. 1987:1067).

In the scenarios the antecedents are commonly "another person is better off" or "losing a lover," but the outcomes are strongly negative, often anger, with none of the sad elements that mix with anger in American English "jealousy" and "envy."

16. "Indecision" clusters (*ragu*)

This cluster is best articulated in Minangkabau Indonesian, where it is a single cluster including "suspicion," "fear–anxiety," and "indecision." The words have fairly strong prototypicality ratings (62%–93%) with unusually little sign of weak fringe words.

The scenarios for the two "indecision" words (*bimbang, ragu*) show strong cultural differences: Although in both languages the antecedents were commonly "torn between two apparently equal choices," the outcomes were different. In speaking Minangkabau, people seem to work over the problem, often asking for advice. But when speaking Indonesian, people avoid the problem by not doing it or giving up on it. Previously, regarding the "Happy" cluster scenarios, it was noted that the strongest cultural differences emerged only when non-cognate words from the two languages were juxtaposed on the same questionnaire. If in this case cross-language elicitations had been done, we might have gotten an even better idea of what is involved in the differences between the two cultures at this point. Why should people have so much less patience in Indonesian than in Minangkabau?

"CONFUSION" AREA

This is a sprawling, intermingled group of clusters with a common thread of "confusion." Taking cues from the Minangkabau and the Minangkabau Indonesian maps, the area can be separated into five clusters:

17.   "Confusion/Stymied" clusters (*kacau*)
18.   "Confusion" clusters (*kacau–campur aduk*)

17. "Confusion/Stymied" clusters (*kacau*)

Even in Minangkabau, where it is clearest, this cluster has only moderately strong prototypicality ratings – the seven words average only 51%.

The scenarios for the only two words examined in this cluster (*bingung, kacau*) closely resemble the "Indecision" cluster scenarios. Here the antecedents are more general problems rather than specific choices, and the outcomes are withdrawal, confusion (mental or physical), and general helplessness.

18. "Confusion" clusters (*kacau–campur aduk*)

These clusters are clearly defined by the mapping procedure but are difficult to discriminate from the "Confusion" cluster (#17). Both sets of clusters have *kacau* (confusion) as the key word. These clusters have somewhat lower prototypicality ratings (percentage in the 30s) than do the previous sets. Scenarios were not elicited for these words, and the dictionary translations alone are of little help.

19. Interstitial "Confusion" clusters

It seems likely that even with more complete data this would not turn out to be a meaningful cluster. At present it appears to be only a curiosity, an artifact of the mapping procedure.

20. "Restless Anticipation" clusters (*resah*)

A well-defined cluster, especially in the two Minangkabau maps, with strong prototypicality ratings averaging 80%. The scenarios are simple: Typically the antecedents involve waiting for someone and the outcomes are restlessness or sleeplessness.

21. "Cajoling" clusters (*rayu*)

These are peripheral words with marginal prototypicality ratings: The Minangkabau average is 25%, the Minangkabau Indonesian average is 18%.

The scenarios for these clusters suggest they are actions taken in response to emotions: cheering up someone else (who is sad) or seducing someone (who is the object of one's own love or desire). Thus they seem to be not so much emotion words as words involved with emotion. Hence their peripheral position in the realm of emotion.

"ANGER" AREA

Although the Minangkabau words form a single cluster, in Minangkabau Indonesian we can disentangle four quite discrete "Anger" clusters:

22. "Anger" clusters (*naik darah*)
23. "Anger/Cruel" clusters (*bengis*)
24. "Anger/Dislike" clusters (*gemas*)
25. "Anger/Trembling" clusters (*gemetar*)

The prototypicality ratings are only moderate. The averages for these four clusters range from 50.0% to 70.5% and the Minangkabau cluster averages 66.7%. Even *marah*, the most obvious "anger" word and the key to this entire "Anger" area, is only 65%.

Scenarios were elicited for only three words, these from the "Anger/Cruel" clusters, which hardly provides enough data to sort out such a large and intricate area. It is striking, though, how much these Minangkabau scenarios resemble American English scenarios for anger. Here the antecedents are hurtful acts by others, especially naughty children, and the outcomes are physical violence and verbal abuse. Indeed, it is quite startling to find so much open reaction in these "anger" scenarios when one might have expected to find strong signs of masking anger. In their actual behavior, Indonesians, even the relatively open Minangkabau, mask most anger, and the open expression of anger is strongly disapproved of and negatively sanctioned. But in this verbal task of constructing scenarios, the Minangkabau do not reflect the real pattern of emotion management.

26. "Cruel" clusters (*kejam*)

These clusters are tied to "anger" in both Minangkabau maps, but the words appear as an isolate in the Javanese Indonesian maps. The mapping does show the clusters clearly, but the prototypicality ratings are fairly low – 4% to 46%. No scenarios were elicited for these words, but the dictionary translations do suggest some emotion content.

27. "Uncertain" clusters (*kilaf*)

These words make up a very definite small cluster in each Indonesian map with a link to "anger" in the Minangkabau Indonesian map and to "confusion" in the Javanese Indonesian map. The prototypicality ratings are low, averaging 25%. The dictionary translations are of little help, and scenarios were not elicited. These are characteristic peripheral clusters.

"ANNOYANCE" AREA

These words are close to the "Anger" area, and on the basis of the Minangkabau Indonesian map we can identify five clusters:
28.   "Annoyance" clusters (*kesal*)
29.   "Revenge" clusters (*dendam*)
30.   "Poignant" clusters (*pedih*)
31.   "Bored" clusters (*bosan*)
32.   "Dirty" clusters (*kotor*)

28. "Annoyance" clusters (*kesal*)

These words make up a clear cluster in Minangkabau Indonesian but are less clearly associated in the other two maps. This is a strong cluster, with percentage of prototypicality ratings in the 80s.

Scenarios for only two words were elicited. Antecedents involve personal failure and bad treatment from others, and outcomes commonly involve negative emotions, especially anger. These are good examples of the "way station" emotions, those emotions that lead to other emotions. This cluster acts in effect as a feeder cluster for "anger."

29. "Revenge" clusters (*dendam*)

Here are two words that act as a cluster in each map and that are linked to the "Annoyance" area. *Dandam/dendam* has very strong prototypicality ratings (80%, 86%) but *kasumaik/kesumat* shows an unusually great spread (28%, 61%).

The scenarios sound very much like the American English "revenge": Antecedents involve someone, often the self, getting hurt and the outcome is getting even. In fact, Minangkabau talk about the fine art of revenge in terms much more subtle than are captured in these scenarios:

Ideally the victims do not even know that they are the subject of the revenge act.

30. "Poignant" clusters (*pedih*)

A small cluster linked to *sakik ati* (of the "annoyance" cluster) in each map, it also has ties to "sad." The prototypicality ratings are around 70% in Minangkabau Indonesian, but in Minangkabau, *padiah* is a very strong 90%.

Unfortunately, no scenarios were elicited for this set, but it seems to correspond closely to the American English "hurt," which Shaver et al. discuss as a blend of sadness and anger (1987: 1082).

31. "Bored" clusters (*bosan*)

This clear four- or five-word cluster appears in each map. The average prototypicality ratings are moderate (52%, 67%).

Scenarios were elicited for two words, *bosan* and *muak,* in each language. The antecedents for *bosan* were repetitiousness, and for *muak,* bad behavior of another. The common outcome was withdrawal, avoidance, disengagement. In his emotion research in Malaysia, Jerry Boucher used *bosan* for the English "disgust" but voiced his uneasiness with the translation. Although in these Minangkabau scenarios there is little hint of "disgust," one can certainly see it in the adjacent *muak.*

32. "Dirty" clusters (*kotor*)

These clusters emerge clearly in the maps and include low prototypicality words as well as moderately strong ones. They include *jijik,* which seemed the best single Indonesian equivalent for the English "disgust." "Disgust" has been considered a basic emotion term in English: it is one of only a few that have a readily identifiable facial expression, indeed, a pan-culturally identifiable facial expression (Ekman et al. 1987); and it has a high prototypicality rating – 3.42 on a 4.0 scale in the Shaver study (1987: 1066). So it is puzzling why both Boucher and I have trouble finding a good equivalent in Malay or Indonesian, and why it has such an insignificant development in these three maps. In the Shaver study, disgust (with revulsion and contempt) is a subcategory of anger. But the Indonesian "disgust," both in this cluster and in the preceding "Bored" cluster, shows little or no trace of anger. There is only one direct link to "anger" on the map, and fewer than 4% of the scenario outcomes of the "Bored" cluster words are "anger."

"COGNITION" AREA

This complex peripheral area has a small cluster embedded in a large branching structure. There is a wide range of prototypicality ratings, from 25% to 90%. On the basis of the dictionary translations, the entire branch can be characterized as dealing with "cognition" (more, apparently, than with emotion). But there are small zones within the branch that are more obviously emotional.

33. "Consciousness" clusters (*sadar*)

A small cluster in each map with links to both "sad" and "annoyance." The prototypicality ratings are moderate, although *insaf* is high in Minangkabau Indonesian (89%).

34. "Depression" clusters (*putus asa*)

There are several neighboring words that, on the basis of their dictionary translations, look as if they should be linked together in a true cluster rather than just as adjacent words on branches. Their prototypicality ratings are moderate (50%) to high (96%).

Scenarios for two pairs (*putuih aso/putus asa, nekaik/nekad*) give a strong picture of depression. The most common antecedent is failure, the outcome is giving up, pondering, withdrawal, even suicide.

It has often happened in this mapping enterprise that sets of words do not quite make clusters in the Minangkabau or the Javanese Indonesian maps but are clearly interlinked as clusters in the Minangkabau Indonesian map. The "depression" words provide a rare instance where even in Minangkabau Indonesian a true cluster does not emerge. Nevertheless, it seems safe to consider that these words do form a "Depression" cluster.

"SHAME" AREA

This is a large interconnected area in Minangkabau Indonesian, although it is less integrated in the other two maps. Five clusters can be recognized:
35.   "Mocking/Disapproval" clusters (*ejek*)
36.   "Outraged" clusters (*sindir*)
37.   "Shame" clusters (*cacat*)

38.   "Lazy" clusters (*enggan*)
39.   "Respectful" clusters (*sopan*)

35. "Mocking/Disapproval" clusters (*ejek*)

These are clusters with very low prototypicality ratings (averages are 18% and 19%). The scenarios suggest that this is a strong reaction to the misbehavior of another or, secondarily, to the physical defect of another, and the outcomes are rejection, even sneering. There is very much a mixture of disciplinary disapproval, and disgust or contempt. It seems to be strong behavior, but not so strong emotion.

36. "Outraged" clusters (*sindir*)

This is another set of low prototypicality clusters. The scenarios show much emotion in the antecedents and also much poor behavior on the part of others. The outcomes run the range from passive withdrawal to fighting, with much emotion in the outcomes as well. There is a strong sense of moral and social disapproval, even more than in the previous clusters. Scenarios often use the important word *sesuai*, which means "harmonious/compatible/fitting/appropriate." It is one of the key Indonesian words used to discuss various sorts of order. Therefore this cluster is a strong, albeit not terribly emotional, reaction to misbehavior. It is not itself very emotional, although it is part of emotion scenarios. As an English label for these clusters, "outrage" hints at too much emotion, but it is better than the dictionary translations.

37. "Shame" clusters (*cacat*)

These are clusters in the two Indonesian maps only. The prototypicality ratings are weak (14.5% average). No scenarios were elicited. The dictionary translations suggest that this would be an important "Shame" cluster, although the most obvious "shame" word, *malu*, is not in this cluster but only linked to it by a bridge (see cluster 38).

38. "Lazy" clusters (*enggan*)

There are comparable small clusters in each map. The prototypicality ratings range from moderate to strong (49%–86%).

The scenarios suggest two rather different emotion zones. At one end of the cluster (*anggan/malas*) the scenarios indicate positive avoidance of unpleasant tasks or demands. At the other end the *malu/segan* pairs bring us into the "Guilt/Shame" area. In English these two words, "guilt" and "shame," are distinguished primarily on the grounds of inner versus public: Guilt is inner self–oriented, whereas shame is a reaction to other people's knowledge. This distinction is not so apparent here, although significantly, the incidence of public knowledge in the antecedents for *malu* in Indonesian is much higher than it is for the *malu* antecedents in Minangkabau (41%–11%).

The antecedents for both words in both languages involve a defect, inferiority, or misdeed by the self. The outcomes are usually withdrawal from or avoidance of, especially for *sagan/segan*, some positive act to remedy the situation. This is another piece of the "shame problem" (see Section 7.11).

39. "Respectful" clusters (*sopan*)

These are strings, not actually clusters, in all three maps, with various ties to "shame," "surprise," "contempt," and "lazy."

Prototypicality ratings are moderate (averages 52%, 49%). Also, *hormat*, although very low in prototypicality at 19%, is used as an examplar of emotion (*perasaan hati*) in the major Indonesian dictionary (Poerwadarminta). These words are clearly in some manner considered emotions by Minangkabau. The scenarios show that these words refer to proper behavior "caused" by proper upbringing (this is particularly true for *sopan*) and the presence of a superior, older, more experienced person (*horomasik/hormat* especially has this status emphasis). The outcomes of this emotion – in English one would almost say "this attitude" – are proper behavior and the respect or appreciation or love of others. If scenarios had been developed from the Javanese subjects, one would have expected a great contrast, since Javanese culture is so much more concerned with respect and status than is the relatively coarse, egalitarian Minangkabau. Indeed, H. Geertz (1959) has suggested that the Javanese cognate, *urmat*, is involved in a fear/shame/guilt area, but nothing comparable has appeared in these Minangkabau data. (Perhaps the form of these questions should have been different: Minangkabau were asked for associations with *hormat*, etc., but not for the consequences of lack of *hormat*.)

40. "Arrogance" clusters (*sombong*)

These words form large isolated clusters in each map. This is the only instance in which the Minangkabau cluster has more words than the

Minangkabau Indonesian cluster (six vs. nine). The prototypicality ratings are low to moderate, percentages in the 30s, but up to 58% to 68% for *tinggi ati/hati*.

The scenarios show only minor differences between the words. In the antecedents the person is superior in some way, quite often in terms of wealth. The outcomes are overwhelmingly social isolation – either the self breaks off relationships or others do. This pattern is different from my own intuitive formulation of the American English pattern in two major respects: Conceit or arrogance are often based on a false estimate of importance, whereas in these Minangkabau scenarios there seems to be always real superiority (at least as measured by wealth). Second, in the American English scenarios the arrogant, snobbish person associates with some but snubs other people, whereas in these Minangkabau scenarios the implication is general social isolation.

We must understand this cluster of words in the context of Minangkabau culture: First, the explicit egalitarian ethos that rejects and resents status differences, especially of wealth; and second, the persisting importance of individuals' embeddedness in the social network. In light of these two features, the type scenario of this "Arrogance" cluster resembles a cautionary tale. In no other scenarios are the outcomes so clearly the punishing or discouraging of a particular emotion, and rarely is the importance of the social life so emphasized.

"CALM" AREA

These are peripheral words in the emotion maps. They seem hardly emotion-like in their English translations, but the average prototypicality ratings for the various clusters are actually in the moderate range. Without scenarios it is difficult to make much more of them at present. There are four sets of clusters.
41. "Patient" clusters (*sabar*)
     Prototypicality rating averages: 69%, 52%.
42. "Calm" clusters (*aman*)
     Prototypicality rating averages: 63%, 63%.
43. "Quiet" clusters (*diam*)
     Prototypicality rating averages: 29%, 36%.
44. "Lonely" clusters (*sunyi*)
     Prototypicality rating averages: 32%, 38%.

7. Conclusions

7.1. The influence of culture on emotion

The central challenge of this study is to specify the extent to which different cultures have different patterns of emotion behavior and to develop the case for that linkage between emotion and culture in either causal or holistic terms. In fact, convincing causal links are notoriously difficult to establish. It is unlikely that climate, population density, gene pool, or the like will turn out to have a causal effect on local emotion behavior. But holistic interrelationships can be described. For example, an Indonesian configuration of "anger" can be related to an overall pattern of conflict avoidance.

The study was designed to contrast Minangkabau and Javanese; Minangkabau speaking Indonesian with Minangkabau speaking Minangkabau; males with females; and, in a less direct comparison, these Indonesian languages and cultures with American English and European patterns.

But what can we expect to find? Our expectations can be based on one of three main schools of thought:

1. The *pan-cultural universalism* of those who simply ignore the possible effect of different cultures. Here are found especially psychologists who investigate emotion with "American" subjects on the implicit assumption that the differences among the cultural patterns within the United States are insignificant. And also those (like Jerry Boucher) whose studies generalize to the point that cultural differences are smoothed over, with the result that there is an apparent pan-cultural uniformity in facial expression and physiological concomitants of emotion. To the extent that these psychologists recognize cultural differences they characterize them as mere ethnographical epiphenomena.

2. The *cultural relativism* of those who simply ignore or reject the pancultural findings of the facial expression research, and extrapolate from

the studies of culture that show great and genuine variations in many realms. To the extent that they recognize pan-cultural similarities they characterize them as far too abstracted and generalized to be of use in understanding behavior. Here I include most ethnographers (e.g., Lutz 1988).

3. The *compromise positions*, such as Ekman's, of those who hold that pan-cultural facial expressions are mediated by cultural display rules (e.g., 1977); or Shaver et al., who "expect that the basic level of the emotion hierarchy will look more or less the same across cultures, whereas the subordinate level will look rather different" (1987: 1083).

It is easy enough to reject the first two extreme positions and to laud the reasonableness of the compromise position. But when the compromise position is driven by theory and logic alone, not data, even it may be in trouble. For example, Shaver et al. cast doubt on Catherine Lutz's culture-specific claim for Ifaluk emotions by showing that four of her five basic level clusters are much like their American English clusters. They proceed to impeach Lutz's report, saying: "Only Lutz's fifth cluster, which she called *emotions of inability*, fails to correspond to one of ours, but it is also, by her account, the least 'unified' and so may prove unreliable" (1987: 1083).

Further, they suggest that Lutz's small sample size (thirteen informants) may be responsible for the anomalies of the fifth cluster (Shaver and Schwartz, forthcoming). Of course, these anomalies could be outcomes of research design. But they may also accurately reflect culture-specific patterns. Rather than simply reject them out of hand on methodological grounds, it makes more sense to consider them as potential clues to culture-specific emotion behavior.

This study was begun with the assumption that although a major part of emotion behavior is pan-cultural, a significant minority reflects culture-specific patterns. An 80%–20% split seemed intuitively about right, but this was just a guess, not a finding.

Now, however, on the basis of the results from this study, where the same methodology was used for the three sets of data, we can conclude that the culture-specific is not limited to the level of details or of the emotion words. Instead, in this uneven landscape of emotion, there are some words that do match across cultures, and some clusters and even larger areas that match across cultures. But there are other examples, in the same emotion realms, where not only words but also clusters and areas do not match. Here, where the same methodology was used for each of the three maps, we cannot dismiss the results as artifacts of different research methodologies. It is to these mismatches, errors, or anomalies, that we can fruitfully look for the effect of culture.

Such culture-caused differences, then, can be expected to be relatively minor, and easy to overlook or ignore if the basic mindset is pan-cultural to begin with. And not all differences that have turned up in these studies can be attributed to culture. Some are surely the result of research design differences. Especially in cross-cultural research, where linguistic and cultural translation intrudes extra sources of distortion, there can be no questions, or subject groups or answers, that are ever precisely the same. Klaus Scherer and his colleagues have been extremely sensitive to the problems of accounting for cross-cultural differences in their European research. Before claiming cultural influences, they raise the possibility that differences in national responses may be the result of such factors as seasonal variation in emotion (1986:193); in political events (at the time of their study, Great Britain was engaged in the Falklands war, Israel in the Lebanese war [1986:76]); in personal life situations (the high saliency of traffic accidents as antecedents for fear is associated with the fact that their subjects were mainly students in urban universities [1986:80]).

The challenge, then, is great. It is not enough to discover differences in emotion data gathered from different cultural groups, since these may be artifacts of the methodology, or may be the result of myriad other factors that are only vaguely cultural.

The challenge is to be able to relate such differences in emotion to other cultural features. But here is the irony of the ethnographic gap. We rarely know enough about cultures to be able to predict or even explain the specifics of emotion. The work of Scherer et al. (1986) reverberates with this anguish. They have discovered some striking emotion differences among their European samples, but even they, native European behavioral scientists, often do not know quite what to make of these differences. The various country-case studies they present in appendixes as speculative essays do make provocative progress toward laying out cultural principles relevant to emotion behavior. And, of course, here so far we are not even talking about causal explanations, but only about holistic interconnections: the relationships within a particular culture between particular emotion patterns and other patterns of that culture.

We can now summarize the results of the cluster-by-cluster analysis, looking particularly at the surprises, at those instances of striking differences among the three sets of Indonesian data, or between the Indonesian data and American English data.

7.2. The overall characteristics of the three maps

Even before we get to the level of details, a cursory glance at the overall aspects of the three maps shows differences in the degree to which clusters are interconnected and the closeness, or strength of association, between words. (Please refer to Maps 1, 2 and 3, between Parts I and II.)

Minangkabau Indonesian is the most thoroughly interconnected. It is basically a single large unit, with only seven isolates or independent units, and of these all but two are relatively inconsequential two-, three-, or four-word twigs.

In the Minangkabau map there is a major large interconnected unit, but it is smaller than the one in Minangkabau Indonesian and there are nineteen isolated units, of which five are considerable clusters in their own right.

But in Javanese Indonesian the central unit is smaller still and there are thirty-seven isolated units, of which twelve are clusters.

In terms of distances between words, the two Minangkabau maps are similar, while the Javanese Indonesian map is considerably more spread out. This difference is to some extent perhaps an artifact of the mapping procedure in a way that the interconnectedness of clusters is not. But if one looks at the bottom tier of clusters in each map, roughly from "Fear" on the left to "Happy" on the right, the two Minangkabau maps are much more tightly tied together than is the Javanese map by a ratio of about 3:1.

Thus, in terms of number of interrelationships and closeness of those interrelationships, both of the Minangkabau maps are stronger than the Javanese map, and the Minangkabau Indonesian map is stronger than the Minangkabau map.

It will be recalled that one of the original assumptions of this study was that Minangkabau people were more emotionally expressive, or open, than Javanese, and that Minangkabau when speaking Indonesian would be more emotionally open than when speaking their traditional language, Minangkabau.

The evidence of the maps speaks to the related point of cultural consensus. After all, what makes lines on the maps is agreement, and what makes those lines shorter (stronger) is that more of the fifty subjects agree on the relationship between the two words at the ends of the line.

Minangkabau speaking Indonesian show greater cultural consensus about the relationships between the various words of the Indonesian emotion lexicon. Javanese, using the same set of Indonesian emotion words, agree among themselves to a much lesser extent.

Presumably, cultural consensus is the result of overt use of, even discussion of, emotion words. So the maps represent informant agreement that reflects cultural consensus, which is a function of explicit use of words.

The original assumptions had been phrased in terms of general emotional behavior. Now the conclusions from this examination of the maps is that Minangkabau talk about emotion more than do Javanese, and Minangkabau talk about emotion more when they are speaking Indonesian than when they are speaking Minangkabau.

Khaidir Anwar, the London-trained linguist and native Minangkabau speaker, has observed, without elaboration, that "Minangkabau is not an emotive language as compared with Indonesian" (1980a:159). He was not specifically studying emotion when he wrote these words. Rather, they represent the intuition of a sophisticated multilingual scholar. The present study is an exploration of the situation that inspired Khaidir Anwar's insight.

And a prediction: When a comparable map of Javanese words is drawn up, it will complete the statement that "Minangkabau is to Minangkabau Indonesian as Javanese is to Javanese Indonesian," or:

BM : BI(M) :: BJ : BI(J)

That is, the Javanese map will be even more spread out, with even more isolated clusters, than is the Javanese Indonesian map.

Javanese reticence about emotion has often been noted. Clifford Geertz quoted a Javanese informant saying that "one's feelings should be flat, even, always on the same level" (1960:73). Wolff and Poedjosoedarmo, writing about Central Javanese, report that "direct disclosure of one's personal innermost feelings is rarely done by use of Javanese" (1982:64).

They were describing Javanese emotion talk in Javanese, and saying that Javanese switch to Indonesian when they want to be more expressive of their feelings. But these data indicate that it is all relative, and Javanese even in Indonesian talk about emotion less than do Minangkabau speaking Minangkabau (not to mention when Minangkabau are speaking Indonesian).

Finally, it is worth noting that Javanese is one of the most status-marked of languages (see, for example, Errington 1985). In the simplest formulation there are two levels, High (called *kromo*) and Low (called *ngoko*).

Table 10

	Minangkabau	Minangkabau Indonesian	Javanese Indonesian
Words in starter list	206	229	229
Total words in map	309	369	350
Average map words produced by a word in the starter list	1.5	1.6	1.5

In every case where Horne's Javanese dictionary specifies level, the words chosen by these Javanese informants for translating Indonesian words into Javanese is the Low (*ngoko*) word. I have already suggested that this may be an artifact of the research methodology. These words were elicited in a university situation, and through the national language, so it is not surprising that the students would not incorporate the words that mark status so strongly.

A second sort of general observation about the maps is that the two Indonesian maps have more words overall and that specific clusters have more words than do the Minangkabau maps. As it happens, the overall figure is illusory, since it is a function of the size of the original starter lists, as indicated in Table 10.

As the table indicates, the two Indonesian maps have more words, but these maps were based on the longer starter list, and the ratio of starter words to map words is fairly constant across the three maps. The size of the starter lists was somewhat arbitrary. But the fact that the response to the list is constant suggests that for each of the three languages, the total pool of emotion words is about the same.

This evidence has some bearing on the old question of how many emotion words a language has (see Heelas 1986). Various claims have ranged from none to several hundred. On the whole, no single satisfactory answer can be given for any language, for three reasons: (1) esoteric, archaic words can be invoked to expand (or ignored to contract) the total; (2) as demonstrated here (and for American English by Shaver et al. 1987) the category of emotion words is not clearly defined and the decision of where to draw the lines in the weaker fringe areas can drastically effect the size of the total; and (3) the use of "single words" as a criterion for inclusion is convenient but may be somewhat arbitrary. In these Indonesian lists, for example, a few two-word phrases (e.g., *sakit hati, naik pitam*) were included when they showed up regularly as answers in situations where most answers were single words; and (4) in any case, much emotion behavior, even discussion about emotion, goes on without necessarily using the emotion words themselves.

In this case, with the same explicit methodology used for all three sets, we can confidently claim that the pool of emotion words is about the same for each map. This strengthens the significance of the great structural differences already noted in the maps. Although Minangkabau and Javanese speakers are both working with the same size pool of emotion words in Indonesian, the Minangkabau speakers are in relative agreement, and the Javanese in relative disagreement, about how these words are interrelated.

7.3. The metaphor of landscape

These figures are incomplete representations on two-dimensional paper of one sort of thing that people know about emotions. It is easy enough to call the figures "maps." But I also want to take a further step and call this sort of knowledge "landscapes of emotion." This invokes a metaphor to dramatize certain aspects of the situations, but at the risk of overextending or misleading.

The aspects to emphasize are, first, that the relationship between the diagrams and the cognitive understandings are like the relationships between a map and a countryside. The map is not the same as the countryside. It omits and distorts. Yet, it can be a useful guide and within its own conventions can be judged on its accuracy.

The other aspect to emphasize is that the cognitive realm of emotion is most irregular. It is quite unlike the regularly spaced one-dimensional lists of emotion terms printed out on two-dimensional sheets of paper. One can at least allude to peaks and valleys, dry land and tidewater marshland, continents and offshore islands, to represent the irregularity of an emotional space that includes discrete clusters, cluster chains, dense or sparse areas, areas of great emotion prototypicality, and areas where strings of words become successively less emotional.

7.4. Different cluster formations in the three maps

In a few cases the maps differ in the actual formation of associations. A word or a small set of words that is strongly tied to one cluster in one map is part of another cluster in another map. For example:

1.   *Angek ati* (hot heart) is in the "Happy" cluster in Minangkabau, but

its cognate *panas hati* is in the "Anger" cluster in both Indonesian maps.

2. *Bangga* and *berbesar hati* (both proud) are tightly tied into the "Happy" cluster in both Minangkabau maps, but in Javanese Indonesian they form an isolate.

3. *Suko* in the Minangkabau maps is more closely linked to "Desire," but in Javanese Indonesian it is in the "Happy" cluster, which is an isolate with no links to "Desire."

4. The "Fear" cluster in Minangkabau is in the "Worry" area, but in Javanese Indonesian it is in the adjacent "Confusion" area.

5. *Binguang* in Minangkabau is in the "Indecision" area, but in the Indonesian maps it is in the adjacent "Confusion" area.

6. The "Poignant" cluster in Minangkabau Indonesian is in the "Anger" Area, but in Minangkabau and Javanese Indonesian it is more closely tied to "Sad."

These differences seem minor and could simply be artifacts of the mapping method. However, as a working hypothesis it has been useful to take them to indicate real differences in ways of thinking about emotions. The analyses of the emotion words in Chapter 6, and even more in Part II, attempt to relate these differences to broader cultural features, and certainly this sort of cultural interpretation is one of the continuing challenges for future research.

Powerfully suggestive guides for future research emerge from these results. From Example 1, above, it would appear that the role of "heat" in Minangkabau is different than it is in Indonesian – that "heat" is a property of or an association with happiness in Minangkabau, but not in Indonesian. A hot–cold dimension has been discussed with respect to other Indonesian cultures (see Hollan 1988; Wellenkamp 1988a), but why should the Minangkabau show this rather subtle pattern in the "Happiness" area?

The second example indicates that the Javanese are much more wary, or negative, about even the mildly self-centered "pride" of *bangga/berbesar hati* than are Minangkabau. (Not surprisingly, there is no indication that even Minangkabau view the "arrogant pride," *sombong*, with approval.)

7.5. The prototypicality ratings – membership in the realm of emotion

Not all the words that appear in the maps have equally strong status as emotion words. Not even all the words in the two master lists that generated the maps are equally strongly emotion words. We can sense this from the meanings of the words – from the dictionary translations – but the prototype ratings give an even clearer measure.

We have already discussed the overall prototypicality ratings for these Indonesian lists and compared them with reasonably similar ratings for American English emotion words.

Now, looking at how the prototypicality ratings are distributed on the maps, we find two noteworthy features:

The peak area of emotionality lies in the "Sad" area (see the discussion in Section 6.11). This is dramatically obvious for Minangkabau and only slightly less so for Minangkabau Indonesian (see Figures 10.1 and 10.2 in Part II). In American English, in contrast, the strongest words are more widely distributed: "love," "anger," "hate," "depression," "fear," "jealousy," "happiness," etc. (Shaver et al. 1987:1066).

A second feature the distribution of prototypicality ratings reveals is how the emotion category itself fades out, with lower-rated words around the edges of the maps. Or, put another way, we get some indication of what the adjoining realms are: these as yet unexamined realms with equally nonprecise boundaries adjoining the realm of emotion. It is hardly a surprise to find that the realm of emotion has fuzzy, rather than sharp, boundaries (see, for example, Fehr and Russell 1984), but it is useful to be able to demonstrate it so clearly.

The especial prototypicality of the "nostalgia" words *rindu* and *kangen* can be understood in terms of the importance of temporary out-migration for the Minangkabau (Section 1.6). It is not surprising to find that "nostalgia," the emotion of absent longing, is the ultimate Minangkabau emotion. By extension, it is not surprising to find that the general emotion peak area for Minangkabau is in the "Sad" area. Unfortunately, we do not have data on Javanese prototypicality, although I would now venture to predict that the Javanese, who are especially concerned with harmony and order, would consider the various emotions of the "Confusion" area, including possibly the "Surprise" area, as the most prototypical of all emotions.

7.6. Key words and prototypicality ratings

The key word is that word in each cluster which garners the most namings from the other words. This is a different measure from the prototypicality ratings, which measure membership in the overall category "emotion." In fact, the key word is usually not the word with the highest prototypicality rating in its cluster. This raises questions we cannot answer with the available data: If the key word is the word most referred to in the cluster, but yet not the most "emotion" sort of word in that cluster, how are we to understand these clusters? These prototypicality ratings refer, of course, to membership in the greater category. Perhaps comparable ratings for membership in the category comprising the cluster would clarify matters. But there is at least the suggestion that more is going on with these categories than just the notion of "emotion."

7.7. Translation equivalents and the blue shift

When people were asked for translation equivalents of words between Minangkabau and Minangkabau Indonesian, they gave three different sorts of responses. The least revealing choice was an obvious cognate word in the opposite language. But this choice left open the possibility that people had simply employed the standard sound shift and were not knowledgeably producing a word with equivalent meaning. The second sort of choice is more common, and is more revealing: when the words of one cluster choose the key word of the equivalent cluster in the other language. This provides strong support for the cognitive reality of both cluster and key word, which had previously been determined on the basis of within-language synonym choices. That is, the fact that all the members of a cluster behave in the same way in a task different from the task which originally established the grouping provides independent evidence for the commonality of the grouping. When all the members of a cluster in one language focus on a single word of the comparable cluster in the other language, and that word has previously been identified as the key word on the basis of within-language choices, we have again independent supporting evidence for the identity of that word as key word.

The third possibility, and the most interesting, is the choice of non-cognate, non-key words as translation equivalents in the opposite language. This occurred throughout in a minor way, but in one place – in the "Love" and "Desire" clusters (#6, #3), this third sort of choice was the norm and revealed a strong pattern of shift from intense "love"/ "lust" to less intense "sad"/"want" words.

The dominant translation choice for each Indonesian word is the next milder Minangkabau word, for the choices all step back from the intense center. This confirms the characterization of Indonesian as the stronger language, emotionally speaking, and is suggestive for future research on bilingualism and cultural code-switching in the behavior of these bilingual Minangkabau. The one surprise is that this same phenomenon does not emerge clearly in other areas of the map, nor in the "Love" and "Desire" clusters when translating in the opposite direction, from Minangkabau to Minangkabau Indonesian. If there is a blue shift from Indonesian to Minangkabau, why no red shift in the opposite direction? Probably the answer to both questions is that the strength of cognate and key word choices is so great that it overwhelms this shift pattern, which regularly appears elsewhere. (And there is a suggestion of Minangkabau as the more intense language in Section 5.1).

7.8. Scenario differences between Minangkabau and Indonesian

The emotion scenarios formed by the antecedent and outcome stories provide rich data for comparing words within and between Minangkabau and Minangkabau Indonesian, and have been pointed out in the cluster-by-cluster descriptions of Chapter 6.

For example, within the "Surprise" clusters of both languages, *takajuik* and its cognate *terkejut* are the result of suddenly hearing something, while *tacangang/tercengang* are the result of less suddenly seeing something. But in the "Surprise" clusters there was little difference between the two languages. The cultural implications of this are not immediately apparent.

In the "Happy" clusters, on the other hand, the two languages had quite different scenarios: in Minangkabau, "happiness" was the result of luck and presents from others, but when Minangkabau use cognate words in Indonesian, they understand that "happiness" is the result of personal achievement. There are also strong differences in the outcomes: in Minangkabau they mask their "happiness," while in Indonesian they display it more. Here the cultural differences between the traditional, village-centered Minangkabau and the cosmopolitan Indonesian provide convincing explanations for the differences in emotions (see the analysis in Part II).

7.9. Emotions producing emotions: way stations and end points in the flow of emotion

Most studies of emotion have examined emotions as if they were single isolated events. Prime questions have been along the lines of: What is the meaning of "anger"? (e.g., Tavris 1982). What are the facial expressions and autonomic nervous system concomitants of "anger"? (Ekman et al. 1983). What are the antecedents of "anger"? (e.g., Scherer et al. 1986). Where does "anger" appear in a family tree showing resemblances among emotions? (e.g., Shaver et al. 1987). This isolation of emotions is a valid and productive research strategy so long as it does not deny the obvious fact that actual behavior characteristically involves mixed emotions. For example, one seldom feels anger and only anger; one's face rarely expresses only anger over any period of time. Indeed, there has been considerable research on these complex emotion states evidenced in facial expression blends and other naturally occurring emotion behavior (e.g., Ekman and Friesen 1975; Rosaldo 1980; Lutz 1988).

A very general model that admits the complexity of real emotion behavior recognizes both the simultaneous synchronic combination of several emotions and the diachronic succession of emotions. This is a kaleidoscope model that, like that children's toy, allows for a complicated mixture of emotions changing over time.

Here we shall look at one dimension of the kaleidoscope model, namely, the succession of emotions over time.

One unanticipated finding that emerged from the analysis of the Indonesian and Minangkabau scenarios was the degree to which emotions showed up in the antecedents and the outcomes of other emotions. In other words, to some extent most of these emotions are linked with or dependent on other emotions, either by being caused by other emotions or by themselves resulting in other emotions. An *emotion-genic rating* was used to indicate the percentage of scenarios in which the outcome of one emotion was another emotion. Tables 11 and 12 list the antecedent and outcome emotion-genic ratings for both languages, Minangkabau and Minangkabau Indonesian, by word and also by cluster. It should be noted that these scores reflect only the appearance of emotion words themselves in the scenarios and do not include those instances when emotions may be described without the actual use of the particular emotion word.

In Tables 11 and 12 Minangkabau words are in capital letters; English glosses are in lower case; English approximations of the clusters of Minangkabau emotion words are in quotation marks. In the context of this detailed study of meanings, these English translations are quite unsatisfactory and are included only to provide the non-Minangkabau or -Indonesian speaker with some general idea of what is going on.

The ranges of the scores, both for words and for cluster sets, are similar for the two languages, although Minangkabau Indonesian has a few

Table 11. *Emotion-genic scores for words and cluster sets in Minangkabau (percentages of antecedents and outcomes that are emotion words)*

Antecedents		Outcomes	
Words	Cluster sets	Words	Cluster sets
48% BUJUAK	43% "Touched"	54% TASINGGUANG	
		52% SAKIK ATI	48% "Sensitive"
41% NEKAIK		42% SINDIA, TAGISIA ATI	
38% EJEK		41% CEMBURU	
37% RAYU		38% EJEK, CACEK	37% "Mocking"
			35% "Jealousy"
		35% CAMEEH, KIEH	33% "Teased"
31% KIEH		33% IRI ATI	
		32% SOPAN	
27% SINDIA	26% "Teased"	30% RAGU, DANGKI	29% "Respectful"
26% ANGGAN		29% GALISAH, RUSUAH	
		25% HOROMAIK	24% "Restless Anticipation"
		23% BANDING	
		22% KASUMAIK, MUAK, BINGUANG, SOMBONG	
	21% "Disappointed"	21% RASAH	20% "Touched"

Table 11 (*cont.*)

Antecedents		Outcomes	
Words	Cluster sets	Words	Cluster sets
19% CAMEEH, BANDIANG, KASUMAIK	19% "Mocking"	19% PUTUIH ASO, BIMBANG	19% "Confused"
18% RASAH	17% "Revenge"	18% RISAU, GADANG ATI	17% "Bored"
16% KASIAH			
15% TASIROK, DENDAM, CINTO		15% TACANGANG, KACAU, CAMEH, KASIAH	15% "Arrogance"
		14% CINTO	
		13% ANGKUAH	13% "Revenge"
12% SAGAN	11% "Sad"		12% "Love"
11% TAPARANJAT, SA-DIAH	"Love"	11% TASIROK ANGGAN BOSAN BUJUAK	11% "Happy"
		10% SANANG	10% "Disappointed"
			9% "Indecision"
			8% "Surprise"
7% MALU, HOROMAIK		7% HERAN, BERANG, TAPARANJAT, TAKUIK, SAYANG, GUMBIRA	
6% BANGIH	6% "Surprise"	6% IBO ATI	
5% SANANG		5% SAGAN	

4% GUMBIRA, TACANGANG, TAKAJUIK, BADABOK, MALEH, SAYANG	4% "Anger" "Respectful" "Restless Antici-pation"	4% TAKAJUIK, BADABOK, MALU, DENDAM, SADIAH	4% "Sad" "Fear" "Anger"
3% IBO ATI	3% "Happy"	2% BANGIH	
		1% GARIK	
		MALEH, NEKAIK, RAGU	
0% TASINGGUANG, TAGISIA ATI CAMEH, TAKUIK, GARIK, DANGKI, IRI ATI, CEMBURU, GALISAH, RISAU, BIMBANG, RAGU, RUSUAH, BERANG, BINGUNG, KACAU, GADANG ATI, HERAN, CACEK, SOPAN, PUTUIH ASO, SAKIK ATI, BOSAN, MUAK, SOMBONG, ANGKUAH	0% "Fear" "Jealousy" "Indecision" "Confused" "Bored" "Arrogance" "Sensitive"		

Table 12. *Emotion-genic scores for words and cluster sets in Minangkabau Indonesian (percentages of antecedents and outcomes that are emotion words)*

Antecedents		Outcomes	
Words	Cluster sets	Words	Cluster sets
		71% HORMAT/ respect	
			70% "Respectful"
		68% SOPAN/ respect	
		63% TERSINGGUNG/ sensitive	
56% DENDAM/ revenge			
		50% IRI HATI/ jealous CEMBURU/ jealous	50% "Sensitive"
48% SINDIR/ teased			
43% BUJUK/ flatter	43% "Teased" "Revenge"		
42% ASMARA/ love			
		41% SINDIR/ teased	41% "Jealousy"
40% KESAL/ annoyed			
37% KIAS/ needled		37% EJEK/, mocked TERSENTUH/ touched	
			36% "Teased"
		35% RINDU/ nostalgic	35% "Mocking"
33% EJEK mocked		33% CEMOOH/ scorn	
	32% "Mocking"	32% ANGKUH/ arrogant	
		31% PILU/ sad	
30% CEMOOH/ scorn, KUSUMAT, TERSINGGUNG/ sensitive		30% KIAS/, needled RESAH/ restless	
	29% "Touched"		
			28% "Restless Anticipation"

able 12 (*cont.*)

ntecedents		Outcomes	
ʼords	Cluster sets	Words	Cluster sets
% NEKAD/ reckless		26% GELISAH/ restless BIMBANG/ confused CEMAS/ worried	
		25% ASMARA/ love	
		23% DENGKI/ jealousy	
		22% SOMBONG/ arrogant	20% "Sad"
% GELISAH/ restless	19% "Love"	19% BOSAN/ bored	19% "Longing"
% SOPAN/ respectful			
		16% CINTA/ love	
	15% "Sentitive"	15% SEGAN/, respectful	15% "Bored"
	15% "Respectful"	PUTUS ASO/, lost hope DENDAM/ revenge	15% "Indecision"
% RAYU/, touched CINTA/ love		14% SEDIH/ sad	
	13% KECEWA/ disappointed		13% "Revenge"
% RIANG/ gay			
% MALAS/, lazy HORMAT/ respectful	11% "Restless Anticipation"	11% MUAK/, nauseated, KACAU/ confused, GENTAR/ fear, KESUMAT/ TERCENGANG/ surprised	11% "Love"
% KASIH/ love–pity			
% SENANG/ happy		8% ENGGAN/ dislike,	8% "Disappointed"

Table 12 (*cont.*)

Antecedents		Outcomes	
Words	Cluster sets	Words	Cluster sets
		SAYANG/ love-pity, SENANG/ happy, RIANG/ gay	
7% ENGGAN/ dislike, MALU/ ashamed, SEGAN/ respectful, MARAH/ angry, GENTAR/ fear		7% TERKEJUT/ surprise, MALAS/ lazy, RAYU/ touched, GEMBIRA/ happy	7% "Happy" 7% "Confused" 7% "Fear"
6% SAYANG/ love–pity		6% MARAH/ anger	6% "Surprise"
	5% "Anger"		
4% HERAN/ surprised, TERKEJUT/ surprised, TERPERANJAT/ surprised, RESAH/ restless, CEMBURU, jealous	4% "Happy"	4% HERAN/ surprised, TERPERANJAT/ surprised, MALU/ ashamed, BINGUNG/ confused, RAGU/ confused, KANGEN/ nostalgic	4% "Anger" 4% "Deceived"
3% KESAL/ dejected	3% "Surprise"		
1% GEMBIRA/ happy	1% "Fear"	1% TAKUT fear	
	1% "Jealousy"		
0% CEMAS/ worry, TAKUT/ fear NGERI/ fear, SEDIH/ sad,	0% "Arrogance" 0% "Sad"	0% NEKAD/ reckless, BERANG/ anger, BUJUK/ deceived, NGERI/ fear,	

Table 12 (*cont.*)

Antecedents		Outcomes	
Words	Cluster sets	Words	Cluster sets
KACAU/ confused, PILU/ sad	0% "Bored"	KASIH/ love–pity	
TERSENTUH/ touched,	0% "Indecision"		
TERCENGANG/ surprised,	0% KACAU/ confused		
PUTUS ASO/ lost hope, BOSAN/ bored, BINGUNG/ confused, DENGKI/ jealous, IRI HATI/ jealous, SOMBONG/ arrogant, ANGKUH/ arrogant, RINDU/ nostalgic, KANGEN/ nostalgic, MUAK/ nauseated, BERANG/ angry, BIMBANG/ confused, RAGU/ confused	0% "Longing"		

examples with higher scores than any of the Minangkabau words have. The emotion-genic scores are lower for antecedents than for outcomes: For both languages the mean is 4% for antecedents, 15% for outcomes. That is, emotions are more likely to be reported as outcomes of other emotions than as antecedents to other emotions.

We can characterize the two positions in the flow of emotion as way

Table 13

Minangkabau	Minangkabau Indonesian
4% "SAD," "ANGER," "FEAR"	4% "ANGER," "DECEIVED"
8% "SURPRISE"	6% "SURPRISE"
9% "INDECISION"	7% "FEAR," "CONFUSED," "HAPPY"
10% "DISAPPOINTMENT"	8% "DISAPPOINTMENT"
11% "HAPPY"	11% "LOVE"
12% "LOVE"	

stations and end points. Those emotions with high emotion-genic scores in their outcomes, which produce other emotions, are way stations. Those with low scores are end points. Let us look just at those eight clusters with the lowest outcome scores for each language, that is, the clusters that are most strongly end points (Table 13).

English glosses for these clusters are given in quotation marks to emphasize that the English words are only approximate indications of the meanings of the several Minangkabau or Indonesian words in each cluster. However, for the present argument these glosses are quite adequate to show a startling pattern: those emotions that are the end points in the flow of emotion for the two Indonesian languages resemble those that have been recognized in American and European research as the "basic" emotions: In their eight-culture European study, Scherer and his colleagues (1986) used Joy, Sadness, Fear, and Anger. In a cross-cultural study on the recognition of antecedents, Boucher and Brandt (1981) used Anger, Disgust, Fear, Happiness, Sadness, and Surprise. Ekman and his collaborators, in their ten-culture study (Ekman et al. 1987), used the same six emotions, and there is good additional evidence for Contempt (Ekman and Heider 1988). Shaver et al. (1987), in their American English study, produced prototype scenarios for Fear, Sadness, Anger, Joy, and Love. Izard and Buechler (1980:168) claim Interest, Joy, Surprise, Sadness, Anger, Disgust, Contempt, Fear, Shame/Shyness, and Guilt. It would seem too much to expect a definitive determination of what is and what is not a "basic pan-cultural emotion," but these studies do suggest strong agreement on some of the more basic, more pan-cultural of the emotions. And of the eight emotion clusters that are most strongly end points in the two languages (those with the lowest emotion-genic scores), five or six are the previously identified "basic" emotions.

Turning to the six clusters with the highest scores – clusters we are

Table 14

Minangkabau	Minangkabau Indonesian
48% "Sensitive" (TASINGGUANG)	70% "Respectful" (SOPAN)
37% "Mocking" (EJEK)	50% "Sensitive" (TERSINGGUNG)
35% "Jealousy" (DANGKI)	41% "Jealousy" (DENGKI)
33% "Teased" (SINDIA)	36% "Teased" (SINDIR)
29% "Respectful" (SOPAN)	35% "Mocking" (EJEK)
24% "Restless Anticipation" (RUSUAH)	28% "Restless Anticipation" (RUSUH)

calling the "way stations" in the flow of emotions because they produce other emotions with the greatest frequency – we find a very different set of emotions (Table 14).

Again, these English glosses are reasonable approximations for the words in the Minangkabau and Indonesian clusters. First we can note that six of these eight are the same (or close cognates) in the two languages, and six of the top six are the same (or close cognates). This is strong testimony both to the similarity of the two languages used by the Minangkabau and to the power of the methodology.

That there are such end points and way stations in the flow of emotion is not really surprising, for it accords well with our own intuition; but because most American and European emotion research has been focused on only a few emotions, and those the ones that are both "basic" and end points, we have had less need to think about emotions as way stations in the flow of emotion.

These six clusters, whose words most strongly produce other emotions, are certainly complex emotions. There has been no suggestion that they are associated with specific facial expressions as are some "basic" emotions (Ekman, et al. 1983). In fact, except for "Jealousy" they do not correspond easily to clusters in the English category of "emotion" (see, for example, Shaver et al. 1987).

We can now turn to the prototypicality ratings, shown in Table 15, for these way station emotion words. The words in question range greatly in their prototypicality ratings, or membership in the Minangkabau and the Minangkabau Indonesian realms of emotion. That is, the way station words, producing other emotions, are not "basic," but some, especially those in the "Sensitive" and "Restless Anticipation" clusters, are strongly prototypical emotion words for these Indonesians.

Table 15. *The six "way station" emotion clusters*

Minangkabau	Minangkabau Indonesian
1. "Sensitive" cluster	
TASINGGUANG/sensitive	TERSINGGUNG/sensitive
P:85%; E:50%; 11/14 to "anger"[a]	P:71%; E:63%; 13/14 to *MARAH*/ anger
TAGISIA	TERSENTUH/touched
P:83%; E:42%; 8/11 to "sad"	P:57%; E:37%; 5/10 to "sad"

Emotion-genic examples for "Sensitive" cluster words in Minangkabau Indonesian:

Karena dia TERSINGGUNG, dia marah kepada kakanya.
Because she was sensitive, she was angry at her older sibling.

Karena dia TERSENTUH, dia sedih hatinya.
Because she was touched, she felt sad (in her heart).

2. "Mocking" cluster (EJEK)	
CEMOOH	CAMEEH/scorn
P:20%; E:34%; to several clusters	P:11%; E:33%; to several clusters
EJEK	EJEK/mock
P:18%; E:38%; to several clusters	P:11%; E:37%; to several clusters
CACEK	
P:15%; E:38%	

Emotion-genic examples for "Mocking" cluster words in Minangkabau Indonesian:

Karena dia MENGEJEK, dia dimarahi oleh para gurunya.
Because she was scornful, her teachers were angry at her.

Karena dia MENGEJEK, dia senang hatinya.
Because she was scornful, she was happy.

Karena dia MENCEMOOH, dia dibenci orang.
Because she was scornful, she was hated by people.

Karena dia MENCEMOOH, dia gembira.
Because she was scornful, she was happy.

3. "Jealousy" cluster (DENGKI)	
DANGKI	DENGKI/jealousy
P:58%; E:29%; to negatives	P:63%; E:23%; 5/6 to BENCI/hate
IRI ATI	IRI HATI/jealousy
P:73%; E:33%; to negatives	P:82%; E:50%; 5/6 to BENCI/hate
CEMBURU	CEMBURU/jealousy
P:85%; E:40%; 6/11 to "anger"	P:93%; E:50%; 8/13 to "anger"

Emotion-genic examples for "Jealousy" cluster words in Minangkabau Indonesian:

Karena dia DENGKI, dia selalu membenci orang itu.
Because she was jealous, she always hated that person.

Karena dia IRI HATI, dia tidak senang melihat orang itu.
Because he was jealous, he didn't like to see that person.

Table 15 (*cont.*)

Minangkabau	Minangkabau Indonesian

Karena dia CEMBURU, dia marah pada pacarnya itu.
Because he was jealous, he was angry at his girl friend.

4. *"Teased" cluster (SINDIR)*

Minangkabau	Minangkabau Indonesian
SINDIA	SINDIR/teased
P:15%; E:42%; to negatives	P:71%; E:41%; to negatives
KIEH	KIAS/needled
P:8%; E:35%; to negatives	P:11%; E:30%; most to negatives
BANDIANG	
P:10%; E:23%; to negatives	

Emotion-genic examples for "Teased" cluster words in Minangkabau Indonesian:

Karena MENGIAS, dia merasa puas terhadap perbuatannya.
When he teased, he felt comfortable about it.

Karena dia MENYINDIR, dimarahi orang tua itu.
Because she teased them, her parents were angry with her.

5. *"Respectful" cluster (SOPAN)*

Minangkabau	Minangkabau Indonesian
SOPAN	SOPAN/respect
P:23%; E:32%; 5/9 to "love"	P:39%; E:67%; 9/19 to "happy"
HOROMAIK	HORMAT/respect
P:na; E:25%; to positives	P:19%; E:71%; 10/20 to "respect"

Emotion-genic examples for "Respectful" cluster words in Minangkabau Indonesian:

Karena dia HORMAT, dia disegani oleh kawan dan lawannya.
Because he was respectful, he was honored by friend and foe.

Karena dia SOPAN, dia disenangi oleh semua orang.
Because he was respectful, he was liked by all.

6. *"Restless Anticipation" cluster (RESAH)*

Minangkabau	Minangkabau Indonesian
RASAH	RESAH/restless
P:88%; E:21%; 3/6 to "not calm"	P:75%; E:29%; 8/27 to "not calm"
GALISAH	GELISAH/restless
P:90%; E:28%; to negatives	P:96%; E:25%; to negatives
RISAU	
P:100%; E:17%; to negatives	
RUSUAH	
P:100%; E:28%; 4/8 to "sad"	

Emotion-genic examples for words of the words of the "Restless Anticipation" cluster in Minangkabau Indonesian:

Karena die GELISAH, dia menjadi ketakutan tidak menentu.
Because of his restlessness, he felt a general fear.

Karena dia RESAH, dia kelihatan tidak tenang.
Because of his restlessness, he seemed ill at ease.

[a] "11/14" means 11 out of 14 references are to "anger."

Table 15 shows the six cluster sets, called the "way stations," that have the highest emotion-genic outcomes (they are the same in both Minangkabau and Minangkabau Indonesian). For each cluster, each word and its very approximate English gloss is given (these words, because of their very complexity, are especially difficult to translate satisfactorily with a single English word). The table also indicates, for each word, the prototypicality rating (P), as well as the emotion-genic outcome score (E), which is the percentage of outcomes involving emotion words. Finally, the table describes the sorts of emotions given as outcomes (with, in some cases, the fraction of the emotion words that are concentrated on one cluster or word).

The table also indicates which other emotions are given as outcomes to these words. In a few cases, one of these words is a way station to a specific other cluster. For example, *tasingguang/tersinggung* (sensitive) feeds into "Anger." But in the same cluster, *tagisia* and *tersentuh* (also sensitive) both result in "Sadness." For the most part, the outcome emotions are not limited to a single other cluster but at best can be characterized as to tone (generally negative or, in just one case, positive).

In some cases the scenarios described by these Minangkabau informants refer to only a single actor. In other cases the outcome emotions, the ones produced by the first emotions, are the emotions of another person. In the example "Because she was jealous, she hated that person," the subject feels hatred as an outcome of her own jealousy. But in another example, "She felt scornful, causing her teachers to be angry with her," her scorn has caused anger in others. Even though the form of the first part of the elicitor sentence suggested focusing on only one person ("When she was *X*, she . . ."), when the Minangkabau respondents completed the sentences they often took advantage of the easily available passive form to introduce the emotions of a second person into the scenario.

Thus, the emotion scenarios described by the informants may involve a single person or may be explicitly interactional. This option in talking about emotion appears also in research traditions, where we find some scholars treating emotion as a single-person event (e.g., much of Paul Ekman's work, such as Ekman et al. 1988), while others (e.g., de Rivera and Grinkis 1986) emphasize its interactional nature. There have also been attempts to characterize emotion styles of some cultures as interactional or noninteractional (Lutz 1982). Certainly the distinction between interactional and individual-centered behavior is illuminating for some spheres of behavior. But the data now at hand demonstrate that emotion behavior has both interactional and individual aspects and that either can be emphasized in casual talk as well as in research approaches.

It is worth noting that in her study of Ifaluk emotion, Lutz has discussed the ways in which one emotion produces another emotion in another person. Her examples are of how "justifiable anger" causes "fear," or how "happiness/excitement" causes "excitement/jealousy" (1988:167, 212). In the Ifaluk examples, however, both way stations and end points seem to be basic, whereas, of course, in this Minangkabau case it is more often the non-basic emotions that cause other emotions.

The occurrence of emotions in the antecedents and the outcomes of scenarios for other emotions argues for a model of emotion behavior that is complex synchronically, diachronically, and interactionally. In the normal flow of behavior, emotions occur simultaneously with other emotions, emotions cause other emotions, and the emotions of one actor trigger other emotions of other actors.

The concept of "basic" emotions is supported by these data. Actually, the basic emotions used in Western research are not given uniformly high prototypicality ratings in Indonesia. But they are strongly identified by their uniformly low emotion-genic scores: They are end points, not way stations, in chains of emotion behavior.

The ease with which Minangkabau describe emotions both as individual-centered and as interactions suggests that these two qualities, although conceptually important, are not mutually exclusive but rather are different aspects of the same complex phenomenon, emotion.

Similarly, both sides of the pan-cultural versus culture-specific debate are supported by these data. In one area of emotion behavior, namely the end points of the emotion chains, we find these Indonesian data resemble closely American and European results. In the area of way stations, however, we find words that hardly seem emotion at all from a Western standpoint and that thus argue for a strong culture-specific pattern.

In short, these data make a strong case for a recasting of the terms of contemporary debate on emotion. We cannot look for answers to individual versus interaction or culture-specific versus pan-cultural simply by considering emotion systems as wholes. Rather, intensive and extensive examination of particular systems reveals the heterogeneity of the internal structure and dynamics. The questions might better be: Where in an emotion system is the individual, where the interaction? Where is the pan-cultural, where the culture-specific?

7.10. Indonesian languages versus American English

Although we do not have precisely comparable American data to set against these maps and scenarios from Indonesia, there are several obvious differences:

1. In these Indonesian scenarios, the words of the "Surprise" cluster are strongly negative (see Chapter 1). In American English, surprise itself tends to be a positive experience. In the scenarios Davitz developed for Surprise, the elements are all positive (1969:84). Intuitively I would say that his methods have resulted in an exaggeratedly positive tone. Most surprises are indeed pleasant, but one can easily think of unpleasant surprises. But if we think of the more general cluster of "Surprise," there are clearly other, more unpleasant members: "startle," "shock," "alarm." Although in the analysis by Shaver et al. (1987:1067) Surprise is grouped only with Amazement and Astonishment, two other positive emotions, yet on the whole we can say that Surprise tends to be a positive experience in America but a negative one in Indonesia. This reflects the different cultural attitudes toward order and disorder. For Indonesian, disorder is both important and negative. For American and Europeans, "a slight disorder" can be positively stimulating.

2. The *tersinggung* cluster has the meanings of "sensitive" and "(physical) touching," and is for Indonesians quite negative, whereas "touching" in American English can be either positive or negative. Here we do not find comparable emotion scenarios to help, but we can turn to proxemic research. O. Michael Watson (1970) has distinguished between high contact cultures (e.g., Italian) and low-contact cultures (e.g., Polish). It is difficult, however, to characterize the United States in these terms because the various American subcultures run the gamut from high to low contact (Carucci et al. 1989).

Nevertheless, all cultures calibrate personal space, which is the distance between people, so that there is an optimal zone as well as distances too close or too far for comfort (Hall 1959). In American English, this space can be described with either positive or negative terms (snuggling vs. pawing). But in the Indonesian scenarios the comfortable distance seems to be overwhelmed by a negative cast to the whole subject of space. We can generalize by saying that "touching" in Indonesia is mainly negative, whereas in American English it may be either negative or positive. But since this *tersinggung* cluster is one of the least translatable of emotion terms, comparison is difficult. So we can further observe the following:

3. In addition to *tersinggung*, there are several other clusters that, although strongly emotional in Indonesia, are not even counted in the "emotion" category in American English ("Seriousness," "Honesty," "Indecision").

4. "Pride," in American English, covers a great deal of ground that in Indonesia is found in two unrelated clusters:

a. happy pride (*bangga*) and
b. arrogant pride (*sombong*)

5. The emotions in Indonesia that are most "emotional," those with the highest prototypicality ratings, are in the "Sad" area, especially in Minangkabau. Although Sad is an important emotion in English, it does not have the same saliency. On the other hand, Anger, which is very salient as an emotion in English, and certainly refers to important behavior in Indonesia, as much for its supression as for its expression, is not very salient as an emotion.

6. The cluster with the highest prototypicality rating is "Longing" (*rindu* and *kangen*). This is the emotion of longing and nostalgia for what was left behind. In addition the hallmark of Minangkabau culture is *merantau*, going to distant lands to seek fortune and experience. I did not anticipate such an obvious fit, but it is hard to dispute these findings that *rindu* is the prototypical emotion for Minangkabau.

7. "Fear" (*takut*) has a very strong secondary sense of "guilt," something that is not totally farfetched for an American English speaker, but certainly guilt does not play such an obvious role in the immediate scenarios of American English fear (see Davitz 1969:54). However, Philip Shaver, in a personal communication, reports that "fear of getting caught" did appear in his 1987 data on fear.

8. In the English scenarios for Jealousy and Envy, a possible outcome is sadness in addition to anger (Davitz 1969:68), but Indonesians react to "jealousy" and "envy" with more unalloyed maliciousness.

9. Several sets of words that form good and normal clusters in the Indonesian maps are not easily translated by a single English word. *Takut*, because of its mixture of fear and guilt, is an example, but nevertheless I have called it "Fear." For *risau*, I have used the phrase "Restless Anticipation"; for *tersinggung*, I have tried "Sensitive."

10. The scenarios for "Arrogant Pride," *sombong*, indicate that the

person is in fact superior, whereas the arrogantly proud person in American English may be superior but is more often merely imagining superiority.

7.11. The crucial issues

Finally, these data allow us to address several important issues dealing with emotion in general and particularly with emotion in Indonesia:

1. Do these Indonesian data confirm the hypothesis that Indonesian emotions are more socially oriented, less concerned with inner states?

2. Does the strong Indonesian cultural concern with order versus disorder show up in emotion behavior?

3. Are display rules – those cultural norms for the management of public emotion – reflected in these data?

4. Do these Indonesian data confirm the hypothesis that Indonesians are concerned more with guilt than with shame?

5. Are those emotions that have been recognized as basic in the European research tradition also basic in Indonesia?

And finally, the most important question, lying behind all the others:

6. How does (Indonesian) culture influence emotion behavior?

The question of inner states versus interaction

There is good reason to say that Minangkabau and other Indonesian cultures place more emphasis on social interaction and social relationships than they do on internal states of autonomous individuals.

This argument relies not on an absolute distinction between some sort of ideal types of "interaction cultures" and "individualistic cultures." Instead, in many areas where Western cultures tend more to emphasize autonomous individuals, Indonesian cultures emphasize social interaction (Heider 1984). A dramatic example is the way in which marriages are determined: by the man and woman themselves, or by negotiations between family groups. A more banal example is the final freeze-frames of sentimental movies. American movies end with the two lovers, alone. Indonesian movies end with the two families, reunited (Heider 1991). To be sure, people investigating American emotions (e.g., de Rivera and Grinkis 1986; Shaver and Schwartz, forthcoming) have found it useful, even necessary, to look at them as social interaction and bridle at claims that interaction is particular to the "Them," or other, exotic, cultures (e.g., Lutz 1982). But even after all the necessary qualifications – They do have feelings inside; We do have social relationships – it is a reasonable and useful proposition that in their talk and in their behavior Indonesians emphasize relationships more than do Americans.

It can further be hypothesized that for Minangkabau this interaction emphasis will be stronger when they are speaking Minangkabau than when they are speaking Indonesian, since the language spoken at any particular time is not chosen at random but reflects the nature of the behavioral setting, whether traditional/home or national/cosmopolitan.

But to what extent does any of this show up in the emotion data?

The emotion scenarios for "Happy" do strongly support the Indonesian versus Minangkabau part of the hypothesis. There, the antecedents for happiness in Indonesian are primarily attributed to personal achievement, whereas in Minangkabau the "Happy" antecedents give slightly stronger emphasis to luck and gifts than to personal achievement.

"Sad," the strongest, most prototypical Minangkabau and Indonesian emotion area, greatly emphasizes interaction in its antecedents, but so does the Sad scenario reported by Shaver et al. for American English (1987:1077).

The "Surprise" area is on the whole not concerned with interaction and the outcomes are strongly negative. But one pair of words in Minangkabau, *tasirok* and *badabok*, are unusual in having much interaction in their antecedents and being (at least *badabok*) positive in their outcome. This suggests support for the hypothesis, formulated as: noninteraction is negative, interaction may be positive.

On the whole, though, the evidence is not overwhelmingly strong, and Indonesian interaction scenarios are not greatly more prevalent than the emotion scenarios reported from American and European sources.

The most dramatic evidence appears in the outcome for "Arrogant Pride" (*sombong*): Although the person is usually in fact superior, when they feel *sombong* the outcome is very explicitly social isolation. *Sombong* people remove themselves or are removed by others from society and social ties.

The question of order versus disorder

Certainly every culture is perforce concerned with order and disorder, but in Indonesia and Minangkabau in particular there is an unusually strong emphasis on creating and encouraging order, and an aversion to disorder. (Wellenkamp 1988a discusses a similar pattern among the Toraja of South Sulawesi, Indonesia.) So it is reasonable to expect this concern to appear in the emotion behavior.

"Surprise" is a prime emotion of disorder – of the unexpected, the disorienting – and in both Minangkabau and Minangkabau Indonesian the outcomes are strongly negative. On balance, in American English, unmarked or unqualified surprise is more likely to be a positive, happy emotion, and is highly valued. But in Indonesian, where disorder is anathema, "Surprise" is overwhelmingly negative.

Further, there is a large area in all three maps that could be called the "Zone of Disorder," comprising the areas of "Confusion" and "Indecision," with outliers of "Fear" and "Jealousy," the whole sandwiched between "Sadness" and "Anger." In English, confusion and indecision are hardly emotions at all. They do not appear in the Shaver et al. list of American English emotion words (1987:1066), and the American English areas of "Fear" or "Anger" or "Surprise" at most only hint of confusion or indecision. The extent and the centrality of these emotions of confusion in Indonesian and Minangkabau, then, strongly reflect cultural concerns with order and disorder.

The question of display rules

Paul Ekman's concept of "display rules" has been an invaluable contribution to understanding the relationship between the cultural and the pan-cultural in emotion (Ekman and Friesen 1969), but as yet display rules are referred to more anecdotally, or invoked to explain anomalies. No one has yet drawn up a systematic description of the display rules of any language or culture.

We would expect evidence of display rules in these emotion scenarios, but the evidence is surprisingly sparse and unexpected.

The most important display rules in Indonesian – perhaps in any culture – concern the control and masking of anger. There are variations among the regional cultures of Indonesian, with Javanese representing the extreme of masking, and Minangkabau lying more toward the open, unmasked end of the scale. (Unfortunately here we do not have emotion scenarios from Javanese to compare with the Minangkabau data.)

From the Minangkabau scenarios in both Minangkabau and Indonesian (see Table 16) the display of anger is very frequent, the masking of anger is not mentioned at all, and at best we can count withdrawal as a way of not showing anger. Clearly, when the Minangkabau subjects gave their scenarios for Anger, they did not offer a masked, Javanese-like display rule for that emotion.

The best evidence for a display rule is in the "Happy" cluster, where happiness is strongly masked in Minangkabau outcomes but not in the

Table 16. *Number of scenario outcomes involving display of anger versus concealment of anger for six sets of scenarios for four Anger words in Minangkabau and Minangkabau Indonesian*

	Showed anger (%)	Concealed anger (%)
Minangkabau:		
BERANG (of 27)	74	0
BANGIH (of 27)	52	7
BANGIH (of 60)	55	25
Minangkabau Indonesian:		
BERANG (of 27)	37	19
MARAH (of 27)	59	4
MARAH (of 60)	62	7

Indonesian outcomes. This is in line with the prediction and is surprising only because it does not appear in the "Anger" area as well.

The question of shame versus guilt

Considering how popular shame and guilt are as topics in anthropological writing, it is strange that they should be so difficult to locate in these maps. Other emotions do not pose this problem: such important American English emotions as Sad, Anger, and Fear have readily recognizable counterparts in Indonesian and Minangkabau. However, we have already mentioned some instances where the Indonesian clusters do not have a precise equivalent in English. Shame and Guilt may well be examples going the other way, where clear American English concepts are more difficult, diffuse, and problematical in Indonesian.

Shame is an easier case. Certainly the single-word translation equivalent, Shame = *malu*, is obvious. But according to expectations, *malu* is so salient in Indonesian thinking that it should be the center of an important cluster. Instead, it is peripheral in each map: a dead-end twig in Minangkabau; in Minangkabau Indonesian, linked to three small clusters but member of none; and on a twig in Javanese Indonesian. Some of its neighbors seem to be also "Shame" words, but there is no convincing cluster.

And at the same time the scenarios for the *tersinggung* cluster (belittling talk by a friend) look very much like "Shame" antecedents, yet this cluster is far from *malu*, and they have no links.

The situation for guilt is even more problematical. No good Indonesian or Minangkabau words for guilt showed up during the compilation of the master lists, nor did any appear in the final elicitations. Yet *takut*, in the "Fear" cluster, has the strong secondary scenario that looks like "guilt."

It is not possible to resolve the status of Shame and Guilt with these data. At present we can best say that we have identified some emotion terms and clusters that are clearly defined in one language but do not have clear counterparts in the other.

The question of basic emotions

In the course of research on emotion a few emotions have been identified that seem to be basic. They are salient (Fehr and Russell 1984; Shimanoff 1984); they are associated with specific facial expressions (Ekman 1977) and even autonomic nervous system activity (Ekman et al. 1983); and they show great stability across cultures (Ekman et al. 1987). The evidence for the pan-cultural nature of at least a few emotions is very strong, particularly in terms of their association with specific facial expressions (e.g., Ekman et al. 1987). The utility of these basic emotions in cross-cultural research has been recognized often (e.g., Scherer et al. 1986).

Here we can turn to the variations, to ask from the Indonesian perspective just how good do these basic emotions look.

In their eight-culture European study, Scherer and his colleagues (1986) used Joy, Sadness, Fear, Anger. In a cross-cultural study on the recognition of antecedents, Boucher and Brandt (1981) used Anger, Fear, Happiness, Sadness, and Surprise. Ekman and his collaborators, in their ten-culture study used the same six emotions, and there is good additional evidence for Contempt (Ekman and Heider 1988). Shaver et al. (1987), in their American English study, produced prototype scenarios for Fear, Sadness, Anger, Joy, and Love. We cannot expect a definitive determination of what is and what is not a "basic pan-cultural emotion," but these studies suggest a list of eight emotions to think about.

The evidence from the Minangkabau subjects who have taken part in the cross-cultural experiments dealing with each of these emotions except Love clearly support the basic cross-cultural nature of the emotions in general terms (see Ekman et al. 1987; Ekman and Heider 1988). But the Minangkabau and Minangkabau Indonesian versions of these eight emotions show goodness-of-fit with the pan-cultural expectations more or less in this descending order:

Sadness, Anger, Happiness, Surprise, Love, Fear, Disgust, Contempt

For the first four on the list, Minangkabau and Minangkabau Indonesian are quite close to the pan-cultural pattern. The others are increasingly problematic, showing stronger and stronger culture-specific features.

Love in both of these Indonesian languages is mixed with Pity, and in the maps is close to Sad, not, as in English, close to Happy.

Fear has a secondary scenario of Guilt, which appears to be absent in English. (However, Philip Shaver, in a personal communication, has suggested that with a different methodology, the guilt element would emerge in American English fear scenarios.)

But these first six words each have obvious single-word translation equivalents in Minangkabau and Indonesian and each is part of a clear and obvious cluster of words. Disgust and contempt, however, are difficult to translate into Minangkabau and Indonesian and do not form good clusters. Single words for disgust would be *jijik* in Indonesian, and *jajok* in Minangkabau, but *jijik* is part of a minimal triangle cluster with "Dirty" (*kotor*) in both Indonesian maps, whereas *jajok* is not part of a cluster at all in Minangkabau.

Contempt can be translated as the phrase *memendang rendah*, literally "to look down on," in Indonesian, but that phrase did not emerge clearly at all in any of the three maps. Certainly the Minangkabau subjects in the experiments (Ekman et al. 1987; Ekman and Heider 1988) had no trouble recognizing and using these terms for contempt and disgust. From the test results there would be no reason to suspect anything unusual in the Minangkabau concepts for these two emotions. The evidence of the maps, however, clearly suggests that they are less clear, less discrete, in Indonesian than they are in English.

The best accounting for this puzzle seems to be along the lines used to explain the differences between the Minangkabau and the Javanese maps themselves (see Section 7.2). The maps represent cultural consensus. In a cluster like "Arrogant Pride" (*sombong*) most of the informants produce the same synonyms; as a result, the map shows many words close together. But the areas of "Contempt" and "Shame" evidence much less consensus. For the earlier argument I suggested that Javanese simply discuss emotions less. They know the words but they do not openly puzzle over them.

Here it looks as if even Minangkabau, who do reach strong agreement on many areas of the emotion landscape, back off when it comes Contempt, Shame, and the like. It is certainly not possible to argue that

Table 17

Emotion	Named by (of 14)
Anger/rage	12
Fear/terror/panic	12
Joy/happiness	8
Disgust/aversion	8
Sadness/dejection/grief	6
Surprise	5
Love	4
Contempt	4
Shame	3
18 others	2 or 1

these are obscure or unimportant emotions. But it does appear that of all the major emotions, these are the most sensitive and so the least discussed openly.

A new body of evidence supporting the idea of pan-cultural basic emotions has emerged from the scenario analysis, in which emotion "end stations," which do not themselves result in other emotions, closely match the previously identified basic emotions (see Section 7.9 above). If this pattern holds up in replications with other cultures, it will provide a powerful new criterion for basic emotions.

The concept of basic emotions has been criticized by Ortony et al. (1988:25) on the grounds that there is much disagreement as to what they are, and that there are no criteria for determining "basic emotions." Both criticisms are ill-founded. Even the table provided by Ortony et al. (1988:27), which lists those emotions claimed as basic or fundamental by fourteen studies, is maximally confusing. If it is rearranged, though, it is clear that there has been remarkable consensus (Table 17).

But even more crucial is the fact that there are the criteria of facial expression, autonomic nervous system activity (ANS), prototypicality, and now positions as end stations, or nonproducers of other emotions in the flow of emotion. In short, there is a good deal of fairly suggestive evidence for some basic emotions. But even as this Minangkabau study supports the idea of basic emotions, it offers evidence that these basic emotions are not precisely the same cross-culturally.

The work that produced the list of basic emotions was done mainly in English, or at least by speakers of closely related European languages.

Despite the strength of the findings, there is always the nagging suspicion that this work has been influenced however subtly by the European patterns of emotion. Here we can address the question of whether the Indonesian data suggest any other "basic" emotions that might have been overlooked in the Western research traditions.

Reviewing those words with the highest prototypicality ratings, one might suggest – for Minangkabau Indonesian, at least – the small but strong "Longing" cluster (with *rindu* and *kangen*). In both languages the high prototypicality ratings, as well as the large clusters, suggest that "Confusion" in the "Confusion"/"Indecision" areas would be basic. This would be further supported by the presence of "Indecision" clusters in both languages at the low end of the emotion-genic scale, that end which has the expected basic clusters of "Sad," "Anger," "Fear," "Surprise," "Happy," and "Love."

In short, it seems a fair guess that in addition to the clusters that are expected on pan-cultural grounds to be "basic," in Indonesian and Minangkabau Indecision is a basic emotion and in Indonesian, Nostalgic Longing is basic. However, there is no evidence at all to suggest that either emotion is associated with particular facial expressions or ANS patterns.

In summary, the data of this study generally support the notion that there are a few pan-cultural basic emotions. In fact, here we have found an unexpected new sort of evidence for basic emotions. More importantly, however, the results show how thoroughly and intricately the basic emotions have culture-specific shadings.

7.12. The final question: the influence of culture on emotion

The aim of this book is to show the culture-specific features of emotion behavior against the pan-cultural background. Between English and Indonesian much is similar but some is different; between the Indonesian of Minangkabau, the Indonesian of Javanese, and Minangkabau even more is similar, but still there are differences. To the extent that we have tied these differences to other cultural features we can claim with some confidence to have identified culturally influenced emotion behavior, and to have addressed the question, "How does culture influence emotion?"

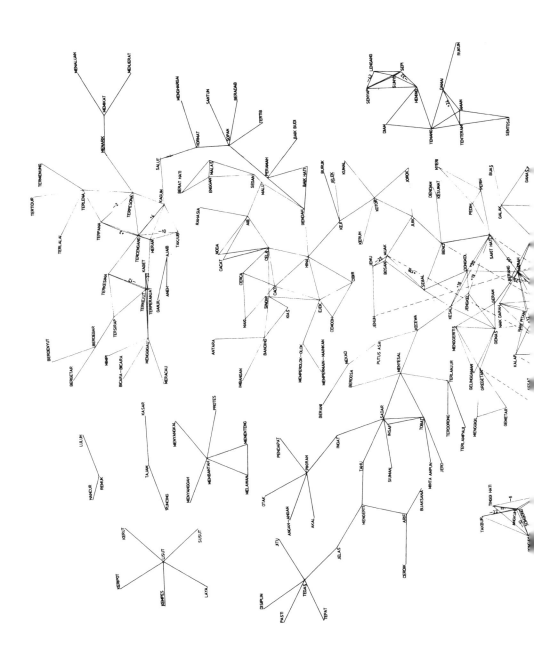

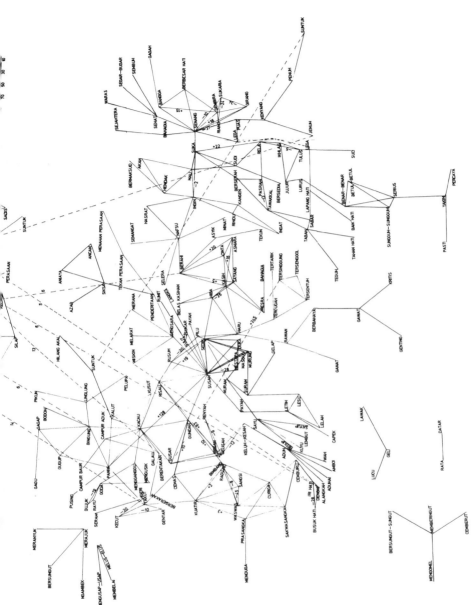

Map 1. A cognitive map of the landscape of emotion in Minangkabau.

Map 2. A cognitive map of the landscape of emotion in Minangkabau Indonesian.

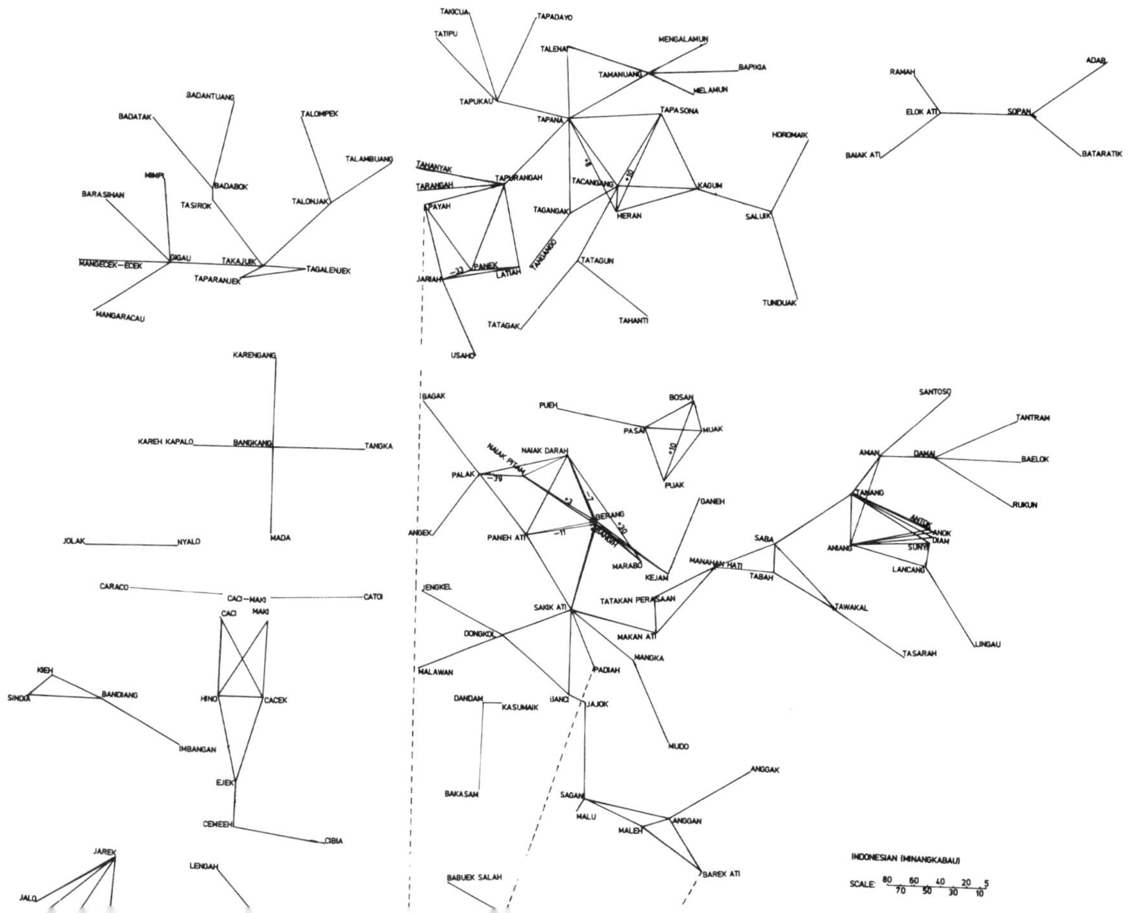

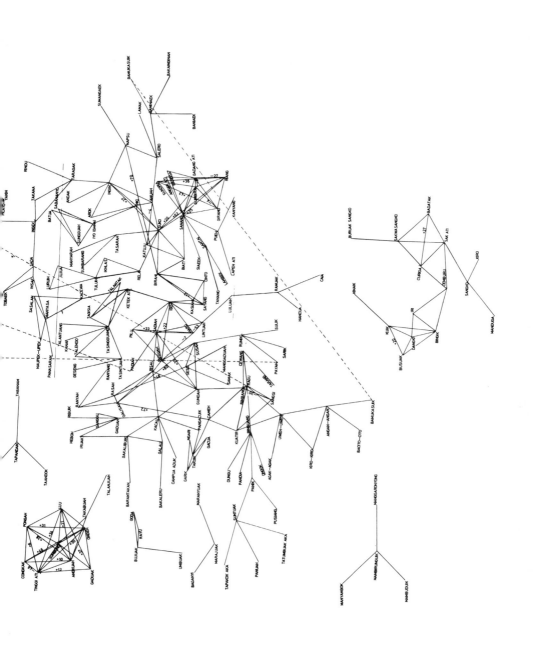

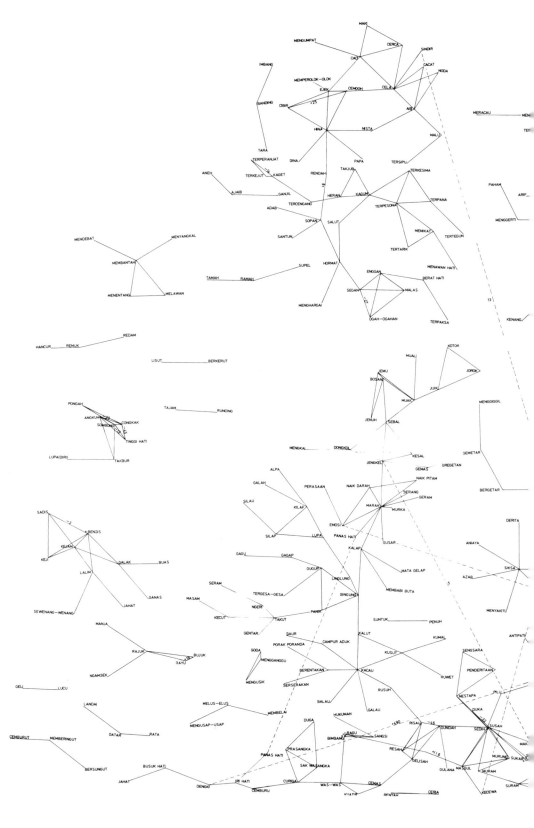

Map 3. A cognitive map of the landscape of emotion in Javanese Indonesian.

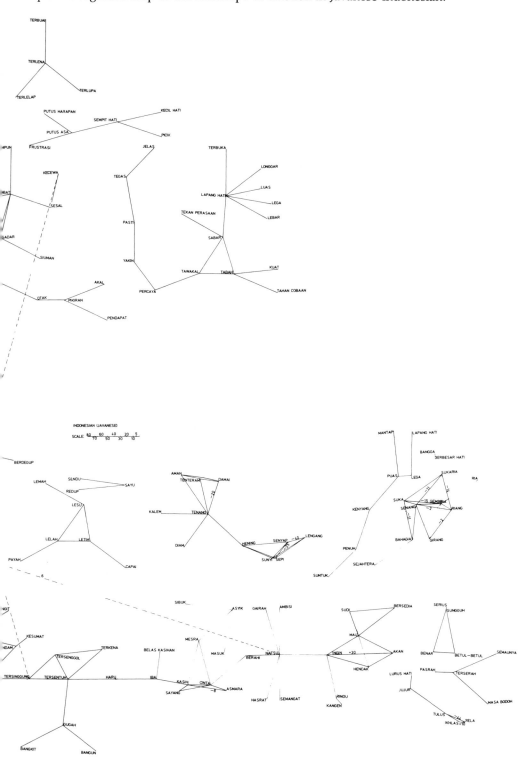

A cluster-by-cluster analysis of the composite maps of emotion terms

The 44 clusters

Each of the 44 clusters is discussed in turn, following this general outline:

1. "Cluster #—. "————"

A.   Defining the clusters
B.   Key words (see Section 2.3)
C.   English glosses
D.   Membership in realm of emotion: prototypicality ratings (see Chapter 3)
E.   Translation equivalents among the three languages (see Chapter 5)
F.   Scenarios described in terms of their antecedents and outcomes (see Chapter 4)
G.   The ethnography of the cluster

Abbreviations

The word for "language" in Indonesian is *bahasa,* so the following abbreviations are used throughout Part II:

BM   Minangkabau language
BI(M)   Indonesian language as used by Minangkabau
BI(J)   Indonesian language as used by Javanese

   In reporting the responses that informants gave for antecedents or outcomes of particular emotion words (e.g., Table 1.3), 19/27 means 19 out of 27 responses.

Introduction

This section considers in turn each emotion cluster across the three maps (Minangkabau, Minangkabau Indonesian, and Javanese Indonesian). The first step is to identify and define clusters that contain the same words or their cognates in each map. Because the three maps represent such similar languages, we do not face the problem of determining correspondences that might (assuredly would) arise if the maps represented unrelated languages.

As it happens, in most parts of the emotion space, the map for Minangkabau Indonesian – BI(M) – is the most elaborate of the three. It shows the most and closest connections between words, as well as the most elaborate clusters. Therefore, it is logical to use the most "complete" cluster as a standard by which to identify the corresponding configurations in the other maps. Occasionally there are discrepancies across the three maps where words or cognates turn up in different parts of the emotion space. We can assume that such discrepancies represent real cultural differences, not some sort of cognitive errors, and treat them as important clues to the cultural influences on emotion.

We begin, quite arbitrarily, with the "Surprise" clusters simply because they happen to fall at the top of the maps.

Indonesian, Minangkabau, and Javanese words are italicized in the text, capitalized in tables and figures. When reference is to both Minangkabau and Indonesian words, the Minangkabau is always given first; English translations of those words are in quotation marks to indicate the tentative and approximate nature of such translation. In the interests of comprehension for an English-speaking audience, this analysis often refers to Minangkabau and Indonesian words with their English glosses. Thus, the *tacangang/terkejut* clusters will be called, loosely, the "Surprise" clusters. This is theoretically somewhat difficult to justify, of course. *Tacangang/terkejut* are roughly similar to "surprise, startle, shock," but the point of the study is to move away from such approximations and to specify just what *tacangang/terkejut* does mean, how it differs from "surprise," and, indeed, how Javanese Indonesian *terkejut* differs from Minangkabau Indonesian *terkejut* and how they differ in turn from Minangkabau *tacangang*. Because it is impractical to write this analysis in Indonesian and Minangkabau, I trust the reader will remain as uneasy as the author is in thinking of these *tacangang/terkejut* clusters as "Surprise," and will withhold final cognitive appreciation until the nuances have been explored.

In the end, however, this is an impossible task. By using "Surprise" as the English label for the first cluster, we tip off the non-Indonesianist as to what, generally speaking, is going on; but we also create an ethnocentric (Anglo-centric, actually) expectation of what the scenarios should contain. If every Indonesian word were accompanied by an English gloss from the beginning, I fear that the purpose of this study would be compromised; if there were no English glosses at all, most readers would give up in weariness. Hitting the best compromise is an old challenge in anthropological writing. The text in Part I leaned a bit more toward glosses, but Part II leans a bit away from their use. Generally in these maps, English dictionary glosses are given for the Indonesian words but not for the Minangkabau words. There are no Minangkabau–English dictionaries, and it seemed that to work through Dutch or Indonesian would simply have added another layer of obscurity.

Finally, in the scenario responses, people almost always answered in the language of the question. But on rare occasions, Indonesian words slipped into the response to a Minangkabau question, for example, the stray BI(M) *marah* among the emotion word outcomes of some Minangkabau emotions.

1. "Surprise" clusters *(terkejut)*

A. Defining the clusters (see Figs. 1.1–1.3)

> In BM there are three clusters with 11 words and three focals: *takajuik, tacangang, talena*
> In BI(M) there is one cluster with 13 word members, and the focal word: *terkejut.*
> In BI(J) those same words form four clusters with 12 words and five focals: *terkejut, kagum, terpesona, and tertarik/memikat*

Anomalies. a. There is a *latiah/letih* group or cluster in each map. In Minangkabau only it is linked to one of these "Surprise" clusters. It is included in each map segment here for reference but will be considered and analyzed later.

b. In Minangkabau these clusters are isolated. In Minangkabau Indonesian and Javanese Indonesian there is a bridging link from *kagum* to *hormat, salut,* and *sopan.* (Their cognates in Minangkabau, *horomaik* and *saluik,* are dead-end twigs from *kagum.*)

Interpretation. Minangkabau Indonesian has more links, fewer clusters, than Minangkabau, and both Minangkabau maps have more links than BI(J), which is the least linked, most fragmented.

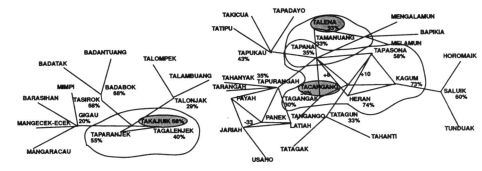

Figure 1.1. "Surprise" clusters BM

B. Key words

In Figure 1.2, the clusters are circled; the key words are circled and shaded. The key words are:

> Minangkabau – BM – *takajuik, tacangang, talena*
> Indonesian spoken by Minangkabau – BI(M) – *terkejut*
> Indonesiam spoken by Javanese – BI(J) – *terkejut, kagum, terpesona*

C. English glosses

In Figures 1.2, 1.3, and 1.4, English glosses are entered for words in the two Indonesian maps. These are simply the first definitions given in the two Indonesian-English dictionaries.

D. Membership in the realm of emotion: prototypicality ratings

In Figures 1.1 and 1.2, prototypicality, or membership in the realm of emotion for the starter words in Minangkabau Indonesian and Minangkabau, shows clines in the clusters.

In Minangkabau, from a peak, or ridge, of *takajuik–tasirok–badabok*, all at 68%, the starter words decline rapidly to the 20s and then the eight dead-end twigs. *Takajuik* is also the key word for this cluster, so there is good coincidence between key word and emotion intensity.

For the *tacangang* cluster in Minangkabau, *tacangang* is also the strongest member at 75%, with the triangle of *tacangang, kagum* (73%), and *heran* (74%) as a peak area, declining to the 30s and then the dead-end twigs. The triangle cluster *talena* is weak, in the 30s.

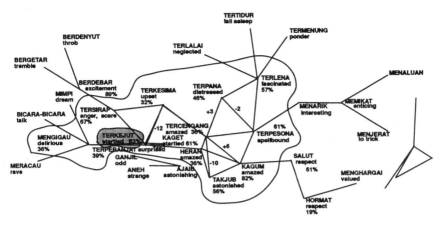

Figure 1.2. "Surprise" clusters BI(M)

So, in Minangkabau key words show highest membership and thus coincide well.

In Minangkabau Indonesian, however, where there is only a single large cluster, the key word *terkejut* is only 63%, whereas *berdebar*, on a branch, is 89% and *kagum* is 82%; *tersirap* (67%) and *heran* (64%) also are higher than the key word *terkejut*.

How does one interpret this? If the two measures in fact have the meanings we are assuming they have (namely, that the key word is the strongest common denominator in the cluster, and that the percentage measures membership in the emotion realm), then this suggests that something else other than emotion is involved with *terkejut* and its cluster. Note also that the closest words to *terkejut*, which are *kaget* and *terperanjat* (also "surprised, startled"), are only 61% and 39%. The suggestion is definitely that more is going on in the cluster than merely emotion (i.e., *perasaan hati*).

E. Translation equivalents

Minangkabau–Indonesian. When Minangkabau subjects responding to the Minangkabau emotion word list were asked for the Indonesian equivalents, and those responding to the Indonesian emotion words were asked for Minangkabau equivalents, the results are not particularly striking at the cluster level. The translation links always join the obvious cognate clusters in the two languages.

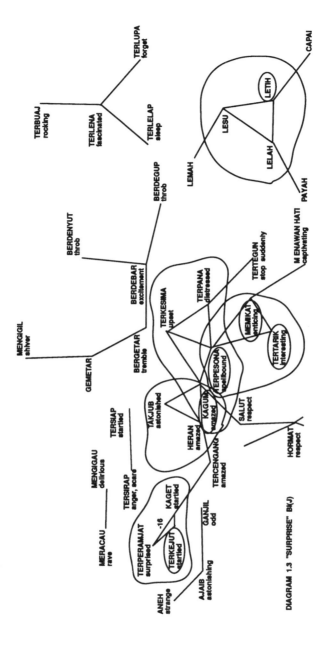

Figure 1.3. "Surprise" clusters BI(J)

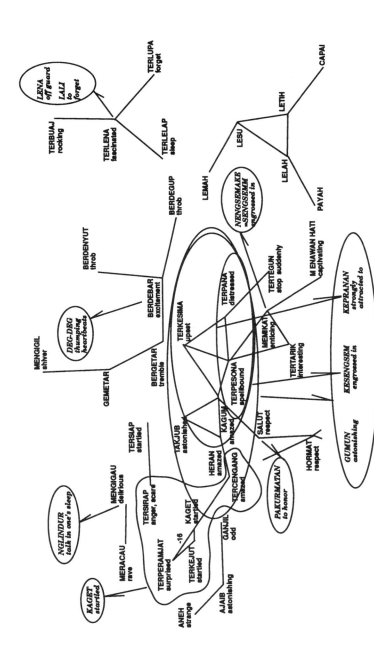

Figure 1.4. Translation equivalents between Javanese Indonesian (in block letters) and Javanese (in italics).

The translation patterns do reconcile one difference between the clusterings in the two languages. In Minangkabau Indonesian one major cluster includes all these "surprise" words, whereas in Minangkabau they fall into two unrelated clusters. The translations reinforce the separateness. Even the single cluster in Minangkabau Indonesian acts like the separate clusters in Minangkabau, for there is no crossover traffic. This suggests that the two links in Minangkabau Indonesian, *terkesima–tercengang* and *terperanjat–heran*, are a bit illusory – that they are better considered double bridges between two clusters rather than integral parts of a single cluster.

At the individual-word level, however, there is a strong tendency for all words in one cluster to focus in on the key word of the opposite cluster. This supports the idea that the key words have special cognitive status. We have already seen that these key words are originally recognized within their own language as the words most frequently named as synonyms for the other words.

Now we see that when subjects are asked for translation equivalents for words in the "Surprise" cluster, they tend *not* to name the obvious cognate in the other language, although there usually is such a cognate. If they had named only the obvious cognate, the results would be hard to interpret. One might say that the subjects were simply making an automatic phoneme shift, regardless of meaning – an act of linguistic laziness that leads to the *faux amis* problem of deceptive cognates. (In fact, this is the way people make their way through languages like Dutch and Minangkabau when they are considerably more fluent in their closely related neighbors, German and Indonesian: They invent plausible words by making the standard phoneme shifts.)

Actually, these subjects eschew the cognate for the key word in the appropriate cluster of the other language. This indicates not automatic phoneme-shifting but a more significant cognitive effort.

I have been careful to insist that there is no direct evidence that Indonesians explicitly recognize either clusters or key words as I have laid them out here. But the pattern of translation equivalent choice shown here argues for an implicit knowledge: People are acting at least *as if* they had these cluster mappings in mind. This is also strongly suggestive support for the claim (by Shaver et al. 1987) that such clusters of associated emotion words are real categories, and that such key words are prototypical examplars of the categories.

From Javanese Indonesian to Javanese (Fig. 1.4). The Javanese translation equivalents that were elicited from Javanese informants using the Indonesian master list offer a basis for a master list of emotion words in Javanese, which will be developed and used in the next stages of this overall research project. For the moment, we can simply show on the figure the most common Javanese words mentioned, together with their English glosses from the Horne (1974) Javanese–English dictionary. There is little to go on, but there seem to be no unusual shifts in this "Surprise" area.

F. Antecedent/outcome sentence completion tasks

In the "Surprise" clusters, the antecedents/outcomes sentence completion tasks were performed for two sets of words, each consisting of two pairs (one pair in Indonesian, and the cognate pair in Minangkabau); and one pair of words in Minangkabau (not matched with its Indonesian counterparts). All five of these pairs are within-language pairs. As it happens, no between-language pairs were done in this area.

a. Analysis of the set consisting of two pairs, *takajuik–taparanjek* (in Minangkabau) and *terkejut–terperanjat* (in Minangkabau Indonesian): As Table 1.1 shows, there are no great differences between languages, but clear differences between words: *Takajuik* and its Indonesian cognate *terkejut* are much more likely to be the result of something heard than are *taparanjek* and its cognate *terperanjat*.

Table 1.2 indicates the great range of antecedent events offered for each word. Again, there were no dramatic differences between languages (Table 1.5), but *taparanjat* and its cognate *terperanjek* (but not the other two) had some recurring specific antecedents, especially (1) being suddenly hit from behind by someone, often a friend; and (2) seeing, hearing, or feeling a wild creature, usually a snake, dog, or insect (Table 1.3). Also, as Table 1.13 shows, the antecedents for both pairs are strongly negative, often neutral, rarely positive.

Table 1.1. *Manner of perceiving the antecedent event*

	Saw	Implied visual	Heard	Implied audible
BM(27)				
TAKAJUIK	3	1	15	2
TAPARANJEK	1	1	3	3
BI(M) (27)				
TERKEJUT	3	1	15	3
TERPERANJAT	3	3	1	3

Table 1.2. *Most common antecedent events*

	Surprised/hit (usually by friend) from behind	Hit	Hit by car	Other	
				Snake	Creature
BM					
TAKAJUIK	1	0	2	2	0
TAPARANJEK	5	2	0	4	3
BI(M)					
TERKEJUT	1	0	1	1	0
TERPERANJAT	5	0	3	3	5

Table 1.3. *Percentage of antecedents that were clearly sudden occurrences (or suddenly perceived)*

BM		
TAKAJUIK	19/27	70%
TAPARANJEK	17/26	65%
BI(M)		
TERKEJUT	22/27	81%
TERPERANJEK	22/27	81%

The generally uncomfortable tone of these outcomes in Table 1.4 is consistent with the negative tone of the antecedents.

To anticipate a contrast with Gerber's Samoan data (1985), where she found both antecedents and outcomes of emotions described in social terms, it should be noted that very few of these antecedents or outcomes are of a social or interactional nature. The outcomes are mainly overt acts like jumping, or screaming or running, or they are physical reactions like fainting, turning pale, or palpitating.

b. Analysis of the set consisting of two pairs, *tacangang–heran* (in Minangkabau) and *tercengang–heran* (in Minangkabau Indonesian).

There are no great differences between the languages in Table 1.5, but *tacangang* and its Indonesian cognate *tercengang* are overwhelmingly the result of visual perception.

Unlike the set analyzed in Tables 1.1 through 1.4, there were no recurring antecedents (Table 1.6). The analysis was more successful at a higher level of generality:

Table 1.4. *Outcomes*

	Jump	Scream	Faint	Pray	Pale	Run	Chest heave	Stare	Other internal sensation
BM									
TAKAJUIK	3	6	4	2	2	3	1	2	1
TAPARANJEK	5	6	2	1	2	4	3	1	2
BI(M)									
TERKEJUT	2	4	10	0	1	3	2	0	1
TERPERANJEK	6	3	1	3	2	5	1	2	0

Table 1.5. *Manner of perceiving the antecedent event*

	Seeing	Hearing	Other
BM			
TACANGANG	17	2	7
HERAN	9	2	15
BI(M)			
TERCENGANG	20	0	
HERAN	2	7	

Table 1.6. *Nature of the antecedent events*

	Moral violations	Counterexpectations	Unusual	Interesting
BM				
TACANGANG	0	3	15	10
HERAN	3	6	4	9
BI(M)				
TERCENGANG	0	4	10	6
HERAN	3	3	8	1

Moral violations: where *X* happened, although it was wrong (e.g., someone was slandered).

Counter expectations: where *X* turned out to be *Y* (e.g., the lazy child was first in his class).

Unusual: where *X*, although rare, happened. (e.g., a falling star).

Interesting: *X*, more intense than normal (e.g., a beautiful view).

There is a slight hint of moral quality to the two *herans*, while *tacangang/tercengang* were more unusual or interesting.

This set, described in Table 1.7, is certainly less sudden than the preceding set in Table 1.3.

Positive/negative. The antecedents of this set are overwhelmingly neither positive nor negative, but neutral (see Table 1.13).

Clearly, the outcomes (Table 1.8) of this set are cerebral, with none of the negative physical agitation of the previous set. One might think of these words as close to "puzzled interest."

c. Analysis of the Minangkabau pair, *tasirok–badabok*.

The manner of perceiving most of the antecedent events was ambiguous, although Table 1.9 shows that *tasirok* was more often the result of seeing something than was *badabok*

To elaborate on Table 1.10, *tasirok* interaction includes: a girl loves him, met friend or lover, saw lover. Noninteraction includes: received news, theft, saw a thigh, or an old woman.

Badabok interaction includes: met lover, or friend. Noninteraction includes: received news, took an exam, heard an explosion, was robbed.

The most striking feature of the antecedents of this pair is the high degree of interaction events, compared with the two previous sets.

This set in Table 1.11 falls between the other two in terms of suddenness of antecedents. Compare Tables 1.3 and 1.7.

Positive/negative. This set has a majority of negative antecedents, but also a high number of positive antecedents (22%, 35%) compared with the other two sets, where positive antecedents range from 0% to 6% (see Table 1.13).

Considering how positive the antecedents are, the outcomes in Table 1.12 are strongly negative. Also, they are strongly physiological, with few signs of interaction.

Overview of meanings. We can now summarize the picture of these "Surprise" clusters. The sentence completion data have given considerable information on the antecedent events – how they are perceived, how suddenly they occur, and whether they are positive or negative as well as on the nature of the outcomes.

This approach has not turned up differences between the two languages, Indonesian and Minangkabau, in this "Surprise" area. So, for

Table1.7. *Percentage of clearly sudden*
antecedents

BM		
TACANGANG	0/27	0%
HERAN	4/27	15%
BI(M)		
TERCENGANG	3/27	11%
HERAN	3/27	11%

Table 1.8. *Outcomes*

	Want to understand	Watched	Raise brows; frowned; shook head
BM			
TACANGANG	1	7	0
HERAN	7	2	8
BI(M)			
TERCENGANG	4	3	1
HERAN	10	2	8

Table 1.9. *Manner of perceiving the antecedent event*

	Seeing	Hearing	Ambiguous
BM			
TASIROK	9	4	15
BADABOK	3	4	19

Table 1.10. *Most common antecedents*

	Surprised (not hit) by someone	Saw lover	Met old friend	Bad news	Theft	Interaction	Non-interaction
BM							
TASIROK	5	5	3	3	3	17	7
BADABOK	2	7	3	0	0	16	15

Table 1.11. *Percentage of antecedents that were clearly sudden occurrences or suddenly perceived occurrences*

BM		
TASIROK	18/27	66%
BADABOK	14/26	54%

Table 1.12. *Outcomes*

	Paled	Rub chest	Sweating chest, heart beating	Pray	Smile	Mouth gape	Interaction
BM							
TASIROK (30)	5	4	6	3	1	1	3
BADABOK (21)	0	2	6	1	1	1	2

Table 1.13. *Positive, negative, and neutral antecedents*

	Positive		Negative		Neutral	
BM: TAKAJUIK–TAPARANJEK	2	4%	41	73%	13	23%
BI(M): TERKEJUT–TERPERANJAT	0	0%	35	65%	19	35%
BM: TACANGANG–HERAN	2	4%	8	15%	43	81%
BI(M): TERCENGANG–HERAN	3	6%	8	15%	42	79%
BM: TASIROK–BADABOK	22	35%	34	55%	6	10%

this area, we can say that Indonesian and Minangkabau meanings are very similar.

However, this approach does reveal a diversity of meanings within the clusters. The tendencies are shown in Table 1.14.

There are regularities: Some antecedents are sudden, unpleasant, with negative physiological outcomes; some antecedents are not sudden, are neutral, with puzzled cerebral outcomes.

Tasirok and *badabok* are remarkable (unfortunately, there are no data on their Indonesian cognates, *tersirap* and *berdebar*). They have high

Table 1.14. *Scenario meanings within the "Surprise" clusters*

	Perceived	Antecedent	Sudden	Pos/neg	Outcome
TAKAJUIK + TERKEJUT	heard	various	70–81%	neg: 35–73% pos: 0–4%	neg physiol
TAPARANJEK + TERPERANJAT	various	hit see creature	65%–81%		
TACAN-GANG + TERCENGANG	seen	unusual	0–11%	neutral pos: 2%–6%	Cerebral puzzled
HERAN + HERAN	various	various	15–11%		
TASIROK		interaction	66%	neg: 34–55% pos: 22–35%	neg physiolog
BADABOK		both interact + noninteract	54%		

membership ratings in the emotion realm, although they are marginal in terms of cluster formation and thus neither is a key term. They are the only terms whose antecedents include any amount of interaction, and they are the only terms with even a strong minority of positive antecedents (35%).

One cannot make a neat single, unitary picture of these clusters beyond saying that such emotions are the result of unusual or unexpected events, usually negative, with outcomes that are usually unpleasant physiological events.

G. The ethnography of the cluster

The Indonesian implications of surprise are discussed in Section 6.1.

2. "Happy" clusters (*gembira*)

A. Defining the clusters (see Figs. 2.1–2.3)

In Minangkabau (BM), there is a core cluster of 9 words around the focal *sanang; suko* is included because, although it is the focal word in the adjacent "Desire" cluster, it also has three ties to words in this cluster. *Biati* is included because it has two ties to words in this cluster. Three branches and twigs from *sanang* are also counted in this cluster. *Suko*

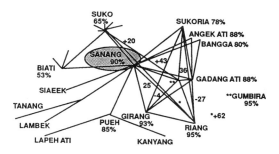

Figure 2.1. "Happy" cluster BM

and *biati* are hinge words between the "Happy" and the "Desire" clusters.

In Minangkabau Indonesian – BI(M) – there is a core cluster with 7 words around the focal word *gembira*, plus branches and a triangular cluster and branch from *senang* plus a twig from *bangga*. External connections: a bridge from *senang* in the "Happy" cluster, to *suka* in the "Desire" cluster; a bridge from *lega* in the triangular cluster, to *lapang hati*; a four-bridge chain from *puas* in the triangular cluster to *kalut*.

Javanese Indonesian – BI(J) – unlike the other two maps, which were well interconnected in the "Happy" area – has three isolates:

the 7-word *senang* cluster with two twigs
the *bangga–berbesar hati* isolate pair
the *puas–lega* branch

Interpretation. The basic *sanang/gembira–senang* areas are similar across the three maps, with cognates and identical words:

BM	BI(M)	BI(J)
SUKO	—	SUKA
SANANG	SENANG	SENANG
GUMBIRA	GEMBIRA	GEMBIRA
GIRANG	GIRANG	GIRANG
RIANG	RIANG	RIANG
SUKORIA	SUKARIA	SUKARIA
GADANG ATI	BERBESAR HATI	—
BANGGA	BANGGA	—
—	—	BAHAGIA

A noteworthy anomaly is in Minangkabau, where *angek ati* appears in this "Happy" cluster. It means, literally, "hot heart," and its literal

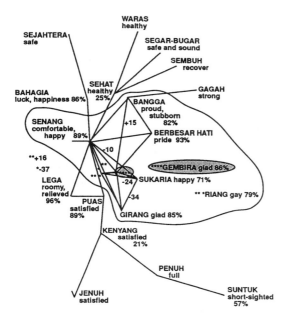

Figure 2.2. "Happy" cluster BI(M)

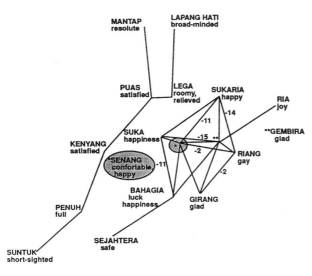

Figure 2.3. "Happy" cluster BI(J)

translation in Indonesian, *panas hati*, is in the "Anger" clusters of both Indonesian maps.

A second anomaly is that although *suko/suka* is strongly tied into the "Desire" cluster in both Minangkabau and Minangkabau Indonesian, and shows secondary links to the "Happy" clusters, its situation in Javanese is different: There, it is firmly tied to the "Happy" cluster and shows *no* ties to the "Desire" cluster.

In general, the links are all about the same across all three maps, but, as usual, Javanese Indonesian has fewer links, resulting in the two un- attached units instead of the single connected structure that appears in the other two maps: Specifically, in Javanese Indonesian, 4 words *(puas, lega, bangga, berbesar hati)* are not linked to the main cluster, and the main cluster is not linked to the rest of the map.

B. Key words

In Figures 2.1 – 2.3 the key words are circled:

BM	*sanang*
BI(M)	*gembira*
BI(J)	*senang*

The core cluster is circled in BI(M). The sets of words used in the antecedent/outcome tasks are:

in Minangkabau: *sanang–gumbira–gadang ati*
in Minangkabau Indonesian: *senang–gembira–riang*
between languages: BM – *sanang*, BI(M) – *gembira*

The key words are:

Minangkabau – BM – *sanang*
Indonesian spoken by Minangkabau – BI(M) – *gembira*
Indonesian spoken by Javanese – BI(J) – *senang*

C. English glosses (see Figs. 2.2, 2.3)

Even with this general hint at meanings, it is clear that Javanese speak- ers keep the "pride" words *(bangga, berbesar hati)* separate, while Min- angkabau see them as closely tied to "happy." There is an "Arrogance" *(sombong)* cluster, which is analyzed below (cluster 40), but the Javanese do not go so far as to put these "pride" words in that cluster. It looks as if they attend more to the stubborn implications of pride, while the Min- angkabau use these words with the "happy–pride" connotation. An an- tecedent/outcome sentence completion task here, contrasting Javanese and Minangkabau uses of the same Indonesian words, would be a test of this hypothesis. In English, of course, the single word "pride" includes both sorts of meanings.

Also, Javanese keep the "satisfaction" branch separate, whereas Minangkabau tie these "satisfaction" words to *senang*, in the "Happy" cluster. In this instance, Minangkabau seem to be more aware of the "comfortable" meaning of *senang*, while the Javanese do not respond to it.

D. Membership in the realm of emotion: prototypicality ratings

In Figures 2.1 and 2.2 the measure of membership in this "emotion" category is indicated for each of the starter words in Minangkabau and Minangkabau Indonesian.

BM: This is a strongly emotional cluster, with 6 words at 88% or higher. Although the key word, *sanang*, is 90%, it is still less strong than 3 other words in the cluster. In other words, prototypicality in reference to the realm of emotion itself is not the same as focality in this cluster.

BI(M): The words are less strong, with only 2 above the 88% mark, and only 1 in the 90s. Again, here the key word, *gembira*, at 86% is less strong than 2 other words in the cluster. Again, prototypicality in the realm of emotion and focality in the "Happy" cluster are not the same.

In both maps the "Satisfaction" area is very strong: In Minangkabau, *pueh*, although only in a branch from *senang*, is 85%; in Minangkabau Indonesian, the cognate *puas* (89%) and *lega* (96%), which form a triangle cluster with *senang* (89%), are stronger than the "Happy" cluster itself.

In the BI(M) map the degree of emotionality on the branches drops off quickly into the 20s.

In Minangkabau, the words *suko* (65%) and *biati* (53%) – which are included in the "Happy" cluster, but whose stronger identification is with the "Desire" cluster – are weak, perhaps presaging a weak emotionality of the entire "Desire" cluster.

E. Translation equivalents

There are data for:
>   Minangkabau to Minangkabau Indonesian and the reciprocal,
>   Minangkabau Indonesian to Minangkabau;
>   and for Javanese Indonesian to Javanese
>   (but not for its reciprocal, Javanese to Javanese Indonesian)

Between Minangkabau and Minangkabau Indonesian we can look at the most popular choice of words in the other language for each starter word.

In Minangkabau, with 11 starter words from Indonesian,

sanang gets 6/11, 55%

cognates get 4/11, 36%

others get 2/11, 18%

BI(M) *senang*'s most popular choice was *sanang*, so this counts as both key word and cognate.

In BI(M), with 9 starter words from BM,

gembira gets 6/9, 67%

cognates get 4/9, 44%

others get 1/9, 11%

Again here, *gumbira* choosing *gembira* counts as both key word and cognate.

The strongest trend in each language is to make the translation choice be the key word of the opposite cluster. The key word had previously been determined as the most popular synonym choice by other informants who did the within-language task. The fact that these informants, who are working from the other language, point to the key word, supports the identification of the key word. Further, it supports the concept of cluster, epitomized by that key word.

Second, the relative weakness of the obvious cognate as a choice of translation equivalent speaks for the thoughtfulness of the subjects. If the cognates were routinely chosen, it would be difficult to decide whether the cognates were actually the best equivalents or whether subjects just didn't understand the instructions and simply performed the formal phonetic shifts, rather than identifying the lexical equivalents.

The non-key, non-cognate choices would be evidence for systematic shifts, but in this cluster there are so few that there is little apparent shift. Of the three examples in the two languages, two are the same: In each language, the first choice for *bangga* ("proud" in both languages) is *berbesar hati/gadang ati*, literally "big heart." This hints that *bangga* and *berbesar hati/gadang ati* are in some manner like a cluster, with *berbesar hati/gadang ati* the key word. In both languages, these words are thoroughly linked to the "Happy" cluster, but it is interesting to note that in Javanese Indonesian they are isolated as a pair. One might think of them as being, for Minangkabau, a sort of proto-cluster, while for Javanese they form a true isolate.

From Javanese Indonesian to Javanese. Javanese informants overwhelmingly choose *seneng* (happy), the obvious cognate to the Javanese Indonesian key word *senang*, and presumably the key word of a Javanese "Happy" cluster.

In Javanese, the 11 starter words in BI(J) choose:

seneng 7/11, 64%

cognates 2/11, 18%

others 3/11, 27%

Of these three others, the isolate pair *berbesar hati* and *bangga* both chose *mongkog* (not in Horne 1974), strengthening the discreteness of this "pride" pair for Javanese thinking.

F. Antecedent/outcome sentence completion tasks

For this cluster, in Minangkabau, *sanang*, *gumbira*, and *gadang ati* were chosen; for Minangkabau Indonesian, *senang*, *gembira*, and *riang*; and for the between-language pair, the two non-cognate key words, *sanang* (BM) and *gembira* (BI[M]) were chosen.

The Minangkabau set: sanang–gumbira–gadang ati. First, aggregating the total of 80 responses for the antecedents of these 3 "happy" words:

Reasons for being happy:

50%	because of achieving a personal goal
30%	involved kin or friends
18%	involved interaction
14%	because of receiving present, praise
8%	because of having money
4%	because others achieved their goals
4%	because someone came home

1 each: saw something; found something lost; escaped danger; got well.

There was little difference in the responses for the 3 words, except that:

gadang ati had 7/11, 64% of the "received a present"

sanang had 5/6, 83% of the "having money" responses

The high frequency of the personal goal achievement responses is somewhat unexpected. This category included passing examinations, succeeding in business, and some slightly more ambiguous responses that might be personal achievement or might possibly be more luck or windfall, such as getting a gift or having a wish granted.

Gender differences do show up here: 27 of the males, but only 13 of the females, gave the personal goal achievement response. However, for the opposite, the socially oriented responses, there was no significant difference between genders:

Interaction responses	9 males, 5 females
Kin/friendship responses	11 males, 13 females
	(chi square = 1.2076)

Outcomes. The aggregate picture of the 78 outcome responses was as follows:

26%	physical: jumped, ran, walked, cheered, clapped;
26%	facial: smiles, laughed, etc.
12%	involved any interaction
12%	involved kin or friends
15%	were happy or some other positive attitude
6%	treated their friends to a meal
5%	became quiet
5%	thanked God
3%	did good (gave alms)

1 each ate, masked all feelings, was lazy

Again, there was little difference between the 3 words, except that:

gumbira got 10/13, 77% of the laughs

gadang ati got 9/12, 75% of the jumping

There is even less sociability in the outcomes than in the antecedents.

The laughing, jumping, running, dancing, and singing is a syndrome of happiness that does show up reasonably strongly in these responses, and in observed behavior: When our Indonesian cook was exceptionally pleased, she would dance and clap her hands and sing in the kitchen. In the West, this syndrome is perhaps more familiar for adults from the nineteenth century, and today it may be more limited to younger people, although in the Shaver et al. American English scenarios for Joy, one finds "giggling, laughing, being bouncy, bubbly, jumping" all as parts of the outcomes (1987:1079). Certainly here it is claimed for adult Minangkabau.

The Minangkabau Indonesian set: senang–gembira–riang. The aggregate picture of the 74 responses describing antecedents of these 3 Indonesian words indicates that people were happy for these reasons:

41%	because of achieving personal goals
21%	of the antecedents involved kin or friends

Table 2.1. *Personal goal achievement responses*

	Males	Females
Minangkabau	27	13
Minang Indonesian	13	20

Chi square = 5.7666; p = <.025

16%	of the antecedents involved interpersonal interaction
18%	because a present, etc., was received
0%	because of money

The picture also tells us there is little difference between the 3 words.

As to gender differences, 13 males, 20 females gave personal goal achievement as a response, the reversal of the situation in Minangkabau (Table 2.1):

The sociability indicators are:

Interaction responses	males 3, females 9
kinship/friendship	males 13, females 20

Thus, in Indonesian the women have more individual goal achievement than men, but they also have more of the two sociability factors. One would have predicted a negative relationship between these two principles, not a positive one.

Otherwise, the overall difference between the two languages is slight on the basis of these two tasks.

Outcomes. For Indonesian, *senang–gembira–riang*, of 69 responses:

30%	were physical – jumping, running, cheering, singing
29%	were facial expressions – smile, laugh, etc.
20%	involved kin or friends
15%	involved interaction
10%	involved positive feelings

There was little difference among these three words, except that *riang* had all ten of the "jumping" responses.

About the same amount of interaction existed as in the antecedents.

There was not much gender difference, although males were more interactional than females, but females were more expressive, as indicated in Table 2.2:

Finally, there was little difference between the languages in this approach to outcomes.

Table 2.2

	Males	Females
Kinship/friends	10	4
Interaction	6	4
Jumped	3	10
Sang	1	6
Cheered	1	3
Facial expression	2	4

Table 2.3

	Personal achievement		Luck or gift	
Indonesian–BI(M)	24	40%	11	18%
Minangkabau–BM	12	20%	15	25%

Chi square = 3.643; $p = <0.1$

Between-language antecedents/outcomes task. Differences between languages were directly attacked by asking subjects to complete the antecedent and outcome sentence completion tasks comparing and contrasting the key words for "happy" in the two languages, Minangkabau *(sanang)* and Minangkabau Indonesian *(gembira)*. Although each word has an obvious cognate in the other language *(sanang/senang, gumbira/gembira)*, the evidence of both within and between language tasks indicated that these words were not only the respective key words but the preferred translation equivalents for each other. The 60 responses were analyzed first for whether they explained "happiness" as the result of personal achievement or the result of something outside the individual (luck or a gift) (Table 2.3).

The results are at least suggestive: In Indonesian, happiness is much more powerfully the result of personal achievement, whereas in Minangkabau happiness is more likely to be the result of luck and presents from others.

We now turn to the sociability factors, which presumably are the opposite of the individual personal achievement, since the two are mutually exclusive:

Indonesian – BI(M)	kinship/friendship	19
	interaction	15

Table 2.4

	Physical: jump, clap, sing, whistle	Facial expression: smile, laugh
Indonesian	12	18
Minangkabau	3	3

Minangkabau – BM	kinship/friendship	23
	interaction	18

We do see, albeit weakly, that both social interaction and relationships figure slightly more strongly in Minangkabau reasons for happiness than they do in Indonesian antecedents.

Outcomes. The 60 between-language-task outcomes are shown in Table 2.4.

In overt physical acts, body activity, singing and whistling, and facial expressions, it is clear that Indonesian is much stronger than Minang-kabau. This is strong evidence for the cultural response rule of masking emotions, of muting the felt emotion in facial expressions and other behavior. Here there are two matters of interest: First, it is a bit surprising to find such a strong masking of happiness. That anger is strongly masked is well known, and we expect to find it in the scenario outcomes of the "Anger" cluster analysis. But Happiness is not such an expectable place for masking; and, as it turns out, the Anger outcomes do not show masking (see clusters 22–26, below). Second, the two sets of outcomes are from the very same, bilingual, Minangkabau informants who are being asked to compare the two languages. Thus, this is strong evidence for code-switching not just of the words themselves but of the appropriate cultural display rules for the management of emotion. Bilinguals, and even people who are less than fluent in a second language, often remark that they feel differently when they speak the other language. These data support the intuitive observation that the management of emotion is linked to the language, and presumably, since the two languages are spoken in different contexts, this indicates differences in the emotion–language–culture complex.

There is more evidence of this muting of emotion in Minangkabau, compared with Indonesian: There were four instances in Minangkabau (and none in Indonesian) of "wiping it out of the mind," as in this example:

Table 2.5

	Kinship/friendship	Interaction
Indonesian	10	14
Minangkabau	8	8

Koknyo SANANG, inyo indak ado banyak bapikia lai.

When he is happy, he doesn't have any further thoughts.

Not only is there greater passivity in Minangkabau, there is greater social action in Indonesian (Table 2.5).

However, there was an item counter to this principle of greater masking in Minangkabau: five Indonesian responses said that the outcome of happiness would be a facial expression of *cerah*, and one Minangkabau response said *jerniah* (an equivalent). These words usually mean "clear" (as weather), or "clean" (as glass), and when applied to the face, seem to mean "open, blank," suggesting some masking with a neutral face. There seems to be a comparable concept in Bali, which Wikan describes as "an appearance of grace and composure" (1989:295).

The overall sense of this outcome contrast, however, is to support the differential response rule principle.

Finally, methodologically it is interesting that these differences turned up in the task that demanded direct comparison of the two languages, and the effect was much muted in the aggregate comparisons of the Minangkabau task with the Indonesian task.

3. "Desire" area *(ingin)*

This area lies between "Love" and "Happy" and itself ranges from "Lust" to "Like."

A. Defining the clusters (see Figs. 3.1–3.3)

BM has 8 words in this area that form a single large cluster with *suko* as the key word, and three twigs and two branches. External connections: *Suko* is a hinge word with the "Happy" cluster; *katuju* has a link with Happy, *napsu* has a link with Love, and *bamukasuik* has a link with *ragu*. *Suko* has a link with the *rela* cluster; *nio* has a link to the *iyo bana* "Sincere" cluster, and *ingin* a link to *taragak*.

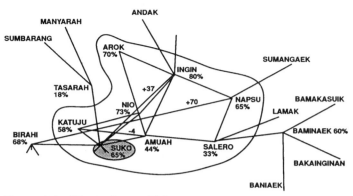

Figure 3.1. "Desire" area BM

BI(M) has three clusters:

The "Lust" cluster, a 3-word triangle cluster with *nafsu* as the key word; two twigs. External connections: *Ingin* is a hinge word with the "Desire" cluster, and has a link to the "Love" cluster.

The "Desire" cluster, a 7-word cluster with *mau* as the key word, and two twigs. *Ingin* is a hinge word with the "Lust" cluster, and there are two links to the "Surrender" cluster. *Rela* is a hinge word with the *ikhlas* cluster.

The "Surrender" cluster, a 3-word triangle cluster with two links to "Desire," and *tawakkal* is a hinge word with the *sabar* cluster.

BI(J) words form two clusters:

A 3-word triangle cluster with *sudi* as the key word

A 4-word cluster with *akan* as the key word, *rindu* and *kangen* on a twig, and a link to *nafsu*.

Here the words in the BI(M) *nafsu* "Lust" cluster do not form a cluster, and the words in the BI(M) "Surrender" cluster form an isolate branch.

B. Key words

The key words are as follows:

BM	*suko*
BI(M)	*nafsu*
	mau
BI(J)	*sudi*
	akan

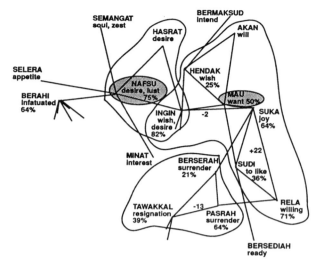

Figure 3.2. "Desire" area BI(M)

C. *English glosses (see Figs. 3.2, 3.3.)*

D. *Membership in the realm of emotion: prototypicality ratings*

BM: *Napsu,* the key word, (65%), is lower than 3 other words in the cluster. The average prototypicality rating for 8 words is 61%.

BI(M): Again here the key words are not the strongest. For the three clusters:

Two words average 79%
Six words average 55%
Three words average 41%

E. *Translation equivalents*

From BM to BI(M)

ingin, napsu choose *ingin*
nio, amuah choose *mau*
katuju, suko choose *suka*
other cognates chosen 2 times

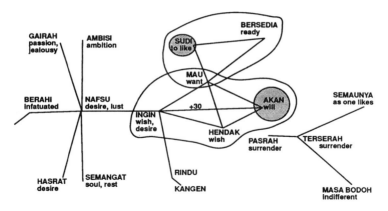

Figure 3.3. "Desire" area BI(J)

From BI(M) to BM

> *hendak, sudi* choose *amuah*
> *suka, mau* choose *suko*
> *nafsu* chooses *ingin*
> *ingin* chooses *nio*
> *rela* chooses *ikhlas*

From BI(J) to Javanese

> cognates chosen 2 times
> *mau* and *sudi* choose *gelem* (to be willing to)
> *hendak* chooses *arep* (to want)
> *suka* chooses *seneng*
> *berserah* chooses *sekarep* (to act as one pleases)

These data are unusual in their diffuseness. There is not the usual pattern of cognate or key word as modal choice. There is, however, in the BI(M)-to-BM direction, evidence for the sort of regular shift noted also in the "Love" cluster: several words that can be so arranged that each chooses not its cognate in the other language, but the next word in the order.

In Table 3.1, there is an apparent break in the pattern where *ingin* chooses *nio*, not the proper next cognate, *amuah*. But *nio* and *amuah* are very close, both in the Minangkabau map (Fig. 3.1) and on the evidence of the translation equivalents where Minangkabau *nio* has as modal choice in Minangkabau Indonesian *mau*, the cognate of *amuah*.

Table 3.1. *Translation shift from BI(M) to BM*

BM	BI(M)
BIRAHI	BERAHI
NAFSU ←	NAFSU
INGIN ←	INGIN
NIO ←	
AMUAH	MAU
SUKO ←	SUKA

Looking at the Minangkabau Indonesian map (Fig. 3.2) in this light, we can say that there are four shifts to the right: *berahi* to *nafsu* to *ingin* to *mau* to *suka*.

As we shall see, this shift is matched by a comparable shift in the adjacent "Love" cluster, where the direction is to the left.

How does one explain this remarkable and unusual pattern? In both shifts the movement is from a stronger, Lust-like Minangkabau Indonesian word to a weaker Happy- or Pity-like Minangkabau word. To anticipate the argument, it appears that in this part of the landscape, and nowhere else, there is a regular shift from stronger, more intense Indonesian words to weaker, less intense Minangkabau words. When Minangkabau bilingual speakers are asked for the equivalent words in Minangkabau, they move away from the strong Indonesian focus.

F. Antecedent/outcome sentence completion tasks

None were done.

G. The ethnography of "Desire"

See discussion in Section 6.3.

4. "Honest" clusters *(ikhlas)*

These words are closely tied to the "Desire" cluster (via *rela* and *suko/ suka*) in both of the Minangkabau maps, but form an isolate in the Javanese map.

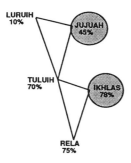

Figure 4.1. "Honest" cluster BM

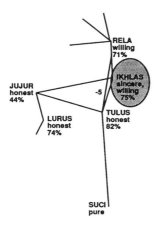

Figure 4.2. "Honest" cluster BI(M)

A. Defining the clusters (see Figs. 4.1–4.3)

> BM: Two 3-word triangle clusters with key words *jujua* and *ikhlas*,
> and *tuluih* the hinge between them. Linked by a bridge to *suko*,
> of the "Desire" and "Happy" clusters.
>
> BI(M): A 4-word cluster with *ikhlas* as the key word, and with one
> twig. *Rela* is a hinge word with the "Desire" cluster; a link from
> *lurus* to *benar–benar* of the "Sincere" cluster.
>
> BI(J): An isolate 3-word triangle cluster, with *ikhlas* as the key word
> and one twig.

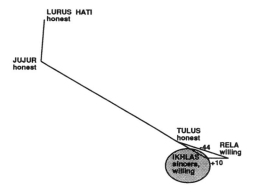

Figure 4.3. "Honest" cluster BI(J)

B. Key words

The key words are as follows:

BM	*jujua*
	ikhlas
BI(M)	*ikhlas*
BI(J)	*ikhlas*

C. English glosses (see Figs. 4.2, 4.3.)

D. Membership in the realm of emotion: prototypicality ratings

In BM, *ikhlas*, the key word, has the highest prototypicality rating. For the two clusters:

For 3 words of one cluster the average is 42%
For 3 words of the other cluster, the average is 74%
For 4 words of the BI(M) cluster, the average is 68%

E. Translation equivalents

From BM to BI(M)

to the key word *ikhlas*	0
to cognate	2
other: *ikhlas > rela*	1

From BI(M) to BM

       to the key word *jujua*   0

       to the key word *ikhlas*   1

       to cognates   3

       other: *ikhlas* > *rela*

             rela > *ikhlas*

From BI(J) to Javanese

       to cognates   2

       to *lili* (willing), presumably

          the cognate in the Javanese

          cluster   2

       other: *lurus* > *jujur*

F. Antecedent/outcome sentence completion tasks

None were done.

5. "Tired" clusters *(letih)*

A. Defining the clusters (see Figs. 5.1–5.3)

      BM: A 5-word cluster with *latiah* as the key word; one twig. Bridge links to both "Surprise" and "Sad" clusters.

      BI(M): A 3-word triangle cluster with *letih* as the key word, and one twig. Two links to "Sad" clusters.

      BI(J): An isolate 3-word triangle cluster with *letih* as the key word, and three twigs.

B. Key words

    BM   *latiah*

    BI(M), BI(J)   *letih*

C. English glosses (see Figs. 5.2, 5.3.)

D. Membership in the realm of emotion: prototypicality ratings

The prototypicality ratings are very low for the words that were tested (Figs. 5.1, 5.2).

   For two words in BM, the average is 16.5%

Figure 5.1. "Tired" cluster BM

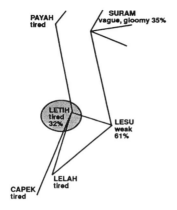

Figure 5.2.   "Tired" cluster BI(M)

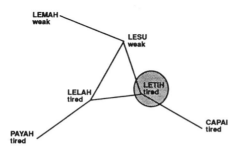

Figure 5.3. "Tired" cluster BI(J)

For two words in BI(M), the average is 47.5%, and one of these, *lesu*, is 61%, which is a moderately high rating

E. Translation equivalents

There are too few starter words to show any patterns.

F. Antecedent/outcome sentence completion tasks

None were done.

These "Tired" clusters make an interesting contrast to the previous set, the "Honest" clusters. On the basis of the English translations alone, neither set seems to fall within the emotion realm. But for the Indonesian languages, the prototypicality ratings suggest that although neither cluster is strongly emotional, the "Honest" clusters are much more strongly within the emotion realm than are the "Tired" clusters.

6. "Love" clusters *(kasih)*

A. Defining the clusters (see Figs. 6.1–6.3)

BM is a neat cluster of 5 words, 2 of which are hinge words:
>   *ibo*, in both "Love" and "Sad" clusters
>   *birahi*, in both "Love" and "Desire" clusters
> BI(M) is more complex, with a basic cluster of 8 words:
>   *Berahi* is linked by one bridge to *nafsu* in the "Desire" cluster and by a long bridge to *naik darah* in the "Anger" cluster.
>   *Hiba*, or *iba*, does not comfortably fit this sort of analysis, but it will be considered as a member of this "Love" cluster, with two bridges to the "Sad" cluster.
>   *Kasih* has one bridge to the "Sad" cluster.
>   *Haru* will be counted in the "Sad" cluster with two bridges back to the "Love" cluster.
>   Also, there are two twigs from the "Love" cluster.
>   *Mesra*, of this "Love" cluster, and *senang*, the key word of the "Happy" cluster, are linked by bridges through *bahagia*.

BI(J) has a core cluster of 5 words. *Berahi*, which in the other two maps is strongly a member of the "Love" clusters, is here slightly closer to

Figure 6.1. "Love" cluster BM

"Desire" and so will not be included in the "Love" cluster. *Iba*, on the other hand, narrowly makes it into this "Love" cluster. But this cluster is not as clearly bounded as its counterparts in the other two maps.

In addition, there is one twig and one branch from this cluster.

In summary, the Minangkabau cluster is simpler than either of the Indonesian maps, where in addition to the basic three – *kasih, sayang, cinta* – found in each map, there are *asmara, mesra,* and *belas kasihan.*

B. Key words

In Figures 6.1–6.3 the key words for each cluster are:

BM   *kasiah*
BI(M)   *kasih*
BI(J)   *cinta*

The core clusters, and the sets of words used in the antecedent/outcome tasks, are:

BM   *kasiah–sayang–cinta*
BI(M)   *kasih–sayang–cinta*
BI(M)   *cinta–asmara*

Between-language: BM *ibo*/BI(M) *kasih*

C. English glosses

Glosses for the Indonesian words in Minangkabau Indonesian and Javanese Indonesian are shown in Figures 6.2 and 6.3.

D. Membership in the realm of emotion: prototypicality ratings

In the figures the measure of membership in the realm of emotion is indicated for each of the starter words in Minangkabau and in Minangkabau Indonesian:

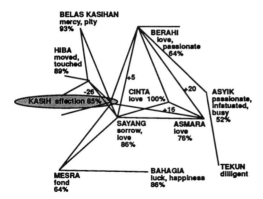

Figure 6.2. "Love" cluster BI(M)

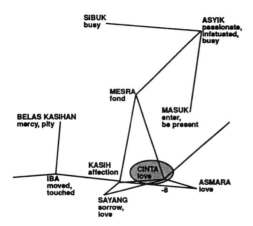

Figure 6.3. "Love" cluster BI(J)

BM: A very strongly emotional cluster, with 4 of the 5 words at 93%–100%. The key word for this "Love" cluster, *kasiah*, is less strongly emotional than 3 others in the cluster. *Birahi*, farthest in the map from the others, is also much lower as an emotion than the others.

BI(M): A strong cluster, although not as strong as the BM equivalent, with most words lower than their BM cognates. Again the key word *(kasih)* is less prototypical as an emotion than 4 other words in the cluster.

The strength of both these clusters corresponds to the situation in English, where the prototypicality ratings of Shaver et al. (1987:1066) show that "love" is the strongest of all 213 English words tested, and that 3 of the strongest 9 words are in the "Love" area.

E. Translation equivalents

To compare Minangkabau and Minangkabau Indonesian we can examine the most popular choices of words in the other language for each starter word.

Into Minangkabau Indonesian, with 5 starter words from Minangkabau, we see that

kasih (the key word) gets 3.5/5	70%
cognates get 2/5	40%
non-key, non-cognates get	
0.5/5	10%

The common pattern appears: The key word strongly outdraws the obvious cognates, and other choices are unimportant.

But into Minangkabau, with 8 starter words from Minangkabau Indonesian, we find an unusual pattern:

kasiah (the key word) gets	
only 2/8	25%
cognates get only 1/8	12.5%
but non-key, non-cognates	
get 5/8	62.5%

This raises a special problem of interpretation. We are able to account for a choice of cognate on the grounds either of lexical ignorance or of merging of the meanings in identical or nearly identical words. We are able to account for choosing the key word in the opposite cluster on the grounds of the cognitive reality of the clusters and the psychological saliency of the key word in the cluster. In most clusters, key words and cognates claim most of the translation equivalent choices. But in this "Love" cluster, when going from Minangkabau Indonesian to Minangkabau (not the other way) we have four out of five choices in the inner cluster that do not go to either key word or cognate. Figure 6.4 shows the first choices of translation equivalents between the two languages. We can disregard the two and a half choices made outside the main cluster (*berahi/birahi*, a hinge term, here reveals its affinity for the "Desire" cluster, and *asyik* for the "busy" sense of that word).

We can reorder the core words as in Figure 6.5, to reveal a regular

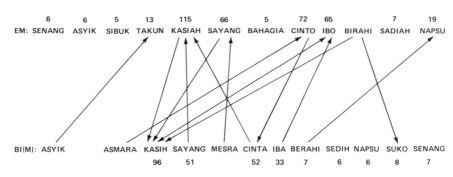

Figure 6.4. *Kasih* cluster. Translation between BM and BI(M).

Figure 6.5. Translation of *kasih* cluster. Regular shift in the BI(M) to BM direction; the BM to BI(M) direction shows the attraction of the key word, *kasih*

shift in choices in the direction of Minangkabau Indonesian to Minangkabau. That is, each Indonesian word chooses not its cognate but the next word to the left. The exception is *cinta*, which "should" choose *mesra*, but because there is no *mesra/masra* in Minangkabau, it is drawn by the key word, *kasiah*. Significantly, *kasih* resists the combined force of key word and cognate, choosing *ibo* instead of *kasiah*.

We have here strong evidence (1) for an ordering of words along a dimension; (2) for a regular shift between languages in terms of this dimension; and (3) that this effect is apparent when thinking from Indonesian to Minangkabau but not the opposite way.

There is no direct evidence to explain this phenomenon. Indeed, one would hardly expect people to be aware of patterning at this level. But we can propose an explanation:

The ordering dimension is a continuum of "Love" cluster words running from "pity" on the left to more pure "love," the Sanskrit word *asmara*, on the right.

The shift makes sense if we assume that people think of the cognate,

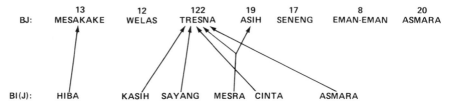

Figure 6.6. *Kasih* cluster translation from BI(J) to Javanese (BJ).

although literally the loosest translation equivalent, as culturally a worse match. For example, a situation, or a relationship that involves more of "love" in Indonesian would involve more of "pity" if discussed, and acted out, on the stage of Minangkabau.

There is independent support for this thesis in the maps themselves. In the Minangkabau map, the "Love" cluster is closer to "sad," while in Minangkabau Indonesian the "Love" cluster is closer to "happy."

These two lines of evidence provide the strongest case for differences between Minangkabau and Minangkabau Indonesian.

In Javanese there is no comparable shift, but there is strong evidence for the attraction of the key word: 4.5 of the 5.0 Indonesian starters have as their first choice *tresna* (Javanese for "love"), presumably the key word in the Javanese cluster. (Fig. 6.6)

F. Antecedent/outcome sentence completion tasks

Four different sentence completion tasks were carried out with these clusters. The word sets were:

a. BI(M)   *cinta–kasih–sayang* with 18 subjects
b. BI(M)   *cinta–asmara* with 26 subjects
c. BM   *kasiah–sayang–cinto* with 28 subjects
d. Between-language   BI(M) *kasih*/BM *ibo* with 18 subjects

a. Minangkabau Indonesian: *cinta–kasih–sayang*

BI(M) *cinta* antecedents from 18 subjects

    14   (saw) a desirable other (beau-
            tiful, wealthy, good person-
            ality, etc)

    2   because the other reciprocated
            love

1	saw an admirable child
3	of these involve interaction

BI(M) *cinta* outcomes from 18 subjects

5	make a sacrifice
2	help the other
2	worship the other
2	want to be near the other
1	of these involves emotion (feels fortunate)

BI(M) *kasih* antecedents from 18 subjects

9	because of suffering other (orphan, poor, in accident, leads disorganized life)
5	because the child is admirable (gentle, lively, good . . .)
1	desirable other
2	other reciprocates love
4	involve interaction

BI(M) *kasih* outcomes from 18 subjects

12	give, grant, help
16	involve interaction
0	involve emotion

BI(M) *sayang* antecedents from 18 subjects

11	because of admirable child (funny, patient, well-behaved, studies hard, etc.)
1	because of desirable other
2	other reciprocates love
2	involve interaction

BI(M) *sayang* outcomes from 18 subjects

4	protect other
5	help other
15	involve interaction
1	involves emotion (happy)

b. Minangkabau Indonesian: *cinta–asmara*

BI(M) *cinta* antecedents from 26 subjects:

16	because of desirable other
6	other reciprocates love

       2   the child was admirable
       0   involve interaction

BI(M) *cinta* outcomes from 26 subjects
       5   make a sacrifice
       4   propose marriage
       2   think of other
       2   want to be near other
       2   value other highly
       6   involve emotion (love, happy,
              respect, indebtedness)

BI(M) *asmara* antecedents from 26 subjects
       7   desirable other
       6   other reciprocates love
       2   involve interaction
       5   involve emotion (falling in love,
              desire, love, flattered, nos-
              talgia)

BI(M) *asmara* outcomes from 26 subjects
       4   thought about others
      10   involve emotions (desire,
              happy, feels fortunate . . .)
       4   involve interaction (desires
              nearness, hold hands, took
              walk)

To summarize these Indonesian words:

	Antecedents	Outcomes
cinta (1)	desirable other	sacrifice, interaction
cinta (2)	desirable other	sacrifice, interaction
kasih	suffering other	helps, interaction
sayang	admirable child	protects, helps, interaction
asmara	desirable other	emotions, interactions

There are no absolute differences among these 4 words, but this would hardly be expected since they are members of a single meaning cluster. On the other hand, the main tendencies are quite divergent: *Cinta* and *asmara* are both caused by desirable others, but *cinta* results in sacrifices, whereas *asmara* results in positive emotions. *Sayang* is caused by the positive attributes of a child, whereas *kasih* is caused by the suffering and misfortune of others, although the outcomes of each are aid and protection.

English is notoriously impoverished in love vocabulary, but *asmara* is closest to "love," whereas *kasih* corresponds more to "pity" and "nurturance" or "sympathy." Although we have no trouble understanding *cinta* and *sayang*, there is no single English word that really means either.

c. Minangkabau: *kasiah–sayang–cinto*

BM *kasiah* antecedents from 28 subjects

14	suffering others
3	desirable others
4	admirable child
6	involve emotion (happy, love, pity)

BM *kasiah* outcomes from 28 subjects

20	gives help
0	sacrifice
7	involve emotion (controls anger, hospitable, well-mannered, pity, shows emotion)
20	(those who help) involve interaction

BM *sayang* antecedents from 28 subjects

10	admirable child
10	suffering others
3	desirable others
1	involves emotions (desire)

BM *sayang* outcomes from 28 subjects

16	gives help
0	sacrifice
5	touches child (kisses, hugs, pats)
2	involves emotion

BM *cinto* antecedents from 28 subjects

15	desirable other
4	admirable child
5	involves emotions

BM *cinto* outcomes from 28 subjects

6	help
5	sacrifice

4   praise
4   wants to be near, to marry
7   involve emotions

The antecedents and outcomes of the Minangkabau words can be summarized as follows:

	Antecedents	*Outcomes*
cinto	desirable other	help, sacrifice, emotion
kasiah	suffering other	helps
sayang	suffering other, admirable child	helps

Comparing this with the summary of antecedents and outcomes of Indonesian words above, it is clear there is little difference between the three corresponding words in each language.

This brings us back to the translation equivalents, where in the Indonesian-to-Minangkabau direction there is a shift away from cognates and key words. Now it appears that the cognates are indeed lexically the closest matches. Therefore, it seems most likely that this translation shift is in fact more sociolinguistic than strictly lexical. That is, people respond to the request for a synonym not with the word that means the same, but with the word that would be used in the same situation.

While claiming this sociolinguistic shift, however, it should be noted how rare it is – in most clusters and indeed in this "Love" cluster when moving from Minangkabau to Minangkabau Indonesian, the choice of translation equivalents is governed by the principles of cognation or key word attraction.

d. For the direct between-language comparison, these "Love" clusters were not ideal because the key words in each language were the cognates *kasiah/kasih*. (I have assumed that between-language comparisons of nearly identical words would not be productive because they would tend to merge into a single dual-purpose word.) Instead, three between-language pairs, each manifesting the translation shift discussed above, were chosen:

Minangkabau	*Minangkabau Indonesian*
ibo	*kasih*
kasiah	*sayang*
cinto	*asmara*

Kasih/ibo:

BI(M) *kasih* antecedents from 78 subjects
43   suffering others
15   admirable child

    8   involve emotion (happy, love,
                pity, reciprocated love . . .)
    1   involved interaction

BI(M) *kasih* outcomes from 78 subjects
    54   give help (15 of these help
                child)
    3   avoid hurt (avoid fight with
                wife, etc.)
        N.B.: the 54 helping situations involved interaction

BM *ibo* antecedents from 78 subjects
    64   suffering other (27 children)
    4   admirable child
    3   involves interaction
    2   involve emotion

BM *ibo* outcomes from 78 subjects
    64   help
    5   involve emotion
    64   involve interaction

These results suggest that *kasih* and *ibo* have virtually the same meaning – mainly the result of suffering; secondarily, the reaction to an admirable child – and that the outcomes are interactive helping or giving.
    Sayang/kasiah:

BI(M) *sayang* antecedents from 60 subjects
    23   admirable child
    12   suffering, unfortunate other
    12   desirable other
    3   emotion (love, reciprocated
                love)
    2   help, gift
    8   involve interaction

BI(M) *sayang* outcomes from 60 subjects
    33   help, make presents (14 to
                child)
    7   touch, pat child
    4   remember
    5   involve emotion (love, happi-
                ness, smile)
    2   concerned with being apart
                from other

BM *kasiah* antecedents from 60 subjects
> 23   suffering, misfortunate other (8 children)
> 16   desirable other
> 8   admirable child
> 8   involve emotion (6 reciprocated love)
> 6   involve interaction

BM *kasiah* outcomes from 60 subjects
> 35   help, protect, give presents (21 to child)
> 6   involve emotion (love, not annoyed)
> 0   involve touching
> 7   involve not parting from other

Asmara/cinto:

BI(M) *asmara* antecedents from 59 subjects
> 30   involve emotions (*cinta* 8; *sayang,* reciprocated love 4; happiness, lust, respect)
> 9   desirable other (6 physical, 3 psychological)
> 4   want to be close to
> 7   other flirted
> 1   arranged marriage
> 1   congenial (*cocok*)

BI(M) *asmara* outcomes from 59 subjects
> 18   involve emotion (happy, lust, jealousy, love . . .)
> 10   desires to be near other
> 13   thinks of other
> 4   confusion (doesn't eat, forgets)

BM *cinto* antecedents from 59 subjects
> 33   desirable other (17 psychological, 11 physical, 2 good family . . .)
> 9   involve emotion (like, happy, love, reciprocated love, 3)

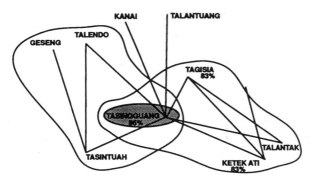

Figure 7.1. "Offended" cluster BM

3	arranged marriage
1	suffering other
1	desires to be near other

BM *cinto* outcomes from 59 subjects

13	wants to be near, not to be parted from other
8	involves emotion (happy, love, nostalgia)
2	confusion
1	thinks of other

G. The ethnography of "Love"

See the discussion in Section 6.6.

7. "Offended" clusters (*tersinggung*)

A. Defining the clusters (see Figs. 7.1–7.3)

> BM: Three overlapping minimal triangle clusters totaling 6 words. *Tasingguang* is a member of all three triangles, *tagisia ati* of two. The cluster includes three twigs. External links: through *ketek ati* to *ibo* in the "Sad" cluster and also through *ketek ati* to *kacewa* in that cluster; linked through *tasintuah* to the *payah* cluster.

> BI(M): a minimal 3-word triangle cluster linked to *haru* in the "Sad" cluster. It includes *tergugah*, which lies along the link to *haru* and has one twig.

> BI(J): a 4-word cluster with one branch. External links: from *tersen-*

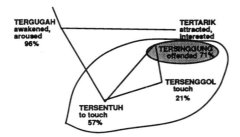

Figure 7.2. "Offended" cluster BI(M)

tuh via *haru* to the "Love" cluster; from *tersinggung* to *sakit hati* in that cluster; and from *tersinggung* via a bridge to *sindir* in that cluster.

All these clusters are comparable in size, in membership, and in external relations in each map.

B. Key words

The key words in this cluster are:
    BM: *tasingguang*
    BI(M): *tersinggung*
    BI(J): *tersenggol*

C. English glosses (see Figs. 7.2, 7.3)

This is a particularly difficult cluster to gloss in English on the basis of the dictionary translations. The emphasis on physical touching and on generalized offense or arousal are of little help, but for the sake of consistency, this cluster can be given the English gloss of "Offended" cluster.

D. Membership in the realm of emotion: prototypicality ratings

Figures 7.1 and 7.2 show the prototypicality measures for the few starter words included in these clusters.

In Minangkabau, the 3 words are between 83% and 85%, making this a relatively strong cluster, while the 4 words in Minangkabau Indonesian show a great range from 21% to 96%, for an average of 61%. It

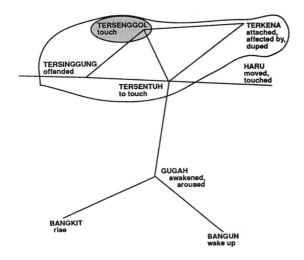

Figure 7.3. "Offended" cluster BI(J)

seems likely that the alternative, nonemotion meaning of physical touching is strong enough to effect the Indonesian but not the Minang-kabau.

In both languages, the key word of the cluster has also the strongest prototypicality score.

The strong Minangkabau scores and the two stronger Indonesian scores are important evidence arguing that this cluster does indeed need to be considered carefully as emotion. (The rarity of these words in common usage and the dictionary vagueness at first suggested that this would not be a significant cluster.)

E. Translation equivalents

In the Minangkabau Indonesian map, the modal choices of each translation equivalent go to the key word of the comparable cluster in the Minangkabau map, not to cognates or others.

BM chooses *tersinggung* (the key word in Indonesian), with only *tas-intuah* choosing *tersentuh*, its cognate, in preference to the key word.

BI(M) chooses *tasingguang* (the key word in Minangkabau).

BI(J) chooses *kesenggol* ("to get touched or jostled unintentionally"; Horne 1974:542), which is presumably the key word of the Javanese cluster. *Kessinggung,* a Javanese equivalent of the key words in the other two maps, is chosen by ten subjects, but this word is not in Horne. It may be an example of illegitimate lazy phoneme shift, creating a logical but nonexistent cognate.

F. Antecedent/outcome sentence completion task

The sentence completion task compared one pair in each language, but no between-language pairs.

BI(M) *tersinggung* antecedents from 27 subjects
- 24 belittling talk or actions
    - 5 tease, ridicule
    - 8 in which a friend is agent
- 2 involve dangerous or awkward travel (e.g., the path is narrow)
- 8 involve negative emotions (contempt: *ejek, caci maki, hina*)

BI(M) *tersinggung* outcomes from 27 subjects
- 17 involve negative emotions (13 *marah*, anger; discouraged, shamed, sad, hate)
- 3 involve avoidance
- 4 involve retaliation
- 1 involves help

BI(M) *tersentuh* antecedents from 27 subjects
- 16 suffering, misfortunate others
- 2 belittling or insulting acts
- 7 undesirable adventures
    - 3 crowds, narrow spaces
    - 4 other danger or discomfort

BI(M) *tersentuh* outcomes from 27 subjects
- 9 gave help
- 3 turned to see the toucher
- 10 involve emotions (4 sad; 2 anger, surprised, gloomy, pity, smiled)

BM *tasingguang* antecedents from 26 subjects
   23   belittling talk
            5   tease, ridicule
            5   friends as agent
    1   crowded situation

BM *tasingguang* outcomes from 26 subjects
   14   negative emotions (11 *berang* or
                naiak darah, anger)
    3   avoidance
    6   retaliate

BM *tagisia ati* antecedents from 26 subjects
   22   belittling talk
            5 friends as agent

BM *tagisia ati* outcomes from 26 subjects
   11   involve emotion (3 sad, 5 cry,
                lazy, irritated, angry)
    8   avoidance
    5   retaliate

The main trends in the antecedent/outcome scenarios of these 4 words can be summarized as follows:

BM key word *tasingguang:* almost the same as *tersinggung.*

BI(M) key word *tersinggung:* caused by belittling talk and actions, often by a friend, resulting in negative feelings, mainly anger, and some retaliation.

BM *tagisia ati:* caused by belittling, shaming talk and actions, often by friends, resulting in sadness, avoidance, and some retaliation.

BI(M) *tersentuh:* caused by suffering/unfortunate other, or undesirable/uncomfortable adventure, resulting in help to the unfortunate or negative feelings, more sad than angry.

G. The ethnography of the cluster

This cluster is difficult to characterize because there is no single appropriate English word for it. *Tersentuh* is much like "pity/compassion," but even it has an anger element. The other three words have a "shame/betrayal" sense, resulting in anger and retaliation (and, for *tagisia ati,* sadness).

In the maps there are links to the "Sad" clusters, and also to "Shame." The antecedents and outcomes contain strong references to anger, too, although this does not show up in the maps.

A secondary meaning pervades these words – a negative reaction to a space problem: crowded, being touched (the Javanese dictionary spoke of "unintentional jostling" and narrow paths). Again, the English "touched" is misleading because when that word is used as an emotion, it suggests pleasant and surprising experiences. Here, clearly, being physically touched or crowded is unpleasant.

A striking feature of these scenarios is the high incidence of emotions as outcomes of emotions. For these 4 words, we find emotions named as outcomes:

tersinggung	63%
tasingguang	54%
tagisia ati	42%
tersentuh	37%

In English, we can see how emotions like Love may produce other emotions like Happiness, whereas Happiness itself does not produce other emotions. Love, then, is strongly emotion-genic, Happiness weakly so.

Comparing emotion-genic scores for words in both languages:

"Love" clusters	15%
tersinggung clusters	49%

The significance of this emotion-genic measure has already been discussed, in Section 7.9.

More socially complex emotions, although they may have as high a ranking *as emotions*, produce more complex, indirect outcomes, and work through the more basic emotions.

It is significant that even the figures for emotion-genicity just cited can be reanalyzed: The emotions produced by the "Love" cluster words, few as they are, are mainly within the "Love" clusters themselves (e.g., "When he is in love, he is infatuated"). This lessens their information value and even raises suspicions that the task was not always performed thoughtfully. On the other hand, the high emotion-genic score of the *tersinggung* words is achieved without *any* words from that cluster. The outcomes of the *tersinggung* words are *always* words from other clusters.

Now we can predict that the pattern of these choices will point to key words in the following clusters, which we shall call "basic emotion clusters."

Figure 8.1. "Longing" cluster BM

8. "Longing" clusters (*rindu*)

A. Defining the clusters (see Figs. 8.1–8.3)

Only in Minangkabau Indonesian – BI(M) – is there a cluster: 4 words, including *ingin*, an important hinge word in the "Desire" cluster.

In Javanese Indonesian, *rindu* and *kangen* simply form a twig from *ingin*; in Minangkabau, *rindu* is a twig from *taragak*.

Because the BI(M) data are so strong, ideally this cluster should have been investigated more thoroughly across the three maps.

B. Key words (see Fig. 2)

In BI(M), *rindu* is the key word.

Antecedents and outcomes were elicited for only one pair, *rindu–kangen*.

C. English glosses (see Figs. 8.2, 8.3)

In this set the dictionary translations of the Indonesian words are quite accurate and do reflect the "longing," "yearning" aspect bracketed between "desire" and "remembrance."

D. Membership in the realm of emotion: prototypicality ratings

There is extraordinary strength: Each word in the core pair, *rindu–kangen*, has 100% prototypicality scores. The only other Indonesian word

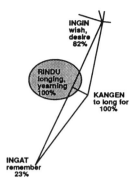

Figure 8.2. "Longing" cluster BI(M)

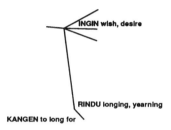

Figure 8.3. "Longing" cluster BI(J)

with 100% is *cinta* (love). *Ingin* at 82% is quite high, and only *ingat*, at 23%, fades out of the emotion picture. Presumably *ingin* is just "remembering," with little trace of the intense nostalgia of the core pair.

E. Translation equivalents

Despite the meager data, there are some strong results from the translation tasks:

In BI(M), *rindu*, the key word, attracts the strongest translation claims from the Minangkabau words.

But in Minangkabau, *taragak* gets the modal choices. It would have been the key word of a well-developed "Longing" cluster. However, its prototypicality score was much lower than the scores of the Indonesian equivalents.

In Javanese it is *kangen*, not *rindu*, that overwhelmingly gets the modal choices from Indonesian.

F. Antecedent/outcome sentence completion task

The only set explored in this area was the BI(M) pair *rindu–kangen*.

BI(M) *rindu* antecedents from 26 subjects

14	not met, or not seen, other
8	involve distance: left, not returned
2	recalling, remembering
9	involve an unidentified other
8	involve a boy/girlfriend
7	involve relatives
2	involve a place

BI(M) *rindu* outcomes from 26 subjects

12	have or intend to meet or reunite with other
6	wrote letter to other
3	looked at photo of other
2	thought about other
6	involve relative
2	involve friend
2	involve boy/girlfriend
9	involve emotions (7 *ingin* desire, cried, *rindu*)

BI(M) *kangen* antecedents from 26 subjects

16	involve distance: left, or not returned
8	not met or not seen
0	recalling
6	involve unidentified other
4	involve boy/girlfriend
5	involve relatives
10	involve a place

BI(M) *kangen* outcomes from 26 subjects

15	met, or intend to meet, went to
3	thought about, recalled
2	wrote, phoned

9	involve place
7	involve unidentified other
4	involve relatives
2	involve boy/girlfriend
0	involve friend
1	involves emotion (love/pity)

Both *rindu* and *kangen* are caused by absence, nonpresence, distance from another person. For *kangen*, a place, usually the home village, can also be important. The identity of the other person is often not specified, but when it is, relatives and lovers are equally important.

The outcomes are the act or the intention to end the separation by closing the distance through travel, or to ameliorate it by writing, calling, or thinking about the other. *Kangen* is more apt to take action, to travel back to the place, while *rindu* is split between reunion and action at a distance.

Neither word is strongly emotion-genic:

Kangen is ¹⁄₂₆, 4%.

Rindu is ⁹⁄₂₆, 35%, but seven of these outcomes use the word *ingin (desire)*, but in the sense more of "intention" and one other is the redundant *rindu*, so *rindu* should be considered ¹⁄₂₆, or 4%, like *kangen*.

G. The ethnography of "Longing"

See the discussion in Section 6.8.

9. "Sincere" clusters (*benar*)

A. Defining the clusters (see Figs. 9.1–9.3)

BM has a 4-word cluster, 3 of which words are cognate with the BI(M) cluster words. This BM cluster has a bridge to *nio*, in the "Desire" cluster. The 3 words of the isolated twig in BM are cognate to the words in the BI(M) branch.

BI(M) has a 4-word cluster with a branch from *serius*, and the cluster is connected by a bridge to *lurus* and then *jujur* in the "Honest" cluster and, eventually, to the "Desire" cluster.

On the authority of the BI(M) map, isolated parts of the other two maps were brought together.

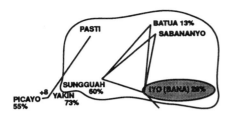

Figure 9.1. "Sincere" cluster BM

BI(J) has an isolated 3-word cluster with a twig, and these are the same 4 words of the BI(M) cluster. The 3 words of the BI(M) branch are found in BI(J) in a long twig coming out of the *sabar* cluster.

B. Key words

The key words are as follows:

BM	*iyo bana*
BI(M)	*sungguh–sungguh*
(BI(J)	*benar* and *betul–betul*

No antecedents and outcomes were elicited for this area.

C. English glosses (see Figs. 9.2, 9.3)

The dictionary translations make this cluster appear not like emotion but like a personal characteristic, one of "serious/sincere." In this case, the European loan word *serius* seems to retain its precise meaning in Indonesian use.

D. Membership in the realm of emotion: prototypicality ratings

With its fragmented appearance in the maps, and its nonemotion English glosses, it is rather surprising to find that in both languages there are words with high prototypicality scores:

	Minangkabau	Minangkabau Indonesian
YAKIN	73%	86%
SUNGGUH	60%	75%
PICAYO	55%	n.a.

Unfortunately there are no data on antecedents and outcomes to flesh out the meanings of these words and these clusters. We are left to choose between two possible but not provable explanations:

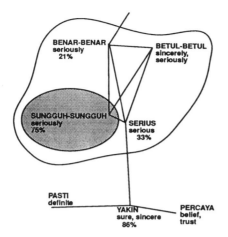

Figure 9.2. "Sincere" cluster BI(M)

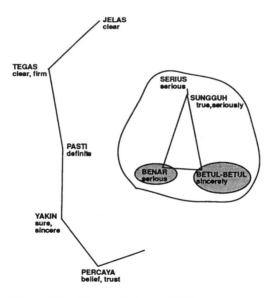

Figure 9.3. "Sincere" cluster BI(J)

1. The realms in English and Indonesian are different: The English realm of "emotion" does not include "seriousness" (e.g., in the Shaver et al. list of 213 prototypicality ratings (1987:1066), neither "serious" nor "sincere," appear at all). But *perasaan hati*, which is a category not pre-

cisely covering the same ground as "emotion," does include the "serious/"sincere" words.

2. On the other hand, the translation problem lies at the level of the emotion words themselves: They are not well translated by the English "serious" or "sincere," and are in fact obvious emotion words. This second situation is similar to what appeared in the "Offended" cluster (*tersinggung*).

Unfortunately, we do not have the data to establish which of these possibilities is more accurate.

F. Antecedent/outcome sentence completion tasks

None were done.

"SAD" AREA (*SEDIH*)

The "Sad" area, centered on the word *sadiah/sedih*, is one of the largest and most complex in the maps. It consists of embedded, overlapping clusters (in Minangkabau Indonesian). Rather than deal with this area cluster by cluster, it seems better to handle it in its entirety. As it turns out, the entire "Sad" area is like other individual clusters in the ease with which it can be identified as consisting of sets of words with maximal mutual connections and minimal external connections.

BI(M). The core of this area in Minangkabau Indonesian consists of three clusters focused on *susah* and *sedih*. Because of the constraints of two-dimensional paper they are superimposed in Figure 10.2, but in Figure 10.3 the mass is pulled apart to show each of the three clusters in isolation.

10. "Difficult" clusters (*sulit*)

This is a 3-word triangle with *sulit* the key word. *Susah* is a hinge word to the other clusters in this "Sad" area. There are two twigs.

There are no external connections.

11. "Sad" clusters (*sedih*)

This is a 9-word cluster with *sedih* as the key word, extending from *risau* to *haru*.

Two branches (one with the *tersinggung* cluster) from *haru*. *Sedih* and *susah* are both hinge words to the other clusters in the "Sad" area, and *risau* is a hinge word to the "Confused" area. External connections: three links from *sedih* and *haru* to the "Love" cluster;

Risau is a hinge word to the "Confused" cluster; and there are two links from *susah* to the "Confused" cluster.

12. "Gloomy" clusters *(murung)*

This is a 5-word cluster with *sedih* as key word. There is one branch to *sayu*; one twig to *gelap*; two links to the *letih* cluster. External connections: one bridge from *sedih* to the "Love" cluster, as just noted.

Branches. A branch from *susah* includes the *ancam* cluster, #13 ("Torture" cluster). But because *susah* is a hinge in the three "Sad" area clusters already described, this branch cannot be definitively attributed to any single one of them.

In summary. The "Sad" area includes 50 words in 5 clusters and various branches and twigs, but it is self-contained, with only five external links plus one hinge word.

BM. In Minangkabau (Fig. 10.1) a core "Sad" cluster with 6 words, *sadiah* being the key word, has a branch from *lintuah* and a twig from *sadiah*.

It also has the unusual complex branch that links a series of clusters. Here, somewhat arbitrarily, and following the pattern of the Minang-kabau Indonesian map, the *tasingguang* cluster is counted as being part of this "Sad" cluster, but the next cluster on the chain, the *manyasa* cluster, will be dealt with elsewhere.

External connections:

  ibo is a hinge word with the "Love" Cluster
  rusuah is a hinge word with the "Confusion" cluster, and *sadiah* has two links with the "Confusion" cluster
  padiah has a bridge to the *sakik ati* cluster
  ketek ati is linked in a chain through three small clusters to the "De-sire" cluster

With 20 words, this is a smaller region than its counterpart in the BI(M) map, and the "Sad" core is simpler.

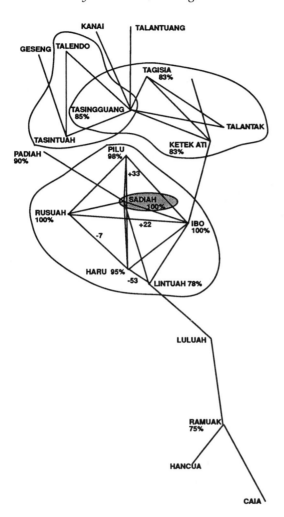

Figure 10.1. "Sad" area BM

BI(J). In Javanese Indonesian (Fig. 10.4) the three core clusters, – 10, 11, and 12. – each involve *sedih* and *susah* as hinge words:

10.　　A 3-word triangle of *susah–*
　　　　sukar–sulit, like the #10.
　　　　"Difficult" cluster in BI(M),
　　　　with *sukar* as the key word.

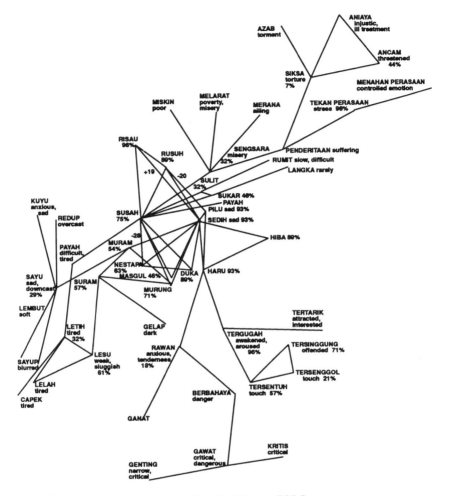

Figure 10.2. Overview of the "Sad" area BI(M)

11.	A 4-word cluster, words that are in the #10. "Sad" cluster in BI(M), with *sedih* as the key word.
12.	A 4-word cluster, 3 of which words are in the #12. "Gloomy" cluster in BI(M), with *sedih* as the key word.

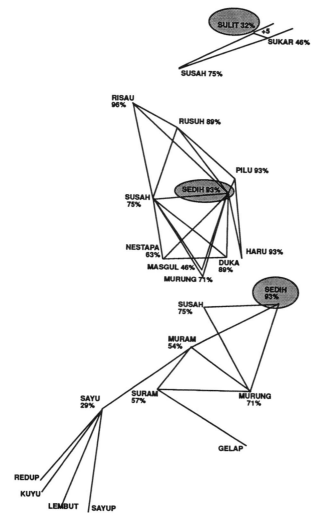

Figure 10.3. Three "Sad" clusters isolated from Figure 10.2 BI(M).

Other features. The *tersinggung* cluster has already been dealt with in the BM discussion.

An isolated 3-word triangle cluster, with four twigs, and *gawat/bahaya* as the key words, corresponds to the BI(M) branch from *haru*. This can be called the "Danger" cluster.

A 3-word triangle cluster with the hinge word *nestapa* is also in the "Sad" cluster, with *sengsara* as the key word.

Two other isolates are also included here because in BI(M) they are linked to the "Sad" clusters:

the isolate twig around *sayu*

the isolate branch around *siksa*

External connections: These five units are not connected to each other as they are in BI(M) and BM. In the main cluster, *susah* has two links, via *pilu* and *makan hati*, to the "Hate" cluster; *makan hati* has one link to the *jengkel* cluster, and *sedih* has one link to the *resah* cluster. *Masgul* has one link to the *ragu* cluster.

In summary. This area in Javanese Indonesian has 36 words, closer to Minangkabau Indonesian. But it is more fragmented, and the main cluster is less clearly defined. These 36 words are considered together, then, on the authority of the Minangkabau Indonesian map, not on the basis of these Javanese responses alone.

B. Key words (see Figs. 10.1, 10.3, 10.4)

For the details, see the preceding section. The major key words for these "Sad" clusters are:

BM	*sadiah*
BI(M)	*sedih*
BI(J)	*sedih*

C. English glosses

Because there was little information from antecedent/outcome sentence completion tasks to help sort out the meanings in this area, we shall have to make do with the dictionary translations.

BI(M). 10. This triangle develops out of the "trouble" – "difficult" sense of *susah*, and could be glossed as the "Worry" cluster.

11. This cluster contains the core "sad" meanings. It contains *sedih* and *pilu*, which will be explored in the antecedent/outcome section. As we shall see, it can be labeled with confidence as the "Sad" cluster.

12. This cluster moves from "sad" all the way to visual darkness, and can be glossed as the "Gloomy" cluster because the words in Indonesian

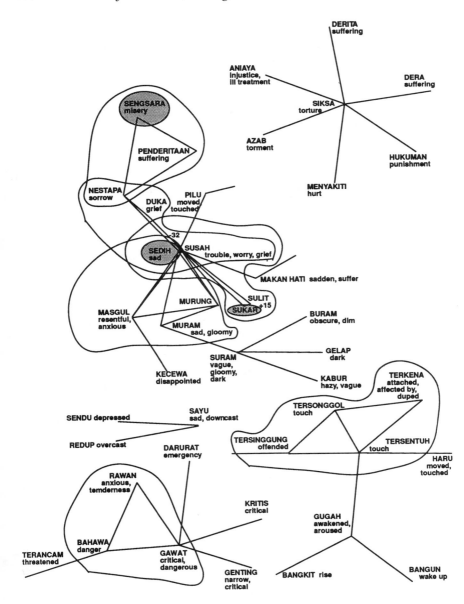

Figure 10.4. "Sad" area BI(J)

have the same double meaning, emotional and physical visibility, as "gloomy" has in English.

The peripheral clusters are the

tersinggung cluster (#7)

letih, or "Tired" cluster (#5)

siksa, or "Torture" cluster (#13)

There are antecedent/outcome data only for the *tersinggung* cluster among these periperals, but from the dictionary data it seems clear that there is a connection with sadness.

Consideration of this area makes it clear how misleading it could be to try to specify how many words are in a particular cluster. Certainly one can say with confidence that in this "Sad" area there are 50 words. If one were to test each word for prototypicality in a "Sad" category, however, then *sedih* would surely be the strongest prototype. But the strength would drop off and the peripheries would be only weakly "sad."

D. Membership in the realm of emotion: prototypicality ratings

In BI(M) there are 6 strong words (89%–96%) in the "Sad" cluster itself, with the rest of that cluster and the other core clusters much weaker. Most of the peripheral words for which there are ratings drop off rapidly, as might be expected from the English glosses. The glosses and the prototypicality ratings give a picture of a very uneven landscape of emotionality.

In BM (Fig. 10.1) the core is stronger than in Minangkabau Indonesian. Three words are 100%. Of the 4 words on the 209-word Minangkabau list that were rated 100%, 3 are here and the fourth, *risau,* is immediately adjacent, a short bridge away from *rusuah.* There are two words at the next level of the Minangkabau list, with a rating of 98%. One of these, *pilu,* is a member of this cluster, and the other, *sayang,* is linked by a short bridge to *ibo,* of this cluster. Of the 4 words at the next level of the Minangkabau list, at 95%, *haru* is here and *cinta* is in the next cluster, the "Love" cluster.

This dominance of "sad" words, or the concentration of the highest rated words across this "Sad" cluster, strongly argues that this area is the prototypical emotion area for Minangkabau.

A similar pattern emerged in Minangkabau Indonesian, where two of the three 100% words are in the small "Longing" cluster, not far from the "Sad" cluster.

If one looks at those words with prototypicality ratings of 93% and higher in the two languages, as listed in Tables 2 and 3 (Section 3.2), it is evident that the weight of both distributions centers on the "sad" clusters. For contrast, compare the Shaver et al. (1987:1066) American English ratings, where the top words are, in order,

> Love, Anger, Hate, Depression, Fear, Jealousy, Happiness, Passion, Affection, Sadness

Perhaps the greatest surprise is that "anger" is not strong in the Indonesian lists, even though it has a large cluster of words. In Minangkabau and in Minangkabau Indonesian it resembles "sad" in both size and complexity.

E. Translation equivalents

Considering how rich and important this "Sad" area turned out to be, it is unfortunate that more words were not used in elicitations of translation equivalents.

From BM to BI(M), the modal choices were to *sedih*, the key, 5/13; but to non-key, non-cognates, 8/13:

rasah	>*gelisah*
susah	>*sulit*
risau	>*rusuh*
seso	>*susah*
galisah	>*resah*
ranyah	>*resah*
lintuah	>*luluh*
lintuah	>*iba*

There is no obvious pattern in these choices, although if we had more choices from more words to fill in the gaps, a pattern might have emerged.

From BI(M) to BM, *sadiah*, the key word, gets 8/12, and non-key, non-cognate words get 2/12:

susah>*sulik*

risau >*rusuah*

From BI(J) to *javanese*, of the modal choices, 6/7 go to *susah*, presumably the key term in the Javanese cluster.

F. Antecedent/outcome sentence completion task

This task was done with the BI(M) set *sedih–pilu;* also, comparable triads were done in each language:

BM	*rayu–bujuak–sadiah*
BI(M)	*rayu–bujuk–sedih*

The two triads were chosen on the basis of early results which linked *bujuk/rayu* closely to *sedih*. This association was supported by dictionary definitions that also suggested close relationships. The maps, however, show no direct links, and neither do the antecedents and outcomes. Therefore, here we shall examine the antecedents and outcomes only for *sedih/sadiah* and *pilu,* and return to *rayu/bujuk* in a later section.

Minangkabau Indonesian: *sedih–pilu:*

BI(M) *sedih* antecedents from 26 subjects

16	suffering ego (life situation, lost other; 12 parted from other, including 7 deaths)
7	suffering other
2	children
8	relative
5	friend, boy/girlfriend

BI(M) *sedih* outcomes from 26 subjects

13	wept
5	thought or pondered
1	was alone
1	with another
4	involved emotion (4 *murung,* gloomy; *iba*)

For comparison and support, here are the *sedih* responses from the *sedih–rayu–busuk* set:

BI(M) *sedih* antecedents from 28 subjects

17	suffering ego, including 9 parted from other, including 3 death
5	suffering other
0	child
7	relative
9	friend, lover

BI(M) *sedih* outcomes from 28 subjects

13	wept
4	thought
4	were alone
1	with another
1	was sick

    4   involved emotion (no *nafsu*,
                passion; *kasih*, pity, 2 sad)
    1   looked for fun
    1   recollected

BI(M) *pilu* antecedents from 26 subjects

    3   suffering others (not stated
                who)
    9   suffering others, including
                5   children
    8   suffering ego
   10   parted from other, including
                3   death
    7   involve relatives
    6   involve lover/friend

BI(M) *pilu* outcomes from 26 subjects

    6   wept
    7   thought, pondered
    4   were alone
    2   helped other
    8   involved emotions (8 sad)

BM *sadiah* antecedents from 26 subjects

    2   suffering others
   16   suffering ego
   11   parted from other, including
                5 deaths, of which 2
                were of pets
    6   involved a relative
    4   involved a lover or friend

BM *sadiah* outcomes from 26 subjects

   13   wept
    4   thought
    2   were alone
    2   asked for help
    2   emotion (*barek ati; sayu* [sad])

These results do not clearly distinguish *sedih* from *pilu*, which is not surprising because the map shows them to be very close: Both are caused by suffering and misfortune, especially being parted from an important other. In *sedih*, the sufferer is more likely to be ego, while in *pilu* ego and other are equally likely. The scenarios involve relatives as much as friends and lovers.

Scherer et al. found that Americans and Europeans differed greatly from Japanese in the prevalence of death as an antecedent to "sadness" (1988). The figures were 22.4% and 22.2% versus 5.2% for the Japanese. They suggest this is the result of different cultural constructions of death.

The composite figure for these Minangkabau in three words in both languages is 17%, much closer to the Euro-American level than to the Japanese level. This could be interpreted as showing that death for the Minangkabau Moslems more resembles death for the Judeo-Christian Euro-Americans than for the Shinto-Buddhist Japanese. In fact, it suggests that further research might be useful.

We can make comparisons with other clusters: Where *kasiah/kasih*, in the "Love" cluster, has been caused by suffering others to the exclusion of suffering egos, and so was close to "pity," these words are more evenly balanced between ego and others.

Comparing these words with the "Longing" cluster (*rindu–kangen*) where there is also much parting/being apart/distance, one sees that here there is much more finality, and often death, in the parting.

The outcomes of *sedih/pilu* are more turbulent – much weeping, especially with *sedih*, pondering, being alone, and much emotion, although the emotions named are almost exclusively other emotions in this "Sad" area.

In contrast, outcomes of the "Longing" cluster are less emotional and characteristically involve rational plans to meet again or to revisit the place.

Sedih looks very much the same in the two Minangkabau Indonesian sets, suggesting that here at least the different lexical contexts did not elicit different aspects of the same word. (That is, if one had asked for a contrast of "gloomy–sad" and the "gloomy–dark," the two scenarios for "gloomy" would be quite different because each would draw on a different meaning of the word. This has not occurred in the present case.)

Sadiah, the Minangkabau cognate, is similar but even more strongly the result of self-suffering, usually because of parting from another relative, lover, or friend, and the outcome is mainly weeping, with some solitary pondering.

As predicted for basic emotions like those in the "Sad" area, the scenarios do not often result in emotions, and when they do, it is invariably another emotion in the same, "Sad," area. Thus, the emotion-genic score for these words is very low.

G. The ethnography of "Sadness" (see also the discussion in Section 6.11)

This area, and the "Sad" cluster in particular, seem to be the focus of Indonesian and, even more, Minangkabau emotion. And the anteced-ent/outcome scenarios involve interpersonal relationships, specifically the severing of those relationships. Again, this is even stronger in Min-angkabau than in Indonesian. Other emotions, such as Love or Happi-ness, are less central and their scenarios show less interpersonal inter-action. "Happy," for example, might logically be considered the opposite of "sad," but it has a prototypicality rating much lower and its anteced-ents are centered on personal achievement, not on what would be the opposite of the "sad" scenarios, namely, being with, or joining, another person. What we label the "Love" cluster, and what might be expected to be about interpersonal closeness, turns out to be in its scenarios strongly "pity" and involves also much attraction from a distance.

Thus, if the hypothesis of Indonesian emphasis on interaction over inner states, with the corollary that in such a culture even emotions are oriented toward interaction, it makes sense that the prototypically strongest emotion area should also be one that emphasizes interaction most. What is unexpected is that these factors should converge on "sad-ness."

These Indonesian scenarios for "Sad" look very much like the Amer-ican English scenarios for sadness described by Shaver et al. (1987:1077), although the typical antecedent events, disruption of an interpersonal relationship, is even stronger in the American than in the Indonesian scenarios, and the outcome of withdrawal is more common in the Amer-ican scenarios. This is unexpected. The prediction would have been that the Indonesian scenarios would be more, not less, concerned with inter-action. But in both weeping is the most common outcome.

Although in some emotion areas there is considerable difference be-tween the cultures, in this "Sad" area there seems to be little cultural difference. If, then, "sadness" and sedih are virtually identical, certainly in comparison with other translation pairs, one is not surprised to find cross-cultural facial expression recognition tasks showing exceptionally high agreement scores in this area.

Such is the case in a ten-culture study on the recognition of Caucasian facial expressions (Ekman et al. 1987). Members of the different cultures, European and Asian, were asked to identify the emotion expressed. Each representation was of a good example of the pan-cultural facial expression for one of six basic emotions. The Minangkabau subjects were lowest or near lowest in percent choosing the "correct" emotion attribution for five of the six emotions, but for Sadness they were tied for second highest. This evidence suggests the hypothesis that when the scenarios of comparable emotions match in two different cultures, facial expressions will also.

However, when we talk about exceptionally high agreement between "sad" and *sedih*, we are talking only about the prototypical "Sad" words. If we consider the entire "Sad" area, then important differences do appear. For example, the position of the "Love" cluster in the Indonesian maps is tangential to "Sad," but in American English it is far away.

So in this instance, the focal emotion is the same cross-culturally, while the broader areas themselves differ.

THE TWO AREAS OF "INDECISION" AND "CONFUSION"

In the southwestern corner of each lexical map (see maps 1–3) lies a large, complex area that must be approached gingerly in order to make sense of its internal structure. Using the Minangkabau Indonesian map as the main authority, we can first isolate two complex areas, one around *kacau*, which we shall call the "Confusion" area, and the other around *ragu*, which we shall call the "Indecision" area. Each is made up of several clusters, and both clusters and areas are fairly discrete in each map. The most extensive external ties occur between the "Confusion" and the "Sad" areas. In this analysis we deal with each area in turn, treating them cluster by cluster.

"INDECISION" AREA

The "Indecision" area in the Minangkabau Indonesian map includes the core cluster, which is the "Indecision" cluster (#16), and two peripheral clusters, the "Fear" cluster (#14) and the "Jealousy" cluster (#15). In the other two maps these same words or their cognates form comparable clusters. The major noncongruence is the "Fear" cluster, which in both Minangkabau and Minangkabau Indonesian lies in this area, but which in Javanese Indonesian is a branch in the adjacent "Confusion" cluster.

14. "Fear" clusters (*takut*)

A. Defining the clusters (see Figs. 14.1–14.3)

"Fear" is a small compact cluster or branch that in Minangkabau and Minangkabau Indonesian is more closely tied to the "Indecision" area but in Javanese Indonesian is a branch in the "Confusion" area.

BI(M) is a cluster of 4 words and one twig. External connections: *Takut*, a hinge word, also figures in the large core "Indecision" cluster. *Takut* is also linked by a bridge to *panik* in the "Confusion" area and to *gregetan* in the "Anger" area.

BM is a cluster of 4 words and a bridge to *pangacuik* (which is linked by a bridge to *kacau* of the "Confusion" area. External connections: from *takuik*, one bridge to the "Indecision" cluster and one bridge to the "Confusion" area.

BI(J) contains 4 words of the BI(M) cluster, but they are less interconnected, forming only a branch. Also, here they are linked only to *panik* in the "Confusion" area, with no links at all to the "Indecision" area. There are no external connections.

Comment. The fact that both Minangkabau maps differ from the Javanese map in where they locate this "Fear" cluster is probably less significant than it first appears, since even in the Minangkabau maps the "Fear" cluster has strong, if secondary, ties to the other area. The difference is that the strong primary links tying "fear" to "indecision" in Minangkabau do not exist at all in Javanese Indonesian.

B. Key words

In all three clusters the same word, *takuik/takut*, is the key word.

C. English glosses (see Figs. 14.2, 14.3)

These clusters seem to include "fear" itself as well as words that primarily describe physical reactions to fear, such as "shudder" and "quiver."

Considering the English glosses for the entire "Indecision" area in Minangkabau Indonesian, it is apparent that although this can be called

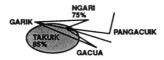

Figure 14.1. "Fear" cluster BM

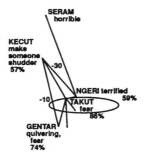

Figure 14.2. "Fear" cluster BI(M)

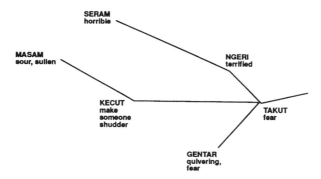

Figure 14.3. "Fear" cluster BI(J)

the "Fear" cluster, the adjacent end of the large "Indecision" cluster also contains some "fear," although the cluster itself is a less homogeneous cluster that reflects many sorts of disorder stretching from "fear" through "indecision" to "jealousy."

D. Membership in the realms of emotion: prototypicality ratings

These clusters are fairly strong, and the key words (*takuik/takut*) are the strongest in their respective clusters. In Minangkabau Indonesian the "fear" end of the core "Indecision" cluster is actually stronger than the "Fear" cluster itself, although *takut*, as the hinge word in both, is strongest of all "fear" words.

E. Translation equivalents

For both Minangkabau and Minangkabau Indonesian the modal choice of each word was the key words, *takuik/takut*, in the other language.

For Javanese Indonesian, however, the unanimous first choice was *wedi*, the *ngoko* word for "fear." Horne does not list a *takut* in her dictionary, so presumably it is not even available to Javanese in Javanese.

F. Antecedent/outcome sentence completion tasks

Antecedents and outcomes were elicited for:

      Minangkabau: *cameh–takuik–garik* from 27 subjects,

      Minangkabau Indonesian: *cemas–takut–ngeri–gentar* from 27 subjects

      Between-languages: BM *garik*/BI(M) *takut* from 78 subjects.

The obvious hypothesis that emerges from the structures shown in the lexical maps is that there are two "fear," one in the "Fear" cluster including *ngeri*, *garik*, and *gentar*, the other in one end of the "Indecision" cluster including *cameh/cemas*, with *takuik/takut* as hinge word sharing in both clusters. Thus, this task was expanded from the usual pair of words to include the hinge word *takuik/takut* and words on either side of it, from each of the two tangential clusters.

For the between-language set the overwhelming key words *takuik/takut* would be the obvious candidates. However, because they are such clear cognates it seemed better to substitute another word. (In retrospect, on the basis of the final mappings, a better choice than *garik* would have been *ngeri/ngari*, much closer to *takuik/takut* but still a non-cognate. Ironically, the results from this antecedent/outcome task suggest that *ngeri* is rather different from the other words in these clusters, and so would have been perhaps an even more deceptive choice.)

      Minangkabau: *cameh–takuik–garik:*

BM *cameh* antecedents from 27 subjects

      9   future or possible misfortune (feared river would flood ego's house, the child was walking in the jungle . . .)

6 failure (ego got low grades; ego did it wrong)

5 sickness

2 sudden negative experience (heard a great explosion)

BM *cameh* outcomes from 27 subjects

6 caution (ego locked the door carefully; ego crossed the narrow bridge carefully . . .)

5 physiological (ego paled, ego's heart throbbed)

4 emotional (*galisah* 2; *rusuah*; *tapakuah*)

2 thought (ego thought about what would happen)

BM *takuik* antecedents from 27 subjects

8 saw a threat

2 from animals (snake, tiger)

2 from supernatural (road is haunted)

4 from other person (saw a crazy person stone a passerby)

5 was alone, deserted (the road ahead was empty; ego had to face the enemy alone)

8 did something wrong

BM *takuik* outcomes from 27 subjects

12 withdrew, avoided (ego ran away fast; ego didn't leave home)

7 physiological reaction (paled, shivered)

6 arranged for company (asked for company, invited a friend home)

2 emotional (*galisah*; not *tanang*)

BM *garik* antecedents from 27 subjects

12   threats to self, including

8 from others (ego was held up; ego's opponent was bigger than ego)

3 from animals (tiger, dog, snake)

1 from supernatural (haunted)

1   threat to other (ego's child was playing on the edge of the water tank)

2 alone

3 saw fight, etc.

1 did something wrong

4 beyond capacity, lack self-confidence (ego couldn't solve that problem)

BM *garik* outcomes from 27 subjects

6   physiological reactions (paled, shivered)

5   withdraw, avoid (didn't go by that place; fled from ego's opponent)

4   arranged for company, help (accompanied a close friend; asked for help)

1   took positive logical action (looked for a stick to kill the snake)

1   gave up

1   emotional (*takuik*)

Minangkabau Indonesian: *cemas–takut–ngeri–gentar*
BI(M) *cemas* antecedents from 27 subjects

16   future or possible misfortune, including

6 someone hasn't returned home yet

4   sickness

3   sudden negative threat

1   inadequacy
1   personal failure

BI(M) *cemas* outcomes from 27 subjects
9   physiological
7   emotional
2   caution
2   ask for help
1   think things over

BI(M) *takut* antecedents from 27 subjects
14   saw threat to self, including
      6 from other person
      4 from nature
      4 from supernatural
7   did wrong
2   alone, deserted

BI(M) *takut* outcomes from 27 subjects
16   avoidance/withdrawal
4   physiological reaction
4   got help
2   emotional (*gelisah; kecut*)

BI(M) *ngeri* antecedents from 27 subjects
9   saw a car/train accident
9   saw a wounded/dead person
3   saw a fight
2   saw a rugged ravine
2   faced an overpowering oppo-
      nent

BI(M) *ngeri* outcomes from 27 subjects
20   avoidance/withdrawal
5   physiological reaction

BI(M) *gentar* antecedents from 27 subjects
21   faced by opponents, including
      12 by overpowering oppo-
         nents
2   emotional (*takut; gugup*)

BI(M) *gentar* outcomes from 27 subjects
13   avoidance/withdrawal

5   physiological

3   emotional (2 *takut; ragu*)

Analysis. These seven words from the two languages can be summarized as follows:

BM *cameh* caused by (1) future or possible misfortune, (2) personal failure and by sickness; outcomes are (1) caution, and (2) physiological, emotional reactions

BI(M) *cemas* caused by (1) future or possible misfortunes, (2) sickness, sudden negatives; outcomes are (1) physiological, (2) emotional, also caution, call for help

BM *takuik* caused by (1) doing wrong, (2) threats, and being alone; outcomes are (1) withdrawal, (2) physiological, get help

BI(M) *takut* caused by (1) threats, (2) doing wrong, being alone; outcomes are (1) withdrawal, (2) physiological, get help

BM *garik* caused by (1) threats, (2) beyond capacity; outcomes are (1) physiological, (2) withdrawal, get help

BI(M) *ngeri* caused by (1) misfortune to others; outcomes are (1) withdrawal, physiological reaction

BI(M) *gentar* caused by having to face an opponent; outcomes are withdrawal, physiological.

Ngeri (BI[M]) is alone in explicitly resulting from passively seeing bad things happen to others.

The other six words all involve the self more directly. Comparing them word for word, across languages, turns up only minor differences: *cameh/ cemas*, which in Minangkabau results in more caution, in Indonesian results in more immediate physiological and emotional responses.

However, to test the hypothesis that there are two different sorts of "fear," with *takuik/takut* being the hinge word in each, we need to contrast the *cameh/cemas* pair from the "Indecision" cluster with *garik* and *gentar* from the "Fear" cluster. Here we can identify a difference: The "Indecision" cluster results from more general anticipated misfortune, plus sickness, whereas the "Fear" cluster is caused by direct threats to the self. The dictionary glosses suggested this, and, of course, all three maps have clearly separated the two. This distinction can be sharpened by calling one the "fear–terror," the other "fear–anxiety." (Indeed, in Shaver et al. [1987:1067] the superordinate "fear" divides into just such specific "fears."

There is a strong incidence of "doing wrong" in the antecedents of *takuik/takut*, but we can deal with that better after looking at the between-language pair.

The between-language pair: BM *GARIK*/BI(M) *TAKUT:*

BM *Garik* antecedents from 78 subjects
- 39   threats, including
    - 13 threats from others, including 10 threats from overpowering others
    - 15 threats from natural sources, including 4 snakes, 2 tigers, 3 dogs
- 8   did wrong
- 6   another angry at ego
- 3   being along
- 3   the place is deserted
- 7   nighttime is negative

BM *garik* outcomes from 78 subjects
- 46   avoidance/withdrawal including
    - 1 physical (shut ears)
- 9   reform one's behavior
- 5   other physical
- 4   request help, company
- 5   takes other positive correctional action (kills snake, lights candle, etc.)
- 4   refuses to do something without help/company
- 1   emotional (*ragu*)

BI(M) *takut* antecedents from 78 subjects
- 26   threats, including
    - 7 from natural sources, including 3 tigers, 1 dog, 1 water buffalo
    - 11 from others, including 4 from overpowering others
    - 4 from supernatural
- 22   from doing wrong, including
    - 2 where superior knew of the wrongdoing
- 8   others angry at ego

7	saw something bad
1	alone
3	deserted path
4	nighttime negative

BI(M) *takut* outcomes from 78 subjects

43	avoidance/withdrawal, including
2	physical (shut eyes)
5	other physiological reactions (shivered, paled)
8	reform behavior
6	request help
0	take other positive action
1	emotional reaction (*takut*)

In both languages, the prime cause is "threats to ego," the prime outcome is withdrawal or avoidance. But having established the difference between the two "fears," we recognize that the two words now do not offer a good contrast because *garik* is at the far end of "fear–terror," whereas *takut* is the hinge word.

The appearance of guilt. What is particularly significant here is the strength of "did wrong" as a secondary antecedent scenario, especially with *takut* in Minangkabau Indonesian and, from smaller samples of subjects described above, with *takuik* in Minangkabau.

To be specific, in Minangkabau Indonesian, combining the two sorts of responses for *takut:*

subjects: 105; threat: 60 (57%); did wrong: 29 (28%)

and for BM *takuik:*

subjects: 27; threat: 8 (30%); did wrong: 8 (30%)

This poses a problem of translation at first, although not for the prime scenario, where *takut* is the emotion caused by danger or threat and results in avoidance or withdrawal: "Fear," in English, fits nicely, and, indeed, any dictionary or moderately bilingual speaker would not hesitate to translate *takut* as *fear*.

But the secondary antecedent, "doing wrong," is more of a puzzle, especially because it almost never appears that the wrong is known by anyone else. Indeed, it looks very much as if this second sense of *takut/takuik* is, in English, more like guilt. A major difference would be that although Guilt produces other emotions like Sadness, or Shame, or Fear, *takut/takuik* has virtually no emotions as outcomes.

One of the most interesting and fruitful lines of thinking about emotions and culture has been the contrasting of guilt and shame. And a commonly occurring claim is that "guilt" is absent, or at least the word for guilt is absent, in a culture (from Ruth Benedict on the Japanese [1946], to Obeyesekere on his own native Sinhalese [1979]). Indeed, in Indonesian or Minangkabau it is hard to find a satisfactory word for guilt. Dictionaries give BERSALAH, which really means to be wrong (*salah*).

Here the antecedent is rarely described as *merasa salah*, which would mean either "felt wrong" or "felt guilty," but it usually is *berbuat salah* or *melakukan salah*, both of which mean to actively do wrong.

Thus, it appears that to some degree fear and guilt are signified by the same word, *takut/takuik*, and have the same sorts of outcomes – mainly, avoidance and withdrawal.

It further appears that *wedi*, the first choice for *takut* in Javanese, has the same mixture of fear and shame. According to Hildred Geertz, "WEDI means afraid in both the physical sense and the social sense of apprehension of unpleasant consequences of an action" (1959:232).

It is that second sense of doing wrong that I identify as a "shame" pattern. Indeed, one of Geertz's examples is "If I borrow some rice from a neighbor and can't pay it back, I feel *wedi* of that neighbor." And Geertz associates *wedi* closely with *isin*, "shame, shyness, embarrassment, guilt." Somewhat farther afield, but still within the Austronesian language family, Flores-Meiser discusses a fear–shame complex from Tagalog in the Philippines (1986:63) and suggests that it is widespread in Oceania. But the Tagalog "fear" word – *takot* – does not itself seem to include both these meanings. Also, from the Philippines, Michelle Rosaldo reported that " 'shame' and 'fear' are not identical, but in Ilongot thought they tend to go together" (1980:87).

In the Australian Aboriginal language, Gidjingali, there is a verb, *-gurakadj-*, that means both "fear" and "shame/embarrassment." Hiatt gives several examples of the use of *-gurakadj-*, some of which might be blends of fear and shame but others of which seem to be only fear (e.g., "a woman says she was ng-gurakadj-ira of encountering a ghost") or only shame ("a man sees a naked woman approaching"). Wierzbicka (1986) has discussed this situation – the association under one label of concepts that in English are two different and, indeed, "basic" emotions as evidence for the culture-specific traps of emotion vocabularies: "If the researchers happened to be native speakers of Gidjingali rather than

English, would it still have occurred to them to claim that fear and shame are both fundamental human emotions, discrete and clearly separate from each other?" (1986:584).

In short, there seems to be evidence from several parts of the western Pacific region for a close association of "fear" and "shame" that is not immediately familiar from English and, indeed, is somewhat counterintuitive for English speakers. The Minangkabau data, which are the most extensive and systematic, give a complex picture: There is one word (*takut*) that denotes both "fear" and "shame," but several other words that refer to one or the other only.

In the analysis of English words by Shaver et al. (1987:1067), "guilt" is in the "Sad" area, and only distantly related to the "Fear" area. In contrast, in these Indonesian maps and scenarios, there is no direct connection between *takut/takuik* and "sad." Also, it is noteworthy that *takut/takuik* is the only word in either cluster with any significant amount of "doing wrong" as an antecedent. Only *garik*, when immediately contrasted with *takut*, turns up any, and then it is just 9 out of 105, or 9% – a level so low that it can almost be explained away as a kind of transferral from thinking about *garik* and *takut* together.

Further, in the carefully constructed scenario for American English "fear" presented by Shaver et al. (1987:1076) there is no sign of this "doing wrong" antecedent. One can imagine a sort of scenario in which a person who has done wrong is fearful of discovery or punishment. But here, and in the Shaver study, we begin with an emotion and ask for an antecedent. The results might have been different if one had asked for the emotion appropriate to the situation "doing wrong."

Boucher (1981) reports "doing wrong" as an important antecedent for *takut* (fear) in Malaysian. In his Level 5, categories "38. Ego caught/accused in punishable offense" and "39. Ego committed punishable offense – not caught yet" account for 34% of the Malaysian antecedents and cover the "ego doing wrong" category that I used.

In other words, the Malaysian antecedents for *takut* (fear) reveal a secondary scenario of "doing wrong" that, at 34%, is very comparable to the Minangkabau 30% and the Indonesian 28%.

But now it is worthwhile following the fate of this secondary "doing wrong" scenario through Boucher's procedure.

At his Level 5 there are three categories, as follows:

	Malay	American
38.	21	11
39.	13	n.a.
40.	2	1

These are collapsed in Level 6 into a single category:

"13.   Ego is faced with punishment."

But the label for this category at this next level is taken from the old Category 40, the least important of the three, and by doing so obscures the "doing wrong" theme.

At Level 6 we have Category 13, Category 14 ("Other assaulted ego"), and Category 15 ("Ego is in a dangerous situation"), all three of which are now combined at Level 7 into the single Category 6 ("Ego may be injured"), which accounts for 92% of the Malay stories and 89% of the American stories. The obvious conclusion is that Malay and American antecedents for *takut* (fear) are nearly identical. In fact, though, the successive stages of aggregation have obscured the important differences. It is hardly an accident that the choices of label in the successive levels made by the American psychologist Boucher move the Malay data strongly in the direction of the "fear" scenario described for American English by Shaver et al. (1987). Fortunately Boucher's meticulous preservation of his data in the three final stages has allowed us to trace the ethnocentric twist to which his methodology has succumbed. It has also allowed us to confirm that in Malay, too, there is a strong secondary scenario of "doing wrong."

What, then, does it mean to discover a secondary scenario of "shame" in the idea of *takut?*

First, it helps contribute to the picture of shame. Given the importance of shame in Indonesian life, it has been particularly surprising to find that the "Shame" area also bleeds into other areas in ways not anticipated.

Second, it poses a real problem for some of the other tasks of this study, which choose a single word, *takut*, for "fear." Because it turns out that *takut* means both "fear" and "shame," the results of these other tasks are likely to be less powerful than if a more single-minded "fear" neighbor of *takut* (say, for example, *nyeri*) had been used.

Third, it provides an excellent example of how the expectations derived from the particular configuration of one culture can lead to distortions in another culture.

15. "Jealousy" clusters (*dengki*)

A. Defining the clusters (see Figs. 15.1–15.3)

This is one of the few instances where there is no clear agreement on comparable discrete clusters across all three maps. As Figure 15.2 shows,

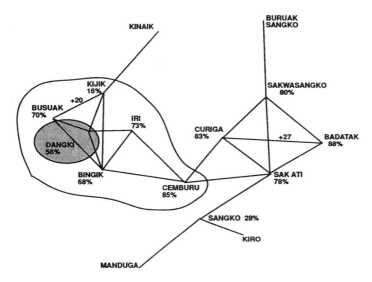

Figure 15.1. "Jealousy" BM

in Minangkabau Indonesian there is a tight triangle cluster, with the key word *iri hati*, linked by a bridge to *cemburu* of the "Worry" cluster. But in Figures 15.1 and 15.3, *cemburu* is more closely associated with the *dengki* group. In this instance we shall go with the authority of the latter two figures and the antecedent/outcome scenarios (described below) in order to include *cemburu* with the *dengki* group in a "Jealousy–Envy" cluster, called the "Jealousy" cluster for convenience.

　　BM: a cluster of 6 words with *dangki* as the key word; and one twig. External connections: *Cemburu* is a hinge word, being in both this cluster and the *curiga* cluster.

　　BI(M): The triangle cluster with *dengki* as key word and including *cemburu*. External connections: In this map, *cemburu* is more closely linked to the "Worry" cluster.

　　BI(J): There is no cluster here, but the words that form the comparable clusters in the other two maps are here strung out as a chain of links. External connections: *cemburu* is linked to *curiga* by a single bridge.

B. Key words (see Figs. 15.1, 15.2)

Dangki/dengki are the key words in the BM and BI(M) clusters (Javanese Indonesian did not form a cluster).

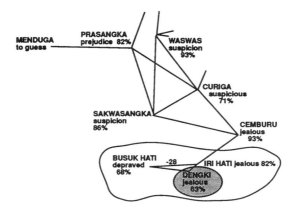

Figure 15.2. "Jealousy" BI(M)

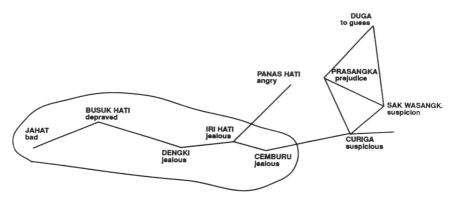

Figure 15.3. "Jealousy" BI(J)

The two sets used in the antecedent/outcome task are *dangki/dengki, iri ati/hati,* and *cemburu.* No between-language sets were used.

C. English glosses (see Figs. 15.2, 15.3)

The dictionary glosses can be refined on the basis of the antecedent/outcome scenarios. The close links to strongly negative words suggested by these dictionary glosses will be supported by the antecedent/outcome scenarios.

D. Membership in the realm of emotion: prototypicality ratings

These clusters show slightly weaker prototypicality than do the adjacent "Worry" clusters. In both Minangkabau and Minangkabau Indonesian the key word *dangki/dengki* is low (58%, 63%) and in fact considerably lower than 3 or 4 other words in its cluster. This is one of the greatest disparities between key word and prototypicality to appear in this study.

E. Translation equivalents

Choices from Minangkabau to BI(M):

4	to the key word *dengki*
1	to the cognate (*cemburu*)
1	to another word (*bingik* > *iri hati*)

Choices from BI(M) to Minangkabau

3	to the key word *dangki*
1	to the cognate *cemburu*

Choices from BI(J) to Javanese:

$1\frac{1}{2}$	to *Meri* (Horne: envious)
$\frac{1}{2}$	to the cognate *dengki*
1	to another word (*cemburu* > *sujana* [suspicious])

The attractive power of the key word *dangki/dengki* is strong in both of the Minangkabau maps, although the Javanese choices are less revealing. In all three, *cemburu* does not get associated with this *dengki* cluster, so by the criteria of this task, *cemburu* would have been left out of the cluster.

F. Antecedent/outcome sentence completion tasks

Minangkabau: *dangki–iri ati–cemburu*

BM *dangki* antecedents from 27 subjects

19	another person better off than ego, including
	7 friends
	1 relative
	in respect to:

   6 material things
   2 money
   2 grades
   1 personal characteristics

BM *dangki* outcomes from 27 subjects
   8   negative emotions (2 *buruak* bitter; 2 *banci* hate; 2 *cacek* contempt; *sakik hati;* not *sanang*, not happy)
   5   slanders
   4   other revenge/hurting other
   3   withdrawal/avoidance
   2   takes from other, wants from other

BM *iri ati* antecedents from 27 subjects
   23 another person better off than ego, including
   8 friends
   5 relatives
   in respect to:
   8 materials things
   4 personal characteristic
   2 money
   2 grades/school

BM *iri ati* outcomes from 27 subjects
   9   Emotions (2 *masam* sour; *sindia* contempt; *berang* anger; *takuik* fear; *cemooh* contempt; not *sanang*, not happy)
   1   slander
   1   revenge/hurts other
   5   takes from other, contests other
   3   withdrawal/avoidance

BM *cemburu* antecedents from 27 subjects
   20 lover, girl/boyfriend, spouse lost
   5 only flirted with another
   7 spouse
   1   another person better off

BM *cemburu* outcomes from 27 subjects

11	emotions (6 *berang* anger; *curiga* suspicion; *mambuduik*; *sakik hati*; weeps 2; *rajuak* 2)
3	revenge/hurts another
5	withdrawal/avoidance
4	watches/ponders

BI(M) *dengki* antecedents from 26 subjects

    21   Another person better off than ego, including

        8 friends

        5 relatives

       in respect to:

        3 money

        2 grades

        2 characteristics of other

        6 other material things

     4   because parent gave things to a sibling

BI(M) *dengki* outcomes from 26 subjects:

6	emotion (5 *benci* hate; *sakit hati*)
2	slanders
2	takes from another
11	other revenge/hurts other
3	withdrawal/avoidance

BI(M) *iri hati* antecedents from 26 subjects

    29   another person better off, including

       12 friends

       7 relatives (including 5 gifts from parent to sibling) in respect to:

       2 money

       3 grades

       4 characteristics

       8 material things

BI(M) *iri hati* outcomes from 26 subjects:

    13   Emotions (4 not *senang* not happy; 3 *benci* hate; *sedih* sad; *sinis* cynical; *marah* anger;

cemooh contempt; *dengki; ejek*
contempt)
2 in which the emotions were
felt by another
3   slanders
3   other revenge/hurts other
5   takes from other, contests
2   withdrawal/avoidance

BI(M) *cemburu* antecedents from 26 subjects
22   lover, boy/girlfriend, spouse
went with another
4 only flirted
1 husband
1   saw others in love
1   was in love

BI(M) *cemburu* outcomes from 26 subjects
13   emotions (6 *marah* anger; 2 *benci*
hate; *sedih* said; *curiga* suspicious; *jengkel* anger; *hati
panas* anger; not *senang* not
happy)
7   revenge/attacks
1   takes positive action
2   passive action

To summarize these 6 words:

Iri ati (BM)
caused by other better off
results in negative emotion
and active counteraction

Iri hati (BI[M])
caused by other better off
results in negative emotion
and active counteraction

Dangki (BM)
caused by other better off
results in negative emotion
and active counteraction

(Dengki (BI[M])
caused by other better off
results in negative emotion
and active counteraction

Cemburu (BM)
caused by losing lover
results in negative emotion
and active counteraction
and passivity

Cemburu (BI[M])
caused by losing lover
results in negative emotion
and revenge
and passivity

These antecedent scenarios clearly distinguish between *iri* plus *dangki*, which result from another person being better off than ego, and which can be translated into English as "envy"; and, on the other hand, *cemburu*, which results from losing (or anticipating losing) one's beloved to another person, and which can be translated as "jealousy."

But although the antecedents are so strongly different, the outcomes are similar: negative emotions, particularly in the "Anger/Hate" area, and revengeful acts.

As hypothesized, both Jealousy and Envy are complex emotions generating other, basic, emotions. The emotion-genic scores are high for all six words:

Minangkabau	Minangkabau Indonesian
iri ati: 34%	*iri hati:* 50%
dangki: 30%	*dengki:* 23%
cemburu: 41%	*cemburu:* 50%

Not only do these emotions actively produce other emotions, the emotions that are produced are strongly negative. In English, Jealousy and Envy both seem highly emotion-genic, but it is debatable whether they produce more Sadness than anger and hate. Davtiz presents scenarios for jealousy (1968:68), although not for envy, and sadness clearly is more salient than anger/hate/revenge, according to his American subjects. Although the Shaver et al. study (1987) did not work up scenarios for Anger or for Jealousy, these two emotions did form a subcluster in their anger group. These Indonesian scenarios look more like the Davitz version of American English. The closest they come to sadness is *tidak senang* (not happy). There are only two *sedih* (sad) in the entire response collection. Shaver, in a personal communication, suggests that these Minangkabau resemble his Denver Americans but not Davitz's New Yorkers.

In summary, this area of the emotion space includes two closely related emotions, one resulting from unfavorably comparing oneself to another, the second resulting from (threatened) loss of a lover. These two are similar to Envy and Jealousy in English. But they have much sharper, more malicious outcomes in Indonesian, with relatively little of the contemplative hurt and sadness, which are the most typical outcomes of at least one version of the American English emotions.

One should not exaggerate the differences between American English and Indonesian in this area; yet the nuances are there. The angry, revengeful element that dominates in Indonesian is certainly understandable and familiar in English. But the reverse is rare: The American English "sadness" is almost nonexistent in these Indonesian responses.

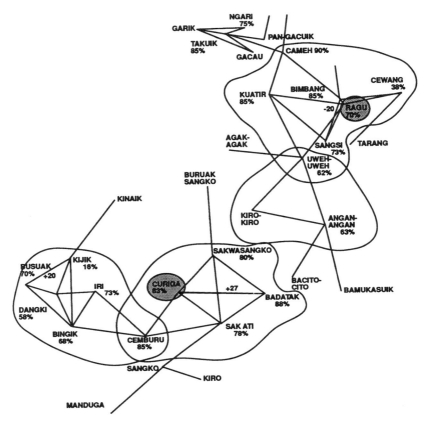

Figure 16.1. "Indecision" BM

16. "Indecision" clusters (*ragu*)

A. Defining the clusters (see Figs. 16.1–16.3)

BM forms two clusters from the words that make up only one cluster in BI(M):

a.   A "Suspicion" cluster: five words with *curiga* as the key word; one twig, one branch. External connections: *Cemburu* is a hinge word with the "Jealousy" cluster (#15). Otherwise "Suspicion" and "Jealousy" are two tangential isolated clusters with no external links.

b.   An "Indecision" cluster – 7 words with *ragu* as the key word; two twigs and a branch, which includes a triangle cluster that was not explored. External connections: A bridge from *ragu* to *barek ati* in

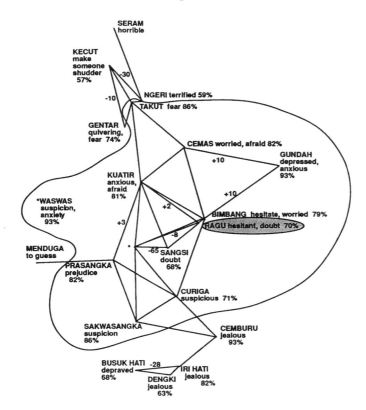

Figure 16.2. "Indecision" BI(M)

the "Anger" area; bridges from *cameh* to *galisah* and from *bimbang* to *gundah*, both in the adjacent "Confusion" cluster.

Anomaly. There is a branch from *ragu* that includes *binguang*. However, in both of the Indonesian maps the cognate, *bingung*, is strongly located with the adjacent "confusion" words. (This branch will be analyzed below with the "Confusion" clusters.)

BI(M) is a long, rambling, but well-defined cluster of 11 words with *ragu* the key word; and two twigs. External connections: This is located between the "Fear," "Jealousy," and "Confusion" clusters.

Gundah is a hinge word with the "Confusion" cluster; *takut* is a hinge word with the "Fear" cluster; and there are two bridges to the "Jealousy" cluster.

Also, *takut* has a bridge to *panik* in the adjacent "Confusion" cluster, and a bridge to *gregetan* in the "Anger" Area.

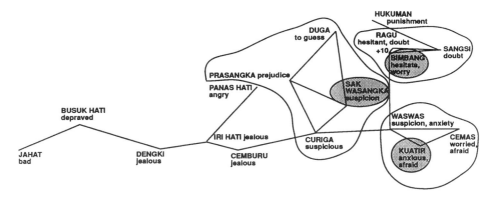

Figure 16.3. "Indecision" BI(J)

For BI(J): the same words in Javanese Indonesian form three connected clusters:

a.   The "Suspicious" cluster, with *curiga* as the key word, comparable to the Minangkabau "Suspicious" cluster, containing 4 words. External connections: bridges from *curiga* to *waswas*, and a long branch into the "Jealous" cluster.

b.   The "Indecision" Cluster, a 3-word cluster with *ragu* as the key word; one twig. External connections: a bridge from *ragu* to the "Sad" area, and a bridge to the "Anxiety" cluster.

c.   The "Anxiety" cluster, a 3-word triangle with *kuatir* as the key word. External connections: a bridge from *waswas* to the "Suspicious" and "Indecision" clusters, and a bridge to the *resah* cluster.

Summary: With the exception of *binguang*, which is in this group in Minangkabau but not in either Indonesian map, all three maps agree on words but not on the degree of relationship between subunits. That is, Minangkabau Indonesian has multiple links between every word; Javanese Indonesian has only single bridges between three subclusters; and Minangkabau has two unconnected clusters.

B. Key words

The key words are as follows:

> BI(M)   *ragu*
> BM   *ragu*
>   *curiga*

BI(J)   *ragu*
             kuatir
             sakwasangka

The antecedent/outcome tasks were discussed in the "Fear" cluster section above, for two sets that overlapped the "Fear" cluster, plus *takut*, the hinge word, plus *cemas* from this "Indecision" cluster.

Also, antecedent/outcome tasks were done for two sets from the center of these clusters:

BI(M)   *bimbang–ragu*
BM   *bimbang–ragu*

C. English glosses (see Figs. 16.2, 16.3)

The serious problems that exist with the English dictionary glosses are discussed in the analysis of the antecedent/outcome scenarios.

D. Membership in the realm of emotion: prototypicality ratings

BM (Fig. 16.1) shows a pattern similar to that in BI(M), below. The range is from 62% to 90%, although one word (*cewang*, 38%) falls far down on the scale. Again, the key word *ragu* (70%) is weaker than 4 of the other 5 words in its cluster, and *curiga*, (83%), the key word in the other cluster, is weaker than 2 of 4 other words in its cluster.

BI(M) (Fig. 16.2) words are fairly strong in prototypicality ratings, ranging from 68% to 93%, with no obvious pattern. Unlike other clusters, this one does not show that sudden drop-off which indicates the incorporation of words that are only marginally or ambiguously emotional.

The key word, *ragu*, is only 70%, and so weaker than 9 of the other 10 words in the cluster.

E. Translation equivalents

The modal choices of translation equivalents go strongly to key words of clusters, but in a pattern that strongly supports the ways in which the maps divide up the "Indecision" clusters. Of course, the same subjects provided both sets of data: one that resulted in the maps, and one for the translation equivalents.

Figure 16.4 indicates with arrows the modal choices of translation equivalents for the starter words in each of the three lists. Thus, Min-

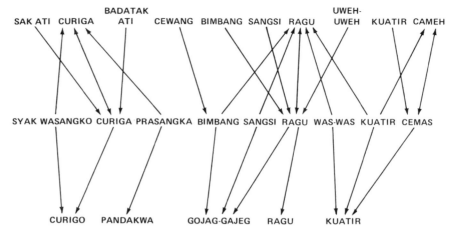

Figure 16.4. "Indecision" Clusters: Between-languages translation equivalents: modal choices.

angkabau starters have modal choices among the Indonesian words; Indonesian words have modal choices back to Minangkabau words (done by the Minangkabau subjects) and to Javanese words (done by Javanese subjects.)

From this one sees clearly that the *curiga* words are separate from the rest. This separateness showed up in the Minangkabau map and in the Javanese Indonesian map, but not in the Minangkabau Indonesian map.

The Javanese subjects, who had produced three clusters of these words in the maps, seem to be choosing translation equivalents on the same principle: There is strong but not total choice of what are presumably the key words of separate clusters in Javanese. Thus, the *curiga* words choose *curigo* (actually, Horne gives it as *curiga* in Javanese); the *ragu* words choose *gojag–gajeg* (Horne's translations of these words do not make sense in this context: *Godjag* is "to wash out [a bottle, etc.] by shaking water in it; *godjeg* "to fool around, laugh and joke"); and the *kuatir* words choose *kuatir* (Horne's *kuatir*, in *ngoko*, "apprehensive, fearful").

It looks as if the strong two-cluster pattern in Minangkabau is projected onto translation equivalents, though not onto the mapping in Indonesian; but a presumed three-cluster pattern in Javanese influences the Javanese Indonesian mapping.

F. *Antecedent/outcome sentence completion tasks*

Minangkabau: *bimbang–ragu:*

BM *bimbang* antecedents from 27 subjects

13	torn between two apparently equal choices
5	leave, left behind another
3	unclear
2	fear failure

BM *bimbang* outcomes from 27 subjects

2	asked advice
6	pondered
5	didn't do it, gave up
5	emotion (2 *barek hati; gelisah; binguang;* 2 wept)
2	made decision, acted

BM *ragu* antecedents from 27 subjects

14	torn between two apparently equal choices
3	involve confusing twins
6	unclear about situation

BM *ragu* outcomes from 27 subjects

9	asked advice
3	pondered
4	didn't do it, gave up
2	wrinkled brow
1	chewed thumb
2	made decision, acted
1	emotion (*rasah*)

BI(M) *bimbang* antecedents from 27 subjects

12	torn between two apparently equal choices
1	leave other behind
5	unclear, ignorant
1	fear failure

BI(M) *bimbang* outcomes from 27 subjects

3	asked advice
4	pondered

12	didn't do it, gave up
7	emotion (2 *ragu;* 2 *rasah;* 4 *bin-gung*)
2	made decisive action

BI(M) *ragu* antecedents from 27 subjects

12	torn between two apparently equal choices
6	unclear situation
2	failure, anticipated failure
2	postdecisional regret

BI(M) *ragu* outcomes from 27 subjects:

2	asked advice
2	pondered
14	didn't do it, gave up
4	repeated query, reread passage
1	made decision
1	emotion (*sangsi*)
1	physical:scratched head

In summary. The antecedents for all 4 words are torn between two apparently equal choices. The outcomes, however, were:

in BI(M), overwhelmingly: didn't do it, gave up

in BM, asked advice, pondered

This pattern is seen in Tables 16.1 and 16.2:

A difference in outcomes does appear between the two languages, much more strikingly for *ragu* than for *bimbang:* In Minangkabau, people are more likely to continue working on the dilemma, asking advice, pondering the situation, whereas in Indonesian they just don't do it or give up altogether.

A second factor splits the two words apart. Cross-cutting languages. This is the emotion-genic score, the percent of outcomes in which the emotion produces another emotion (Table 16.3).

It is not apparent why, in both languages, *bimbang* should be so much more emotion-genic than *ragu,* because in other respects there is nothing to distinguish the words. They both seem equally complex. On the other hand, this is a deceptively high emotion-genic score because those emotions produced by both words are almost entirely from the same "Indecision" cluster or from the very closely adjacent "Confusion" cluster.

Table 16.1. *Bimbang*

	Didn't do it	Advice, pondered
Minangkabau Indonesian	12	7
Minangkabau	5	8

Chi square = 1.89; p = <0.25

Table 16.2. *Ragu*

	Didn't do it	Advice, pondered
Minangkabau Indonesian	14	4
Minangkabau	4	12

Chi square = 9.47; p = <.005

Table 16.3. *The emotion-genic ratings*

	Minangkabau	Minangkabau Indonesian
BIMBANG	19%	26%
RAGU	4%	4%

The scenarios for these words are so consistent and definitive that we must now consider again the dictionary glosses for the words in this cluster and particularly for the ones we have examined: *bimbang* and *ragu*. These two refer to an emotion arising from being faced with two apparently equal choices and not being able to make the choice. The dictionary glosses, "hesitate, worry, doubt," are close but not adequate. "Puzzlement," or "perplexity," or "indecision" are closer.

Turning again to the Shaver et al. prototypicality ratings for 213 English emotion words (1987:1066), we find these three words listed:

WORRY   3.49
DOUBT   2.30
INDECISION   2.02

On their four-point scale, then, "worry" is strongly emotional, "doubt" and "indecision" considerably less so. The dictionary translations have apparently picked English words that are not as accurate lexically, but are more emotional, that is, more prototypical as emotions in English. One hypothesis of the present study is that the emotion space of one culture will not necessarily coincide at every point with the emotion space of another. It is to be expected that the scenarios and the best English translations will not fit English scenarios and expectations, and that the best English translations will not necessarily be words with high emotion prototypicality in the American English emotion realm.

Thus, on examining the scenarios for *bimbang* and *ragu,* we can translate these words as "indecision," but then note that in English the word "indecision" barely makes it into the emotion category. The Indonesian and Minangkabau words, on the other hand, average a robust 78% emotion prototypicality, while in English the word "indecision" is 206 out of the 213 words rated by Shaver et al. (1987:1066).

In short, we have here a concept readily identifiable in both English and the Indonesian languages; in English, however, it may be less emotional, whereas in Indonesian it is certainly emotional.

Some of this may merely reflect the choice of words. "Indecision" is a somewhat formal, subdued word in English. Shaver has suggested (in a personal communication) that if some of the more colorful or metaphorical words had been used – "torn," "conflicted," "hung up," for example – this area would have emerged more strongly emotional in English as well.

"CONFUSION" AREA (*KACAU*)

This sprawling, complex area is located among the "Worry," "Sad," and "Anger" areas. It is reasonably well defined vis-à-vis its neighbors, but internally its constituent clusters often are not precisely comparable across all three maps. Except for a few intense clusters, most of this area has middle to low prototypicality ratings.

Figures 17.1–17.3 give an overview of this "Confusion" area as a whole. Because the Minangkabau Indonesian (Fig. 17.2) map shows the most developed clusters, it will be used as the authority for describing groups of words across all three maps as clusters. It is hard to say whether this apparent minor patterns of inconsistency within the "Confusion" area is intrinsic or whether it would be cleared up with more data. Certainly, this level of research intensity is adequate to reveal consistent clusters across the three maps in other areas of the emotion realms. It is not

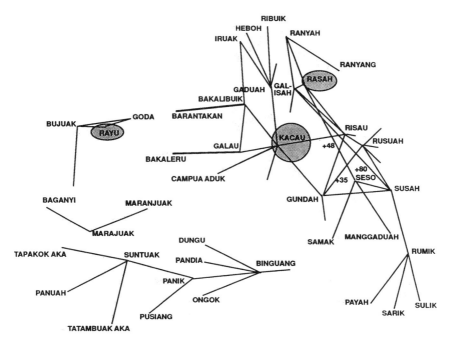

Figure 17.1. Overview of the "Confusion" area BM

really surprising, though, to discover such variation. It may be better seen not as "inconsistency" in this area, but as different degrees of consistency in the different maps. Some parts of the emotion landscapes are solid ground, some are swampy, and the same research instrument will not give us equally firm footing everywhere. And what is adequate to reveal clusters in Minangkabau Indonesian is not strong enough to reveal them in Minangkabau or in Javanese Indonesian. In short, the specifics of the particular research tool – the sorts of questions asked, the size of the subject pool – make a specific cut through reality and give a specific picture of that reality. The specific research tool used in this study shows clearly both variations among different areas within a particular map and also variations among the three maps. It shows that this "Confusion" area is especially indeterminate in each map, and it also has shown a general pattern: that the Minangkabau Indonesian map is more clear, more defined, in all areas than are the other two maps.

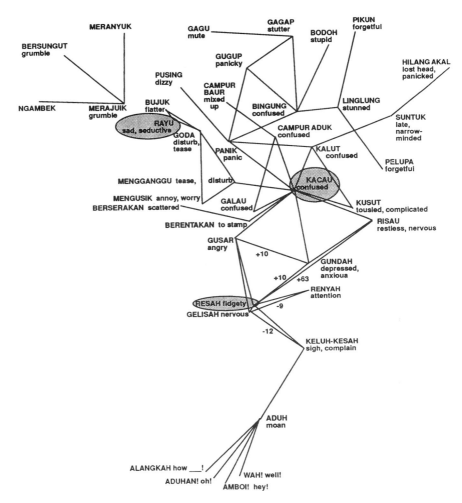

Figure 17.2. "Confusion" area BI(M)

17. "Confusion/Stymied" clusters (*kacau*)

A. Defining the clusters (see Figs. 17a.1–17a.3)

> BM: The words that make up the cluster in BI(M) do not form a cluster here at all, and *binguang,* which in the two Indonesian maps is clearly in this area, is here actually a branch of the adjacent "Indecision" area, as has already been discussed.

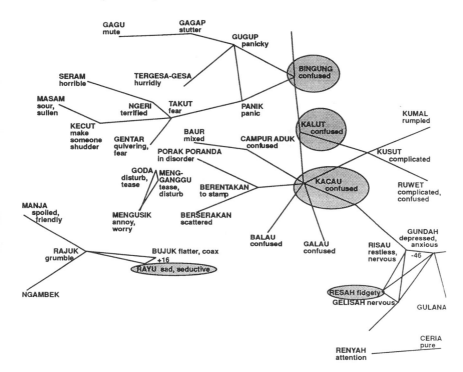

Figure 17.3. "Confusion" area BI(J)

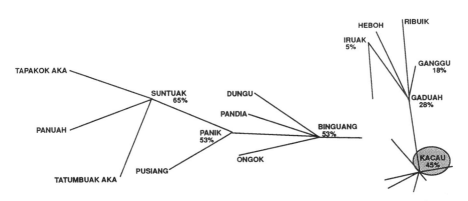

Figure 17a.1. "Confusion/Stymied" cluster BM

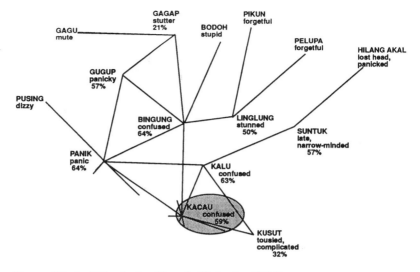

Figure 17a.2. "Confusion/Stymied" cluster BI(M)

BI(M): This 7-word cluster, with *kacau* as the key word, has three twigs and one branch. External connections: *Kacau* is a hinge word with two other clusters in this area, and has a twig to two more. *Panik* has a bridge to *takut*, in the "Fear" cluster; *bingung* has a bridge to *kalap* in the "Anger" area.

BI(J): Here the words form two 3-word triangle clusters, one with *kacau* and *kalut* as the key words, and having two twigs; the other with *bingung* as the key word with two twigs and the *takut* branch already discussed in the "Fear" cluster. External connections: *Kacau* has a link to the *resah* cluster; *bingung* has a bridge to *linglung* that continues to the *lupa* cluster.

B. Key words

The key words are as follows:

BI(M)	*KACAU*
BI(J)	*KACAU/KALUT*
	BINGUNG
BM	*KACAU*

The antecedent/outcome task was done for:

BM	*BINGUANG–KACAU*
BI(M)	*BINGUNG–KACAU*

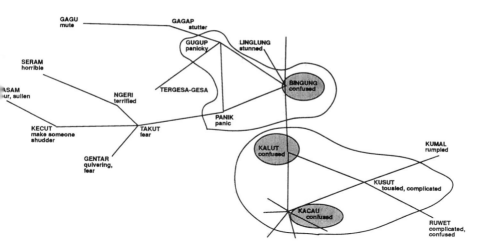

Figure 17a.3. "Confusion/Stymied" cluster BI(J)

C. *English glosses (see Figs. 17.2, 17.3, 17a.2, 17a.3).*

D. *Membership in the realm of emotion: prototypicality ratings*

A relatively weak cluster, with the key word, *kacau*, not the strongest in either map. In BI(M), *kacau* is 59%, weaker than three other words, but these others are only 63% or 64%. The average for the seven BI(M) words in this cluster is only 51%.

E. *Translation equivalents*

From Minangkabau to BI(M)
> the key word (*kacau*) gets 1
> cognates get 2
> non-key, non-cognates get 1 (*panik* > *pusing*)

From BI(M) to BM
> the key word (*kacau*) gets 3
> the other key word (*binguang*) gets 3
> cognates get 5
> others get none

From BI(J) to Javanese
> the apparent key word (*kisruh*, to lose track of things) gets 2
> the apparent key word (*bingung*) gets 3

    cognates get 3
    others get 1 (*panik* > *bingung*)

In summary, there is no strong preference between either cognate or key words, and little choice of non-cognate, non-key words.

F. Antecedent/outcome sentence completion tasks

Minangkabau: *kacau–binguang:*

BM *kacau* antecedents from 27 subjects
    9   difficult problems
        (e.g.: *banyak bana masalah nan diadoinyo* really lots of problems to be faced)
    4   sickness of other
    2   thinking about things

BM *kacau* outcomes from 27 subjects
    9   pondered
        (e.g.: *suko duduak bamanuang seorang diri* he sat thinking it over by himself)
    4   withdrawal/avoidance/attempted escape
        (e.g.: *indak namuah pai kamakama* . . . she didn't want to go anywhere.)
    3   took positive steps
    2   indecision
    4   emotions (*berang* 2; *risau; masam*)

BM *binguang* antecedents from 27 subjects
    5   faced with two choices
    5   didn't know; didn't understand
    5   money problems

BM *binguang* outcomes from 27 subjects
    6   pondered
    5   physical or mental confusions
    1   asked advice

6   emotions (*berang* anger; *hilang aka* lost senses; *maleh; bodoh* stupid; wanted to be *sanang* happy)

BI(M) *kacau* antecedents from 27 subjects

5   faced difficult problems
5   thinking
4   unprepared
4   interpersonal conflict

BI(M) *kacau* outcomes from 27 subjects

3   pondered
3   withdrew/avoided/attempted escape
3   stopped/gave up
1   indecision
1   asked advice
1   took positive steps
3   emotions (*panik; resah; marah*)

BI(M) *bingung* from 27 subjects

9   didn't know/didn't understand
8   faced difficulties
2   faced with two choices

BI(M) outcomes from 27 subjects

5   withdrew
5   physical or mental confusion
6   helpless/fail
3   asked advice
2   pondered
2   tried to solve, learn truth
1   emotion (*galisah*)

In summary, *kacau* in both languages is caused by facing problems and pondering them; the outcome is inaction. This is very similar to the "Indecision" words.

Binguang/bingung is caused by not knowing, or understanding, and also by problems. The outcomes are pondering and confusion.

In BI(M) there is more attempt to solve, asking advice, than there is in BM, but the difference is not dramatic.

On the whole, these sentence completion tasks result in diverse sorts

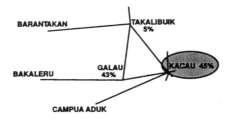

Figure 18.1. "Confusion" cluster BM

of antecedents and outcomes, showing little in the way of general patterns and little positive action. "Confusion" is close to "Indecision," although in the "Indecision" area, analyzed above, there was frequently the response of being unable to make a choice, whereas here it is more general problems that have stymied the person.

18. "Confusion" clusters (*kacau–campur aduk*)

This is a second "Confusion" cluster, which emerges quite distinctly in the mapping but is not distinguishable on the basis of the other data available from the "Confusion/Stymied" cluster just analyzed.

A. Defining the clusters (see Figs. 18.1–18.3)

> BM: a 3-word cluster with *kacau* as the key word. Two twigs, plus the *campua aduk* twig from *kacau*, which is counted here on the authority of its cognates' location in the BI(M) map.
>
> BI(M): a 3-word triangle cluster with *kacau* as the key word, and one twig from *campur aduk*. On the authority of the BM map, the *berentakan* branch from *kacau* is counted in here. External connections: except for the hinge words, *kacau*, this has no external connections.
>
> BI(J): No cluster, but the words established as clusters in the first two maps lie in two twigs and a branch from *kacau*.

B. Key words

In each map, *kacau* is the key word.

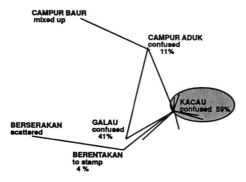

Figure 18.2. "Confusion" cluster BI(M)

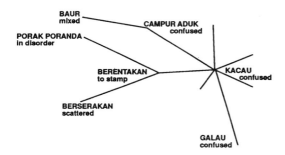

Figure 18.3. "Confusion" cluster BI(J)

C. English glosses (see Figs. 18.2, 18.3)

This seems to be the most consistently translated as "confusion."

D. Membership in the realm of emotion: prototypicality ratings (see Figs. 18.1, 18.2)

These are even weaker than the preceding "Confusion" cluster, in which the 7 words averaged 51%. Here the average for the BM triangle is 31%; for the BI(M) triangle, 37%.

E. Translation equivalents

From BM to BI(M)
    the key word (*kacau*) gets ⅔, 100%

From BI(M) to BM
    the key word (*kacau*) gets ¾, 75%
    another cognate gets ¼, 25%

From BI(J) to Javanese
    the presumed key word (*kaco*) gets ¼
    others get ¾:
    kacau > kisrut
    berentakan > awut–awutan
    campur aduk > campur bawur
    galau > bingung

What is striking here is that although the Minangkabau and Minangkabau Indonesian patterns are quite normal, with most modal choices going to *kacau*, the key word, for the Javanese this pattern does not appear, and non-key non-cognates are chosen. But even there one finds little agreement. The seven choices made between Minangkabau and Minangkabau Indonesian are strong – 15 to 20 (of the possible 50), for an average of 19. But the first choices made by the Javanese have much less agreement – most are 5 or 6, just barely at the acceptable threshold. Two words have first-place ties at 6 each, and only *kisrut*, at 13, is even into the expectable zone for first choices.

This suggests there is something else going on in the Javanese understanding of this "confusion" cluster, but we do not have the data to go any further.

F. Antecedent/outcome sentence completion tasks

None were done for these clusters.

19. Interstitial "Confusion" clusters

This is a sort of interstitial cluster because it consists of words that are all (in Minangkabau and Minangkabau Indonesian) or nearly all (in Javanese Indonesian) hinge words with other clusters. Therefore, with the present data it is not possible to discern any separate identity. Rather, it seems to be an artifact of the mapping, which creates an apparent cluster at the intersections of several other closely related clusters. However, because future investigations may turn up something more substantial here, the data are noted (see Figs. 19.1–19.3).

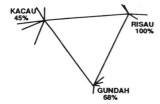

Figure 19.1. Interstitial "Confusion" cluster BM

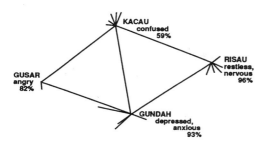

Figure 19.2. Interstitial "Confusion" cluster BI(M)

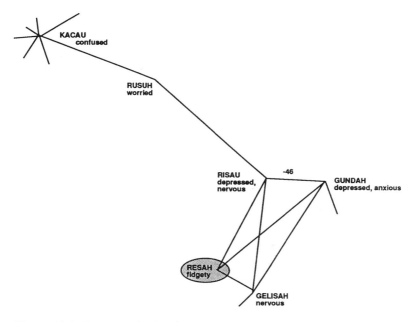

Figure 19.3. Interstitial "Confusion" cluster BI(J)

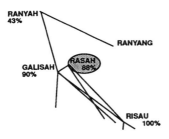

Figure 20.1. "Restless Anticipation" cluster BM

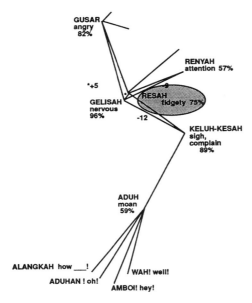

Figure 20.2. "Restless Anticipation" cluster BI(M)

20. "Restless Anticipation" clusters (*resah*)

A. Defining the clusters (see Figs. 20.1–20.3)

This is well defined in Minangkabau Indonesian and in Minangkabau, but in Javanese Indonesian the words are found in different configurations in different clusters.

BM is a 4-word cluster with *rasah* as the key word, and one twig.

External connections: *Risau* is a hinge word in a "Confusion"

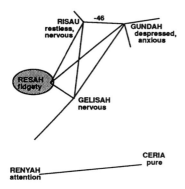

Figure 20.3. "Restless Anticipation" cluster BI(J)

cluster and in the "Sad" area. *Rasah* has a bridge to *seso* in the "Sad" area, and *galisah* has a bridge to *cameh* in the "Indecision" cluster.

BI(M) is a 5-word cluster with *resah* as the key word. One branch from *keluh-kesah*. External connections: *Gusar* is a hinge word with the Interstitial "Confusion" cluster (#19); *resah* has a bridge to *risau*; *gelisah*, a bridge to *gundah* in the Interstitial "Confusion" cluster.

BI(J): Here two of the words are in one cluster, and *renyah* is an isolated twig. The cluster is analogous to what appeared in the other two maps.

B. Key words

The key words are as follows:

BM	*rasah*
BI(M)	*resah*
BI(J)	*resah*

Antecedent/outcome sets were done with:

BM	*rasah–galisah*
BI(M)	*resah–gelisah*

as well as with a set crossing the line between the "Sad" area and the "Confusion" areas:

BM	*rusuah–risau*

C. English glosses (see Figs. 20.2, 20.3.)

D. Membership in the realm of emotion: prototypicality ratings

This is a strong cluster in Figures 20.1 and 20.2. The average prototypicality rating:

> for 4 words in BM is 80%
> for 5 words in BI(M) is 80%.

The key word in BM, *rasah*, is 88%, but still weaker than 2 of the other 3 in its cluster. The key word in BI(M), *resah*, is 75%, but weaker than 3 of the 4 other words in its cluster.

E. Translation equivalents

The first choices of translation equivalents show surprisingly little pattern here, as in the "Confusion/Stymied" cluster (#17).

From BM to BI(M)
> the key word (*resah*) is chosen ¼
> other cognate is chosen ¼
> others are chosen ¾
> *ranyah* > *resah*
> *rasah* > *gelisah*

From BI(M) to BM
> The key word (*rasah*) is chosen ⅗
> other cognates are chosen ⁰⁄₅
> other words are chosen ⅖
> *gusar* > *kacau*
> *resah* > *gelisah*

And from BI(J) to Javanese
> Although *renyah* chooses the cognate *renyah*, each of the other 4 words chose a non-key, non-cognate in Javanese
> *keluh–kesah* > *pasambat* (complaint)
> *resah* > *bingung* (bewildered, confused)
> *gelisah* > *kuatir* (apprehension, fearful)
> *gusar* > *besu* (angry)

F. Antecedent/outcome sentence completion tasks

Minangkabau: *rasah–galisah:*

BM *rasah* antecedents from 28 subjects
> 5   waiting for someone

    4   sickness
    2   facing a problem
    2   hot weather
    1   making a choice
    1   noise
    5   emotions

BM *rasah* outcomes from 28 subjects

    10   restless
    2   pondering
    3   take corrective action
    6   emotions (3 not *tenang* – calm;
            cemas; rusuh; bersalah guilty)

BM *galisah* antecedents from 28 subjects

    12   waiting for someone
    9   negative situation
    2   someone sick

BM *galisah* outcomes from 28 subjects

    12   restless (including 6 can't sleep)
    1   physical reactions
    8   emotions (*berang* anger 2; not
            tenang not calm 2; *maleh; ca-
            meh; bersalah;* not *tenteram,*
            not calm)

BI(M) *gelisah* antecedents from 27 subjects

    15   waiting for someone
    1   someone sick
    2   couldn't sleep
    2   threat of some sort
    2   thoughts
    5   emotions (*bercamuk; bosan; ber-
            salah; ganjal;* not *tenang,* not
            calm)

BI(M) *gelisah* outcomes from 27 subjects

    14   restless, including
            4 can't sleep
    3   physical reactions
    3   action
    7   emotion (*kusut; panik; takut;
            bingung; merobek; kecil hati;*
            not *sabar;* not *keruan*)

BI(M) *resah* antecedents from 27 subjects

5	sickness (including 4 self, 1 other)
1	couldn't sleep
6	waiting for someone
6	thinking about something
4	other threat looms
1	emotion (*gelisah*)

BI(M) *resah* outcomes from 27 subjects

9	restless
1	ponders
2	seeks peace
1	uncertainty
2	takes corrective action
8	emotions (not *tenang* 4, not calm; not *penuh hati*; *bingung; takut*)

To summarize, *rasah/resah* is caused by waiting for someone, or by sickness, or (in Minangkabau) a negative emotion or (in Minangkabau Indonesian) thinking about something. The outcome is restlessness or a negative emotion, particularly "not *tenang*," "not calm."

For *galisah/gelisah*, the causes are waiting for someone or negative situations, and the outcomes are restlessness, especially sleeplessness, and negative emotions.

All 4 words are fairly high producers of other emotions. The emotion-genic scores are:

galisah	8/28	29%
gelisah	7/27	26%
rasah	6/28	21%
resah	8/27	30%

For the Minangkabau set, *risau–rusuah:*

BM *risau* antecedents from 28 subjects

8	waiting for someone
4	thinking, pondering
2	failure
1	lack of something
3	sickness
1	parted from someone

BM *risau* outcomes from 28 subjects

10	ponders
3	restless
2	action
4	diversionary action
2	physical reactions
5	emotion (*marah; binguang; pusing; galisah;* not *tanang*)

BM *rusuah* antecedents from 28 subjects

6	waiting for someone
4	sickness
2	parted from lover, friend
5	lack of money (2 because of theft)
3	bad luck

BM *rusuah* outcomes from 28 subjects

8	ponders
2	restless
2	action
2	diversionary action
8	emotion (*sadiah* sad 4; *rusuah; takuik; marah;* not *tanang*)

These two words have scenarios that closely resemble the *resah–gelisah* sets just described:

They are caused by waiting for someone, or failure, or lack, or bad luck, and their outcomes are pondering, and negative emotions.

They are fairly productive of other emotions:

risau	5/28	18%
rusuah	8/28	29%

Thus, the scenarios are much more definite than the maps in linking *risau* and *rusuah* closely to this "Restless Anticipation" cluster rather than to the "sad" area, although for *risau* and *rusuah* the outcomes are more inaction – pondering, negative emotions – rather than restlessness.

21. "Cajoling" clusters (*rayu*)

This is made up of several words that can be somewhat tentatively lumped together and linked with the "Confusion" area mainly on the authority of the Minangkabau Indonesian map. Their status as emotion words is

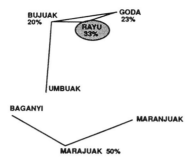

Figure 21.1. "Cajoling" cluster BM

low, and even a satisfactory English translation for the cluster is difficult. This cluster is not central to the emotion landscape, but rather it helps to understand the less determined fringes of the emotion realm.

A. Defining the clusters (see Figs. 21.1–21.3)

> BM: The isolated 3-word triangle cluster with one twig and the *marajuak* isolate.
>
> BI(M): On a branch from *kacau* lie the two tangential 3-word triangle clusters with *goda* as the hinge word joining them. *merajuk* is here an isolated branch.
>
> BI(J): Two isolated 3-word clusters, one with the key word *rayu* and two twigs.

B. Key words

In each map, *rayu* is the key word.
 Antecedent/outcome tasks were done with the close pair from this cluster plus *sedih*, the key word in the "Sad" area:

> BM   *bujuak–rayu–sadiah*
> BI(M)   *bujuk–rayu–sedih*

C. English glosses (see Figs. 21.2, 21.3.)

D. Membership in the realm of emotion: prototypicality ratings (see Figs. 21.1, 21.2)

This is a weak area:
> the 3 words in Minangkabau average 25%

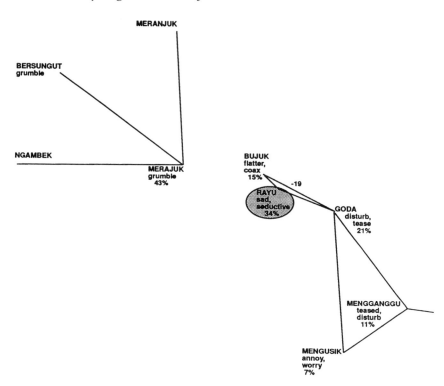

Figure 21.2. "Cajoling" cluster BI(M)

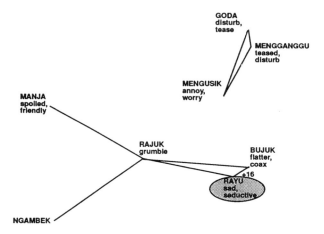

Figure 21.3. "Cajoling" cluster BI(J)

the 5 words in the Minangkabau Indonesian area average 18%
But in this weak company, the key word *rayu* is the strongest in
  both Minangkabau and Minangkabau Indonesian clusters (33%,
  34%).

E. Translation equivalents

From BM to BI(M)
  the key word (*rayu*) gets 3/4
  another cognate gets 1/4

From BI(M) to BM
  the key word (*rayu*) gets 1/5
  other cognates get 2/5
  non-cognate, non-key words get 2/5
  rayu > bujuak
  gusik > manggaduah

From BI(J) to Javanese
  cognates get 2/5
  non-cognates get 3/5
  bujuk > ngrayu and
        ngglembuk (attempt at persuasion)
  rayu > mbujuk
  gusik > nggodha

F. Antecedent/outcome sentence completion tasks

The set of 3 words was chosen at an early stage of the mapping, when
it seemed that there might be direct links between the *rayu* cluster and
the "Sad" area. Also, the dictionary glosses for *rayu* gave "sad" as one
meaning. In the end these links did not appear and the scenarios for
bujuk and *rayu* do not support a "sad" element. Therefore, the "sad"
words (*sadiah, sedih*) have been discussed earlier, with the "Sad" area,
and here only the other two, *rayu* and *bujuk* will be analyzed.
  Minangkabau: *rayu–bujuak*

BM *rayu* antecedents from 27 subjects
    9   wants
        3   wants somebody
        1   wants something

    6   there is a desirable other

    8   is in love

    2   other positive emotion (*sanang* happy; *sayang*)

BM *rayu* outcomes from 27 subjects

    4   got something, someone

    7   flatters someone

    8   emotion (*cinto; salah; mengganggu; suko; namuah* 2; *berang; takalak* smiles)

BM *bujuak* antecedents from 27 subjects

    4   wants something

    1   wants someone

   13   other's negative emotion (12 child crying)

BM *bujuak* outcomes from 27 subjects

    5   flattered another

    5   stopped child crying

    6   gave gifts

    3   emotion (*berang; amuah; kareh hati*)

BI(M) *merayu* antecedents from 28 subjects

   13   wants someone

    6   wants something

    4   negative emotion, attitude

BI(M) *merayu* outcomes from 28 subjects

    5   got someone

    4   got something

   12   talks with good effect, flatters

    2   emotion (*hiba; senang*)

BI(M) *bujuk* antecedents from 28 subjects

   12   negative emotion, attribute

    7   wants something

    0   wants someone

    3   wants to cheer up another

BI(M) *bujuk* outcomes from 28 subjects

    7   cheered up another

    7   gave gift

1   got something
1   got someone

In summary, the antecedents from *rayu* are: wanting, a desire for, especially for someone, and a strong sense of being in love in Minangkabau (less of this in Minangkabau Indonesian). The outcomes are: getting something or someone, and using smooth talk, flattery, and in Minangkabau much emotion.

The antecedents for *bujuk/bujuak* are wanting something, and even more strongly a Sad emotion on the part of another. The outcomes are to give a gift, and cheer someone up.

These are unusual scenarios for emotions, and, indeed, these words have low prototypicality ratings as emotions.

Rayu is glossed in the Echols-Shadily dictionary as "*1* sad, touched, moved, 2 emotional, 3 seductive." Indeed, there is a strong sense of the seductive in the scenarios, but "feeling seductive," although it fits the scenarios, in English seems less like an emotion than a motivation.

Bujuk is glossed by Echols and Shadily as "*1* flattery, smooth words, 2 coaxing, cajoling, 3 deceit," and *bujuk–rayu* as "gentle persuasion, coaxing."

Bujuk/bujuak is really less an emotion in itself and more the reaction to another's emotion of sadness, and it can be translated as "cheering up another." It did not show up as an outcome of the "sad" *sedih/sadiah* scenarios, but this was because the question was phrased "when he/she is sad, . . ." thus asking what a person does when they themselves are sad.

What *rayu* and *bujuk* have in common is talking or other sorts of acting to achieve an end for oneself (*rayu*) or for another (*bujuk*). The emotions involved are ego's own love/desire (*rayu*) or another's sadness (*bujuk*). In this sense, one can see why these words are, however peripherally, found in the emotion landscape.

"ANGER" AREA (*MARAH*) (see Figs. 22.1–22.4)

In Minangkabau the "Anger" area consists of a single cluster, whereas in Minangkabau Indonesian it forms five clusters, all tied to the key word *marah;* and in Javanese Indonesian there are two unconnected clusters. In Minangkabau Indonesian it is closely linked to the "Annoyed" area by hinge words and bridges, but in the other two maps the

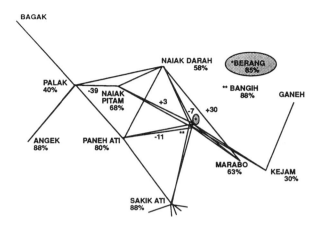

Figure 22.1. "Anger" area BM

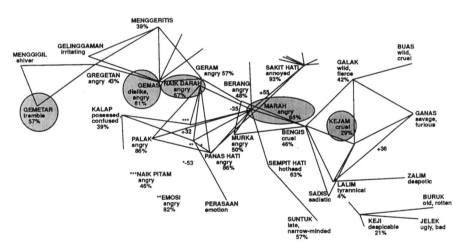

Figure 22.2. "Anger" area BI(M)

links are less strong. To make it easier to follow the analysis, the five Minangkabau Indonesian clusters are shown disentangled in Figure 22.4.

Here we shall examine the single cluster in Minangkabau, one of the two Javanese Indonesian clusters, and the four comparable clusters in Minangkabau Indonesian. (The "Cruel" cluster, #26, is discussed separately below.)

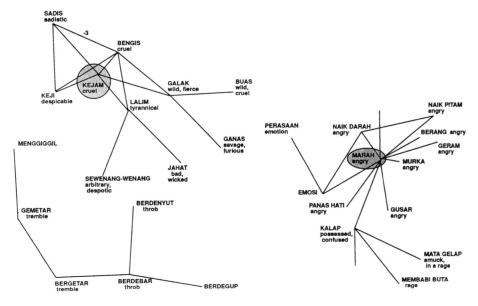

Figure 22.3. "Anger" area BI(J)

In BM, all 9 of the "Anger" area words are incorporated into the single "Anger" cluster; there are also three twigs. The key word is *berang* (although, as we shall see, *bangih* also has some claim to be considered the key word). External connections: Only *sakik ati*, which is a hinge word with the "Annoyance" cluster.

BI(J): a 4-word cluster with *marah* as the key word, plus six twigs and one branch. External connections: *Emosi* is linked by a bridge to *nafsu* in the "Longing" area; *kalap* is linked by a bridge to *kalut* in the "Confusion" area; and *marah* is linked by a bridge to *jengkel* in the "Annoyance" area.

The four entangled clusters in Minangkabau Indonesian (Figs. 22.2, 22.4) are as follows:

22. "Anger" clusters (*naik darah*)

BI(M) (Fig. 22.4): has 8 words, with the key word *naik darah*.

External connections: *Marah* is a hinge word with other clusters in this "Anger" area; *sakit hati* is a hinge word with clusters in the "Annoy-

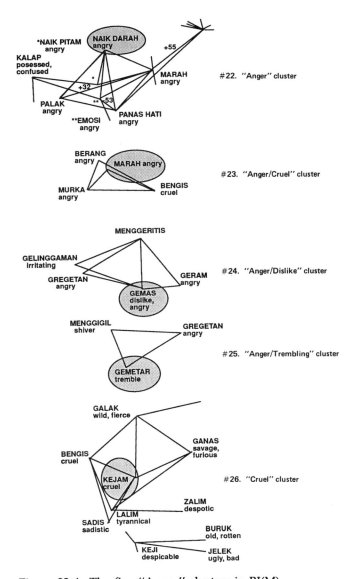

Figure 22.4. The five "Anger" clusters in BI(M)

ance" area; *palak* has a linking bridge to *muak* in the "Annoyance" area; and *kalap* has a linking bridge to *bingung* in the "Confusion" area.

23. "Anger/Cruel" clusters (*bengis*)

BI(M) (Fig. 22.4): A second cluster, "Anger/Cruel," of 4 words with *marah* as the key word.

External connections: *Marah* has many connections; *bengis* is a hinge word with the "Cruel" cluster.

24. "Anger/Dislike" clusters (*gemas*)

BI(M) (Fig. 22.4): The third cluster in this set, "Anger/Dislike," has 5 words, with *gemas* as the key word.

External connections: *geram* is linked to *marah*; *gregetan* is a hinge word with the "Anger/Trembling" cluster and also linked to *takut* in the "Fear" cluster; and *gemas* has two links to the "Annoyance" area.

25. "Anger/Trembling" clusters (*gemetar*)

A. Defining the cluster

> BI(M) (Fig. 22.4): This is the "Anger/Trembling" cluster, a 3-word triangle. External connections: *Gregetan*, a hinge word with the "Anger/Dislike" cluster, also has a linking bridge to *takut* in the "Fear" cluster.
>
> BI(J): Two of the words that appear in the BI(M) "Anger/Trembling" cluster are also found in BI(J) on a 6-word isolated branch, which is included in Figure 22.3.

B. Key words

The key words are as follows:

BM	*berang*
BI(J)	*marah*
BI(M)	22. *naik darah*
	23. *marah*
	24. *gemas*
	25. *gemetar*

Antecedent/outcome tasks were done for only one pair in each language:

BM	*berang–bangih*
BI(M)	*berang–marah*

They were also done for one cross-language pair:

BM: *bangih*/BI(M): *marah*

C. English glosses

The Indonesian word *emosi*, although it is derived from the European word "emotion," is firmly embedded in the "Anger" area (Fig. 22.3) and so can best be translated here as "anger." But, as with many recent loan words, its meaning in speech varies with the consciousness the speaker has of the English/European meaning. (In the dialogue of some modern Indonesian movies, *emosi* is used with the general meaning of "emotion.")

Both *naik darah* and *naik pitam* are glossed as "anger," but it is worth noting that their literal meanings reflect physiological events. *Naik* means to climb, or rise. *Darah* means "blood," and *pitam* means "dizziness," so *naik darah* can be broken down into "rising blood," referring to the flushing of anger, and *naik pitam* to the intensification of blind fury.

D. Membership in the realm of emotion: prototypicality ratings

The ratings for these "Anger" clusters are unexpectedly low.

In BM, the 9 words average 66.7%

In BI(M):

the 8 words of the first "Anger" cluster (#22) average 70.5%

the 4 words of the "Anger/Cruel" cluster (#23) average 52.3%

the 4 words of the "Anger/Dislike" cluster (#24) average 50%

the 2 words of the "Anger/Trembling" cluster (#25) average 50%

The key words are not always those with the highest prototypicality rating:

in BM, berang (85%), is lower than two others

in BI(M) (#22), *naik darah* (67%) is lower than four others

in BI(M) (#23), *marah* (65%) is the highest of the four

in BI(M) (#24), *gemas* (61%) is highest of the four

in BI(M) (#25), *gemetar* is highest of the two

What is most remarkable is the low score of the key word *marah*. Now we see that it is reflected in the low ratings for the entire cluster in Minangkabau Indonesian. Also surprising is that *sakik ati/sakit hati* is the strongest word in both maps.

E. Translation equivalents

From BI(M) to BM
    the key word (*berang*) gets 2.5
    the near-key word (*bangih*) gets 6
    (and of these, three words split their modal choices between *berang* and *bangih*)
    non-key, non-cognate get 2
      palak > paneh
      kalap > silap

From BM to BI(M)
    the key word (*marah*) chosen 6/7
    non-key, non-cognate chosen 1/7
      palak > panas hati

The dominance of *marah* is clear. Also, by this translation criterion, it seems clear that the most salient word in Minangkabau is *bangih,* and not *berang,* which had been identified as the key word on the basis of the within-language choices. This is the only instance of such a discrepancy in the entire study. In every other case, where many words from one language choose a single word from the other language as their modal translation equivalent, that word is also the key word chosen by the other words within that language.

It is also noteworthy that *palak* in each language chooses not the key word but the cognates *paneh ati/panas hati.*

From BI(J) to Javanese
    Nesu (angry), presumably the key word in Javanese, is chosen 9 times
    cognates are chosen 3 times
    there is one choice of a non-key, non-cognate: *gemetar > ndredeg.*

F. Antecedent/outcome sentence completion tasks

Minangkabau: *berang–bangih:*

BM *berang* antecedents from 27 subjects
    7   ego's child was naughty

4	ego was ridiculed, teased, mocked
4	something was ruined by another
3	something was stolen by another
3	ego was accused of something
1	obligation not fulfilled by another
2	challenged/opposed by an inferior

BM *berang* outcomes from 27 subjects

9	did physical violence – hit, ran amuck including 3 hit own child
7	scolded, spoke harshly
4	facial reaction – face red; stared wide-eyed, looked sullen
2	emotion (*naiak darah, naiak piam*)

BM *bangih* antecedents from 27 subjects

12	ego's child misbehaved
5	another didn't fulfill obligation
4	ego was insulted, mocked
3	ego was robbed
1	opinion not listened to
1	belongings damaged

BM *bangih* outcomes from 27 subjects

10	physical violence to another, including
	5 hit her own child
2	hit something
5	withdrew/avoided
2	scolded

Minangkabau Indonesian: *berang–marah:*

BI(M) *berang* antecedents from 27 subjects

5	ego's child was naughty
4	opposed/disobeyed by inferior

3	was teased/ridiculed
2	something was ruined by an-other
1	obligation was not fulfilled by another

BI(M) *berang* outcomes from 27 subjects

7	ego scolded/abused/admon-ished
5	ego left/avoided
3	ego hit someone

BI(M) *marah* antecedents from 27 subjects

6	ego's child was naughty
6	ego was teased/ridiculed/mocked
6	ego was disappointed in/opposed by inferior
5	ego's belongings stole/ruined/seduced away
4	another didn't fulfill obliga-tions
2	a relative was hurt by another

BI(M) *marah* outcomes from 27 subjects

8	hit another including 2 hit own younger relative
7	got revenge, including 3 legal revenge
6	scolded/abused other
2	physical action against a thing
2	emotion (*kalab;* cried)
1	passive withdrawal

Between-language comparison: BM *bangih*/BI(M) *marah:*

BM *bangih* antecedents from 60 subjects

23	ego's child misbehaved
9	another didn't fulfill obliga-tions
7	something was stolen, ruined
5	emotion (*sakik ati* 4; *iri* jealous)

3   opinion or request not sup-
     ported
2   insulted, mocked

BM *bangih* outcomes from 60 subjects
21   hit, pinched another
     8 something
     7 his own child
15   withdrew/avoided/remained
     quiet
12   scolded, spoke harshly
2   emotion (*tasingguang; berang*)

BI(M) *marah* antecedents from 60 subjects
15   ego's own things stolen, ru-
     ined, seduced away
9   ego's child was naughty
8   obligations not fulfilled by other
6   teased/ridiculed by other
6   emotion (*tersinggung* 2; *paba-
     saran; kesal; sakit hati* 2)
4   opposed/disappointed by in-
     ferior
3   a relative hurt by another

BI(M) *marah* outcomes from 60 subjects
22   did physical violence – hit, ran
     amuck
2   physical act against a thing
11   scolded/abused/grumbled
4   withdrew/avoided/passive
3   emotion (*kesal* 2; *naik pitam* an-
     ger)
2   facial expression (eyes turned
     red; *seram* horrible expres-
     sion)

To summarize the antecedents and outcomes of these six sets:

BM *berang* caused by naughty
child, others tease, destroy,
ruin, oppose.

BI(M) *berang* caused by
naughty child, others
tease, ruin, destroy.

Results in: physical violence against other, scolding.
Emotion: 2/27

BM *bangih* caused by naughty child, others fail in obligations, insult, steal.
Results in: violence, withdrawal
Emotion: 0/27

BM *bangih* caused by naughty child, others misbehave, don't fulfill obligations, steal, destroy, insult.
Emotion: 5/60
Results in physical violence, withdrawal, scold.
Emotion 2/60

Results in: scolding, withdrawal, physical violence.
Emotion: 0/27

BI(M) *marah* caused by naughty child, others tease, oppose, steal, ruin, don't full obligations.
Results in: violence, revenge, scolding.
Emotion: 2/27

BI(M) *marah* caused by others steal, ruin, don't fulfill obligations, ridicule, oppose, naughty child.
Emotion: 6/60
Results in violence, verbal attack.
Emotion 3/60

In short, people are angry because of trouble within the family, especially with their children, and because of attacks of various sorts on themselves. And they respond with physical or verbal abuse. It is somewhat surprising that there is so little evidence for a cultural rule about restraining or masking anger, of withdrawing from an anger-producing situation, or of trying to reduce the intensity of anger. In fact, these data from Minangkabau subjects both in Minangkabau and in Indonesian, look remarkably like what would be expected from Americans, or others who do not place such a high value on the concealing of anger.

In the Scherer et al. study of scenarios, one of the strong findings was that "Japanese students are much more readily angered by strangers than by problems in relationship with known others, whereas the opposite is true for Europeans and particularly for Americans." (1988:14) They speculate that in Japan there are stronger rules controlling interaction of people within the same social network and that these rules include a much greater masking of anger (and so, perhaps also the actual feeling of anger). One might add that the dichotomy between known other, one who is closely tied by formal interaction rules, and unknown other, one toward whom there is no social obligation, is especially sharp and wide in Japan. However, these Minangkabau data confuse the issue: On the basis of my a priori theory as well as my field observations,

I would have predicted that the Minangkabau would follow the Japanese pattern. In fact they do not. The most common antecedents for "anger" are the violations of interaction norms: social obligations of others and especially naughty children. The explanations that seem so logical for Japanese culture would have been equally convincing for Minangkabau had the data not turned out the opposite. The value of these comparable data lies in identifying important questions and in forcing deeper analysis of the cultural backgrounds involved.

Actually, in the American scenarios of anger presented by Shaver et al. (1987:1078) the outcomes show about the same level of physical reaction, and a good deal more verbal reaction and more suppression of the anger than do the Indonesian scenarios.

In general, the Indonesian and American scenarios that have been elicited for anger are very similar. This is a surprise, since in their actual behavior most Indonesians mask anger much more than do most Americans. See, for example, Hollan's description of anger management by the Toraja, another Indonesian group (1988).

26. "Cruel" clusters (*kejam*)

This "Cruel" cluster is vestigal, although still in the "Anger" area in BM; it occurs well developed in the "Anger" area in BI(M); and in BI(J) it is well-developed but an isolated cluster.

A. Defining the clusters

> BM (Fig. 22.1) There is minimal evidence of the "Anger/Cruel" cluster in Minangkabau. Here *kejam* is merely a member of the "Anger" cluster with links to both *berang* and *bangih*. *Ganeh* is a twig from *kejam*.

> BI(M) (Figs. 22.2, 22.4): This is 6-word cluster with *kejam* as the key word, and two twigs. *Keji* is included here because of its strong association with this "Cruel" cluster in the BI(J) map. External connections: *bengis* is a hinge word with the "Anger/Cruel" cluster. *Keji* here lies between *kotor* and *ejek* clusters, with one bridge to each. But otherwise the cluster has no external connections.

> BI(J): (Fig. 22.3): This is a 6-word isolated cluster with *kejam* as the key word, and four twigs. Five of the words are also in the BI(M) cluster, so this is clearly the comparable cluster, but it lacks the strong tie to "anger" found in the BI(M) map.

B. Key words

The key words are as follows:

BM	not relevant
BI(M)	*kejam*
BI(J)	*kejam*

C. English glosses (see Figs. 22.2–22.4)

These words seem to describe the physical shaking that accompanies "anger."

D. Membership in the realm of emotion: prototypicality ratings

The prototypicality ratings are relatively low. In both languages *kejam*, the key word, is low (29%, 30%). In BI(M), even counting the stronger hinge word *bengis* (46%), the average for the 4 words is only 30%.

E. Translations equivalents

There are not enough words here to identify patterns, but it is worth noting that 3 of the 4 words in BI(J) choose the Javanese *kejam*, which is presumably the key word in Javanese.

F. Antecedent/outcome sentence completion tasks

None were done.

27. "Uncertain" clusters (*kilaf*)

This is a minor cluster in both Indonesian maps, linked to "Anger" in the Minangkabau Indonesian map but to "Confusion" in the Javanese Indonesian map.

A. Defining the clusters (see Figs. 27.1, 27.2)

> BM: Cognates of the Indonesian starters were not used in the Minangkabau master list, and the words themselves did not appear as responses to other starters, so there are no data for this cluster in Minangkabau at all.
>
> BI(M): This is a 4-word cluster with *kilaf* as the key word and one

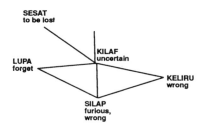

Figure 27.1. "Uncertain" cluster BI(M)

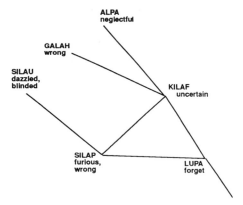

Figure 27.2. "Uncertain" cluster BI(J)

twig. External connections: a bridge from *kilaf* to *kalap* in the "Anger" area.

BI(J): This is a 3-word triangle cluster with *kilaf* as the key word and three twigs. External connections: a bridge from *kilaf* to *bingung* in the "Confusion" area.

B. Key words (see Figs. 27.1, 27.2)

Kilaf is the key word in both Indonesian maps; No antecedents and outcomes were elicited.

C. English glosses (see Figs. 27.1, 27.2)

The dictionary glosses are not helpful in making sense of the relations between these words.

D. Membership in the realm of emotion: prototypicality ratings

Data are for the two starters in BI(M) only. *Kilaf*, the key word, is lower than *silap*, but the two together average only 25% prototypicality.

E. Translation equivalents

The data are inadequate to show patterns, but *kilaf* in both Indonesian versions chooses "forget" (into Minangkabau it is *lupo*, into Javanese it is *lali*). *Silap* from Javanese Indonesian into Javanese splits its modal choice between *lali* and *blering* (blinded by light).

F. Antecedent/outcome sentence completion tasks

None were done.

G. The ethnography of "Uncertain."

There are enough data to be able confidently to place this cluster on the outer limits of the emotion landscape. And there are enough loose ends to suggest the value of further study.

"ANNOYANCE" AREA

This is an area closely tied to the "Anger" area. We can identify five clusters mainly on the basis of the Minangkabau Indonesian map (Fig. 28.2):

28.   "Annoyance" cluster (*kesal*)
29.   "Revenge" cluster (*dendam*)
30.   "Poignant" cluster (*pedih*)
31.   "Bored" cluster (*bosan*)
32.   "Dirty" cluster (*kotor*)

28. "Annoyance" clusters (*kesal*)

A. Defining the clusters (see Figs. 28.1–28.3)

> BM: In this map "Annoyance" is represented by a 3-word triangle cluster with *sakik ati* as the key word and two twigs from *dongkol*.

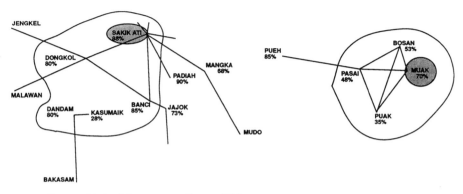

Figure 28.1. "Annoyance" area BM

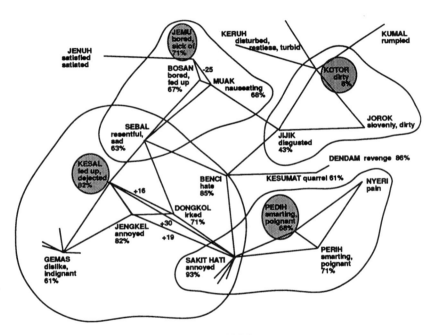

Figure 28.2. "Annoyance" area BI(M)

External connections: *sakik ati* is a hinge word with the "Anger" cluster and has a twig; *banci* has a bridge via *jajok* to the *maleh* cluster.

BI(M): This is a 7-word cluster with *kesal* as the key word. There is

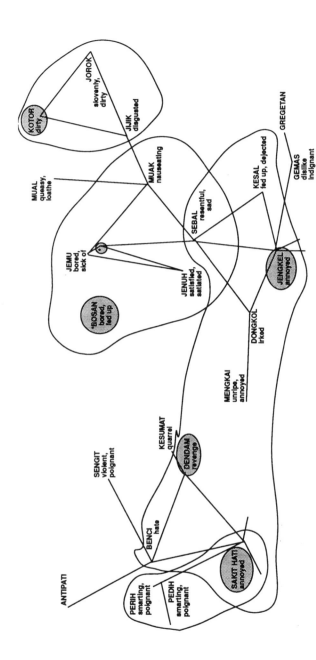

Figure 28.3. "Annoyance" area BI(J)

one twig. External connections: *Sakit hati* is a hinge word with the "Poignant" cluster and with the "Anger" area; *gemas* is a hinge word with the "Anger" area; and *sebal* is a hinge word with the "Bored" cluster. From *kesal* a large branch extends to *kecewa* and beyond. *Benci* has a bridge to the "Dirty" cluster.

BI(J): Here the words are found in two unconnected clusters: a 3-word triangle cluster with *dendam* and *sakit hati* as co-key words, plus four twigs; and a 4-word cluster with *jengkel* as key word, plus two twigs. External connections: the triangle cluster lies far from the "Annoyance" area, but close to "Sad." It is linked by two bridges to the "Sad" cluster and one bridge to the *"tersinggung"* cluster. *Sebal* is a hinge word with the "Bored" cluster.

C. English glosses (see Figs. 28.2, 28.3)

D. Membership in the realm of emotion: prototypicality ratings (see Figs. 28.1, 28.2)

The average prototypicality rating for the 7 words in the Minangkabau Indonesian cluster is 77%; in Minangkabau, the average for the 3-word cluster is 84%, and for the 4-word cluster, 54%.

E. Translation equivalents

From BI(M) to BM
  The key word (*sakik ati*) gets 5/7
  cognate (*benci > banci*) gets 1/7
  non-key, non-cognate gets 1/7
    (*gemas > galinggaman*)
But from BM to BI(M)
  the cognates get 3/3
And from BI(J) to Javanese
  Mangkel (resentful), presumably the key word in Javanese, gets 3/5
  cognate (*sebal > sebal*) gets 1/5
  non-key, non-cognate gets 1/5
  (*sakit hati > lara ati* hurt feelings. *Note: Lara* is the *ngoko*, while in Javanese *sakit* is the *kromo*.)

F. Antecedent/outcome sentence completion tasks

In each language one word from this cluster was paired with words from another cluster in the same area. Now we shall break apart the pairs and present here only the results of the word that is in this cluster, namely:

BM   *sakik ati*
BI(M)   *kesal*

Because these same two words were used as a between-language set, we shall also analyze that between-language set as:

BM   *sakik ati*
BI(M)   *kesal*

BM *sakik ati* antecedents from 27 subjects
  5   was ridiculed
  2   was deceived
  2   wishes, plans, fell through
  1   theft
  1   failed
  1   promise broken
  2   lost lover
  7   other bad treatment

BM *sakik ati* outcomes from 27 subjects
  16   emotions (4 *berang* anger; 2
         marabo anger; 1 *marah* anger;
         2 *banci* hate; 3 *dandam* re-
         venge; 2 *jelek;* not *sanang* not
         happy; cried)
  3   withdrew/avoided
  2   physical assault on something
  1   positive action to repair situa-
         tion

BI(M) *kesal* antecedents from 27 subjects
  5   promise broken
  5   request/desire not fulfilled
  3   fails/errs
  3   waits for someone
  2   ridiculed
  2   disturbed by someone
  2   something stolen/ruined
  1   deceived

BI(M) *kesal* outcomes from 27 subjects

11	emotions (9 *marah* anger; *ejek; jengkel*)
4	grumble/complain
6	withdrew/avoidance/silence
3	physical assault against a thing
2	facial reaction (2 sour)

Between-Language Set: BM *sakik ati*/BI(M) *kesal*

BM *sakik ati* antecedents from 60 subjects

6	slandered
6	ridiculed
5	wishes/plans/intentions not fulfilled
5	failed/low performance
5	promise broken
5	lost lover
4	something stolen/ruined by other
2	deceived
1	was left alone
2	other bad treatment

BM *sakik ati* outcomes from 60 subjects

29	emotions (9 *marabo* anger; 5 *berang* anger; 2 *bangih* anger; *naiak darah* anger; 3 *dandam* revenge; *kecewa; banci* hate; *cimburu; dongkol; buduik; birunguik; muram;* cried)
14	withdrew/avoidance/broke contact
5	takes positive action to repair situation
1	physical assault on something

BI(M) *kesal* antecedents from 60 subjects

9	failure (including 7 school failures)
8	wishes/plans fell though
5	waiting for someone

<table>
<tr><td>4</td><td>someone wasn't good/honest</td></tr>
<tr><td>3</td><td>promise broken</td></tr>
<tr><td>3</td><td>abandoned by someone</td></tr>
<tr><td>3</td><td>emotion (*benci* hate; *dihina* contempt; *jengkel*)</td></tr>
<tr><td>2</td><td>something stolen/ruined</td></tr>
<tr><td>2</td><td>disturbed by someone</td></tr>
<tr><td>1</td><td>deceived</td></tr>
<tr><td>1</td><td>ridiculed</td></tr>
<tr><td>1</td><td>rain hasn't stopped</td></tr>
</table>

BI(M) *kesal* outcomes from 60 subjects

<table>
<tr><td>24</td><td>emotions (16 *marah* anger; 2 ran amuck; 2 *rajuk*; 2 cried; *benci* hate; *sakit hati*)</td></tr>
<tr><td>7</td><td>withdrew/avoidance/silence</td></tr>
<tr><td>7</td><td>took positive action to repair situation</td></tr>
<tr><td>5</td><td>grumbles</td></tr>
<tr><td>4</td><td>physical assault against something</td></tr>
<tr><td>3</td><td>facial reaction</td></tr>
</table>

To summarize, using just the results from the direct comparisons in the between-language sets (although the two 27-subjects response sets are similar):

BM *sakik ati* is caused overwhelmingly by bad treatment from others: slander, ridicule, disappointment, and very secondarily by personal failure. The outcome is negative emotion, mainly in the "Anger" area, and, secondarily, withdrawal (without mention of an emotion), as well as very minor positive action.

BI(M) *kesal* is caused by personal failure, especially in school, and bad treatment from others. The outcome is negative emotion, mainly in the "Anger" area, and withdrawal and positive action.

Both *sakik ati* and *kesal* are emotions that produce emotions. Their emotion-genic scores are high:

sakik ati	29/60	48%
kesal	24/60	40%

G. The ethnography of "Annoyance"

The most striking feature of this cluster is the high degree to which these emotions produce anger. It is as if this cluster is a feeder cluster for the "Anger" area.

Sakit hati is an especially interesting concept. It has a high prototypicality rating in both Minangkabau (88%) and in Minangkabau Indonesian (93%). It is tempting but probably not very revealing to mention that it is a phrase made of two common words: *Sakik/sakit* usually means "sick" or "painful"; *ati/hati* refers to the liver, the seat of emotions, and, of course, also occurs in the superordinate label for this realm of emotions, *perasaan hati*. But it is clear from the scenarios that "Annoyance/ Anger" is a better gloss than some more literal or figurative translation, such as "sickness of heart" or, worse, "sickness of liver."

John C. Spores (1988:64) has pointed out that the English commentators on nineteenth-century Malaya claimed that *sakit hati* was the cause of *amok*, the "sudden mass assault" culture-bound syndrome (see also Simons and Hughes 1985). But it is remarkable that a century later in nearby Sumatra, there is virtually no sign of this *amok* violence in these *sakit hati* scenarios.

29. "Revenge" clusters (dendam)

This is not a legitimate cluster, but the two words *dandam/dendam* and *kasumaik/kesumat* occur together, although in different configurations, in each map, and in the two Indonesian maps they are linked to the "Annoyance" area.

A. Defining the clusters (see Figs. 28.1–28.3)

> BM: *Dandam* and *kasumaik* are on an isolated twig.
> BI(M): *Dendam* and *kesumat* are on a twig from *benci* of the "Annoyance" cluster.
> BI(J): *Dendam* is a member of a 3-word triangle cluster attributed to the "Annoyance" cluster, and *kesumat* is a twig from *dendam*.

B. Key words

In BI(J), *dendam* is a co-key word with *sakit hati*.

Antecedent/outcome tasks were done with the 2 words in both languages.

C. English glosses (see Figs. 28.2, 28.3)

D. Membership in the realm of emotion: prototypicality ratings

BM *dandam* (80%) and BI(M) *dendam* (86%) have strong prototypicality ratings, while *kasumaik*, in Minangkabau, is very weak at 28%; but in Minangkabau Indonesian, *kesumat* is 61%.

E. Translation equivalents

Between Minangkabau and Minangkabau Indonesian the 2 words choose each other; from Javanese Indonesian to Javanese, *dendam* gets 1.5, *mangkel* (resentful) gets 0.5. (*Mangkel* was the presumed key word and most popular choice for the "Annoyance" cluster, described earlier.)

F. Antecedent/outcome sentence completion tasks

Minangkabau: *dandam–kasumaik:*

BM *dandam* antecedents from 27 subjects
>   18   someone was hurt, physically or otherwise, including 12 self was hurt
>   4   emotions (2 was ridiculed; 2 feelings hurt)

BM *dandam* outcomes from 27 subjects
>   13   got even, took revenge
>   7   withdrew, avoidance
>   2   hurt another
>   1   emotion (*berang* anger)

BM *kasumaik* antecedents from 27 subjects
>   8   injuries to ego or other
>   6   something stolen or ruined
>   5   emotions (*sakik ati* feelings hurt 4; *malu*)
>   1   betrayed
>   1   another better off

BM *kasumaik* outcomes from 27 subjects:
>   6   emotions (2 *berang* anger; 2 *banci*

> hate; *paneh ati* anger; not *sanang* not happy)

4	got even
3	killed other
1	hurt other
3	took action to retrieve something
1	facial expression

BI(M) *dendam* antecedents from 27 subjects

15	emotions (9 *sakit hati* hurt feelings; 4 contempt by other; *tersinggung;* not *puas* not content)
9	physical hurt, killing, including 5 where self was victim

BI(M) *dendam* outcomes from 27 subjects

10	got even
6	killed the other
4	emotions (*marah* anger; *benci* hate; not *puas* not content; not *senang* not happy)
3	hurt other
2	withdrew

BI(M) *kesumat* antecedents from 27 subjects

8	emotions (4 *sakit hati* hurt feelings; *dihina* ridiculed; *dikecewakan; iri hati* jealous)
6	physical injury to person 4, or belongings 2
2	opposed/animosity
1	betrayed
1	unjustly accused

BI(M) *kesumat* outcomes from 27 subjects

7	withdrew
4	got even
3	emotions (2 *benci* hate; *sakit* hurt)
2	hurt other
1	killed other

Table 29.1

	Someone hurt	Emotion	E–G score
BM DANDAM	18	4	15%
BI(M) DENDAM	9	15	56%

Chi square = 9.299; $p = <.005$

Table 29.2

	Got even	Withdrew	Emotion	E–G score
BM DANDAM	15	7	1	4%
BI(M) DENDAM	19	2	4	15%

1	opposed other
1	suicide

To summarize, for *dendam* the antecedents are significantly different for the two languages (Table 29.1).

Although the role of emotion (as opposed to physical hurt) is much higher in Minangkabau Indonesian, the outcomes are similar (Table 29.2).

As the low emotion-genic scores show, the outcomes produce not other emotions but action of some sort.

For the other word, there is less striking contrast between languages thoughout (Tables 29.3, 29.4).

This reflects, but to a lesser degree, the role of emotion as antecedent and outcome noted for *dendam/dandam*.

30. "Poignant" clusters *(pedih)*

This cluster, with its key word *padiah/pedih*, is a dramatic illustration of an instance where two-dimensional maps cannot give a good picture of the relations between clusters. In Minangkabau Indonesian there is a solid 4-word cluster in the "Anger"/"Annoyance" areas. In both Minangkabau and Javanese Indonesian, however, *padiah/pedih* pulls *sakit hati* and the "Annoyance" group close to the "Sad" area. This *padiah/pedih* is closely tied to "sad" and "annoyance"/"anger," although otherwise these areas are far apart. At least the maps do show each link, even though the scale is necessarily inaccurate.

Table 29.3

Antecedents:	Someone hurt	Something hurt	Emotion	E–G score (%)
BM KASUMAIK	9	6	5	19
BI(M) KESUMAT	6	2	8	30

Table 29.4

Outcomes	Got even	Withdrew	Emotion	E–G score (%)
BM KASUMAIK	8	0	6	22
BI(M) KESUMAT	8	7	3	11

A. Defining the clusters (see Figs. 28.1–28.3)

> BM: *Padiah* is not in a cluster but has bridges to *sakik ati*, of the "Annoyance" cluster, and to *sadiah* of the "Sad" cluster.
>
> BI(M): This is a 4-word cluster with *pedih* as the key word. External connections: *Sakit hati* is a hinge word with the "Annoyance" and "Anger" clusters.
>
> BI(J): Here also *pedih* is linked to *sakit hati* and, via *pilu*, to the "Sad" cluster, with *perih* as a twig from *pedih*.

B. Key words

In BI(M): *pedih*.

D. Membership in the realm of emotion: prototypicality rating

In BM, *padiah* is strong at 90%. In BI(M), although *pedih* and *perih* are only 68% and 71%, with *sakit hati* as 93%, the cluster average is 77%.

E. Translation equivalents

From BM to BI(M)
> *padiah* names the key word, *sakit hati*

From BI(M) to BM
> both *pedih* and *perih* name *padiah*

From BI(J) to Javanese

> both *pedih* and *perih* name *perih* (hurt, sting), which is presumably the key word in Javanese.

F. Antecedent/outcome sentence completion tasks

None done.

31. "Bored" clusters *(bosan)*

A. Defining the clusters (see Figs. 28.1–28.3)

> BM: an isolated 4-word cluster, with *muak* as the key word, with one twig. External connections: none.
>
> BI(M): a 4-word cluster with *jemu* the key word. External connections: *Sebal* is a hinge word with the "Annoyance" cluster; *muak* has a bridge to the "Dirty" cluster and to *palak* in the "Anger" cluster; and *jemu*, via *jenuh*, is linked to the "Happy" area.
>
> BI(J): a 5-word cluster with *bosan* as the key word, and one twig. External connections: *Sebal* is the hinge word with "Annoyance" and *muak* has a bridge to the "Dirty" cluster.

B. Key words

The key words are as follows:

BM	*muak*
BI(M)	*jemu*
BI(J)	*bosan*

Antecedent/outcome tasks were done:

in Minangkabau:	*bosan–muak–sakik ati*
in BI(M)	*bosan–muak*
	bosan–kesal

D. Membership in the realm of emotion: prototypicality rating

In both maps the key word has the highest prototypicality rating, an unusual circumstance.

> The average for the 4 words of the BM cluster is 52%
> The average for the 4 words of the BI(M) cluster is 67%

E. Translation equivalents

From BI(M) to BM
    to the key word *(muak)* 1/4
    to *bosan* 2/4
    to other 1/4
      (sebal > sakik ati)

From BM to BI(M)
    to the key word *(jemu)* 0/0
    to *bosan* 4/4

From BI(J) to Javanese
    bosan > jeleh
    muak > jijik
    sebal > sebel

Here *bosan*, although not the key word in either Minangkabau map, gets the most first choices in each. This is an unusual situation.

F. Antecedent/outcome sentence completion tasks

In Minangkabau, *bosan–muak–sakik ati* were done; because *sakik ati* has been analyzed already, only *bosan* and *muak* are discussed here.
    in BI(M), *bosan–muak*
    from the *bosan–kesal* set, only *bosan*
No between-language sets were done.
Minankgabau: *bosan–muak*:

BM *bosan* antecedents from 27 subjects
    9   repetitious activities
    7   bad behavior on someone's part
    2   waiting for someone
    1   failure

BM *bosan* outcomes from 27 subjects
    12   withdrawal/avoidance
    6   gives up
    3   emotion (2 *banci* hate; *berang* anger)

BM *muak* antecedents from 27 subjects
    15   bad behavior on part of an- other

3   repetitious activity
2   much work/problems
1   fighting

BM *muak* outcomes from 27 subjects
12   withdrawal/avoidance
6   emotions (*marah* anger; *berang* anger; *marabo* anger; *maleh* lazy; *jajok*)
3   ordered another to behave correctly
2   grumbled
2   hit or broke something

BI(M) *bosan* antecedents from 27 subjects
21   repetitious behavior including
5 at school
4 at work
5 someone talking
2 food

BI(M) *bosan* outcomes from 27 subjects
10   gives up/stops
7   withdrawal/avoidance
6   emotions (2 *malas* lazy; *keluh*; *benci*; *kesal*; not *suka* doesn't like)

BI(M) *muak* antecedents from 27 subjects
11   behavior of other is bad
5   fighting, dispute
4   repetitious activities
2   other's bad attitude toward self
2   work, problems overwhelming

BI(M) *muak* outcomes from 27 subjects
16   withdrawal/avoidance
3   emotions (*benci* hate; *jijik*; *marah* anger)
2   grumbled/growled
1   broke something

BI(M) *bosan* (from the *bosan–kesal* set):

BI(M) *bosan* antecedents from 27 subjects:

13	repetitous activities
	4 someone talking
	3 food
	2 work
	2 school
5	waiting for someone
2	endures long task

BI(M) *bosan* outcomes from 27 subjects

9	withdrawal/avoidance
5	gives up
4	emotions (2 *malas* lazy; *muak*; *benci* hate)
2	goes to the movies
2	complains/objects

To summarize:

BM *bosan* is caused by repetitiousness and someone's bad behavior, and it results in withdrawal and giving up. The emotion-genic score is 3/27, 11%.

BI(M) *bosan* is overwhelmingly caused by repetitiousness, with other's bad behavior negligible. It results in withdrawal and giving up. The emotion-genic score is 10/54, 19%.

BM *muak* is caused by bad behavior of another, and results in withdrawal. The emotion-genic score is 22%.

BI(M) *muak* is caused by the bad behavior of another and results in withdrawal. The emotion-genic score is 11%.

There are few differences between the two languages but considerable differences among the words. *Bosan* is caused by repetitiousness, and means "bored." But *muak* is caused by the bad behavior of another. It is not really "nauseating," as the dictionary suggests, but more "disapproval." In each case the outcomes are withdrawal. The emotion-genic scores are low. These emotions rarely generate other emotions.

32. "Dirty" clusters *(kotor)*

These are unpromising clusters in emotion terms, but they emerged in both of the Indonesian maps and must be dealt with.

A. Defining the clusters (see Figs. 28.1–28.3)

> BM: In this there is only one word, *jajok*, which is linked to *banci* in the "Annoyance" cluster.
>
> BI(M): This is a 3-word triangle cluster with *kotor* as the key word, and two twigs. External connections: *Jijik* is linked to *benci* in the "Annoyance" cluster and to *muak* in the "Bored" cluster; *kotor* is liked to the *ejek* cluster.
>
> BI(J): This is a 3-word triangle, linked to *muak* in the "Bored" cluster. External connections: only the link to *muak*.

B. Key words

Kotor is the key word in both BI(M) and BI(J).

C. English glosses (see Figs. 28.2, 28.3.)

D. Membership in the realm of emotion: prototypicality ratings

Kotor itself, at 8%, is at the low end of the prototypicality scale, but *jijik* (43%) and *jajok* (73%) are stronger.

E. Translation equivalents

BI(M) *jijik* and BM *jajok* choose each other, and *jijik* BI(J) chooses *jijik* in Javanese. *Kotor* chooses *kumuah* in Minangkabau, and *reged* (dirty) in Javanese.

F. Antecedent/outcome sentence completion tasks

None were done.

G. Ethnography of "Dirty "

It includes *jijik*, the best single-word translation for the English "disgust." "Disgust" has figured prominently in emotion research and has often been considered a basic emotion, partly because it has such a distinctive facial expression (Ekman and Friesen 1975:66). In the Shaver et al. study of American English (1987) Disgust is in a cluster under Anger (together with Revulsion and Contempt), and its prototypicality rating is fairly strong (3.42 on the 4.0 scale, thirty-fifth of 213 words). It is surprising to find its Indonesian equivalents in such an inconsequential position in the maps.

"COGNITION" AREA *(KECEWA)*

This area gives an excellent picture of the fringes of the emotion category, where different emotions blend together and where the regular structure of clusters and areas becomes unraveled into dead-end branches and isolated chains of words. It is most clear in Minangkabau Indonesian, where a complex branching structure begins with *kecewa*, a strong emotion with 90% prototypicality rating, and fades out through logical links, finally to reach words that are barely emotions.

A. Defining the Area

> BM: This is mainly a loop of a dozen words that runs from the "Sad" area to the "Desire" area; and on the authority of the words included in the Minangkabau Indonesian branch, we include two isolated chains of 3 and 4 words.
>
> BI(M): Here a single large branching structure includes 32 words. It is connected via *kecewa* to *kesal* in the "Annoyance" area, and has no other connections to any other clusters or areas.
>
> BI(J): A branch of 10 words is linked via *kecewa* to the "Sad" cluster; and, on the authority of the words included in the Minangkabau Indonesian branch, we include four isolated chains of 2,3,5, and 6 words.

33. "Consciousness" clusters *(sadar)*

A. Defining the clusters (see Figs. 33.1–33.3)

> BM: A 3-word triangle cluster with *insaf* as the key word. Here the cluster is on a complex looping structure whose words are tied to "Sad" and "Desire."
>
> BI(M): A 3-word cluster with *sadar* as the key word. It is in the extensive branch leading from the "Uncertain" area via *kecewa*. There are four twigs and three branches.

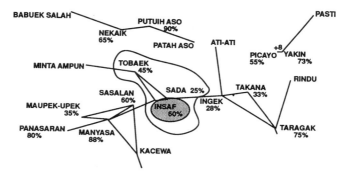

Figure 33.1. "Conscious" and "Depression" clusters BM

BI(J): A 3-word triangle cluster on a branch emerging from the "Sad" area via *kecewa*.

Summary. In two of the maps this cluster is more closely tied to the "Sad" area than to "Annoyance."

B. *Key words*

The key words are as follows:

BM	*insaf*
BI(M)	*sadar*
BI(J)	*sadar*

C. *English glosses (see Figs. 33.2 and 33.3)*

D. *Membership in the realm of emotion: prototypicality ratings*

Although *insaf* is reasonably high in prototypicality rating in both languages (60%, 89%), the average for the clusters is lower:

for the 3 Minangkabau words: 43%
for the 4 Minangkabau Indo-
   nesian words: 62%

E. *Translation equivalents*

In Minangkabau and Minangkabau Indonesian, *insaf* and *sadar* choose the other, while *tobaik/tobat* choose themselves. From Javanese Indone-

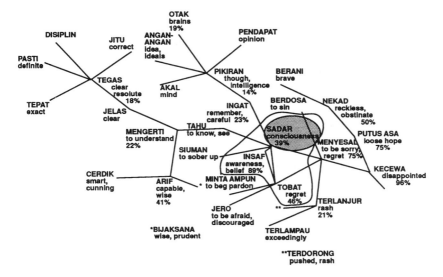

Figure 33.2. "Conscious" and "Depression" clusters BI(M)

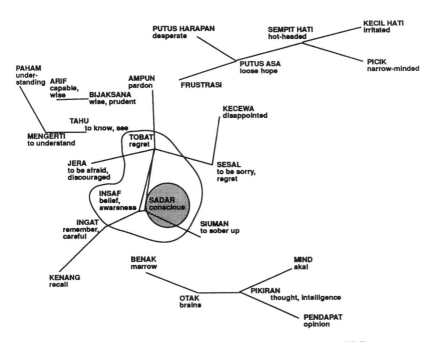

Figure 33.3. "Conscious" and "Depression" clusters BI(J)

sian to Javanese, *tobat* chooses *kapok* (to have learned one's lesson), while both *insaf* and *sadar* choose *eling* (to remember).

F. Antecedent/outcome sentence completion tasks

None were done.

G. The ethnography of "Consciousness"

Sadar is another fringe area cluster that is still clearly emotion. Its occurrence in the same shape in each map argues strongly that it is not somehow an accident of the mapping technique. The English glosses are inadequate to give a good idea of which English cluster it corresponds to.

Now let us return to the "Cognition" *(kecewa)* area as a whole.

34. "Depression" clusters *(putus asa)* (see Figs. 33.1–33.3)

As a rule, clusters are clearly manifested in the maps as a set of words with links among themselves and a few external links to other clusters. Often the cluster is best recognized in the Minangkabau Indonesian map and on that authority projected onto the less orderly data of the other two maps.

In this instance, however, a set of words looks clusterlike, but even the Minangkabau Indonesian map (Fig. 33.2) does not show a true cluster.

On the basis of the dictionary definitions and the scenarios, we can recognize several neighboring words with strong prototypicality ratings that suggest a "Depression" cluster:

kecewa	96%
putus asa	75%
nekad	50%
menyesal	75%
tobat	46%
jero	n.a.

B. Key words

This is not really a useful concept for this sort of branching, rather than clustering, formation.

Antecedents and outcomes were elicited for two pairs, which occur on branches:

| BM | nakaik–putuih asa |
| BI(M) | nekad–putus aso |

C. English glosses (see Figs. 33.2, 33.3)

These dictionary translations give a good idea of how the chains of associated words lead gradually out of the emotion realm.

D. Membership in the realm of emotion: prototypicality ratings

Although there are a few words with very strong prototypicality ratings (in Minangkabau, *putuih asa* at 90%, *manyasa* at 88%; in Minangkabau Indonesian, *kecewa* at 96%, *insaf* at 89%), the ratings drop off rapidly, reinforcing the data of the translations into English.

When comparing cognate words in the two languages, a pattern of sorts does emerge:

Minangkabau	Minangkabau Indonesian
putuih aso 90%	>putus asa 75%
nekaik 65%	>nekad 50%
manyasa 88%	>menyesal 75%
kacewa no data	kecewa 96%
ingek 28%	>ingat 23%
tobaek 45%	<tobat 46%
insaf 60%	<insaf 89%
sada 25%	<sadar 39%

For all 3 words of the "Consciousness" cluster, the Minangkabau Indonesian versions are stronger, but for the 4 others the Minangkabau version is stronger.

E. Translation equivalents

There is little pattern evident with this small sample.

F. Antecedent/outcome sentence completion tasks

Minangkabau: *putuih aso–nekaik:*

BM *putuih aso* antecedents from 27 subjects

    11   failure, including
            4 love
            2 exams

6   hopes dashed/not realized
2   spouse's behavior to self is bad
1   troubled/difficult life

BM *putuih aso* outcomes from 27 subjects
7   gave up
3   suicide/attempted
2   withdrew/avoidance
5   pondered
5   emotion (2 *sadiah* sad; 2 *maleh* lazy; cried)
1   succeeded

BM *nekaik* antecedents from 27 subjects
6   no way out
5   other angry at ego
6   emotion (*panik; sakik ati* hurt feelings; *dihino* humiliated; *dandam* revenge; not *takuik* not afraid)

BM *nekaik* outcomes from 27 subjects
10   withdrew/avoidance
5   suicide
1   didn't know ego
5   take risk, dare

BI(M) *putus asa* antecedents from 27 subjects
18   failure
        3 love
        3 exams
3   hopes dashed
2   troubled life

BI(M) *putus asa* outcomes from 27 subjects
7   withdrew, left
6   suicide/attempted
4   gave up
4   emotion (*frustrasi; sedih* sad; *nekad; rendah diri* humiliated)
1   succeeded
1   found God

BI(M) *nekad* antecedents from 27 subjects
  7   emotion (*emosi* anger; 2 *putus
           asa; gelora; sakit hati* hurt
           feelings; *cinta* love; *kalap;
           dendam* revenge)
  5   failure including
           3 love
  2   blocked from goal
  2   desired a difficult thing

BI(M) *nekad* outcomes from 27 subjects
  7   suicide
  3   mental   forgetfulness/inatten-
           tion
  2   physical violence/outburst
  2   takes a risk
  2   withdrawal/fled
  2   succeeded

To summarize:

BM *putuih aso* caused by failure, hopes not realized. Results in giving up, pondering, suicide, withdrawal.
Emotion-genic score: 5/27,
19%

BI(M) *putus asa* caused by failure, hopes not realized. Results passive: withdrawal,
suicide, gave up.
Emotion-genic score: 4/27,
15%

BM *nekaik* caused by no way
out, emotions of ego or
others 11/27, 41%.
Outcomes: withdrawal, suicide, emotions 0/27; minor
positive action (5/27, 19%).

BI(M) *nekad* caused by failure,
emotions 7/27, 26%.
Outcomes: suicide, with-
drawal, emotions 0/27; minor positive actions (8/27,
30%).

This is very close to the English concept "depression": All four are the
result of failure, and *nekaik/nekad* is unusually strongly the result of negative emotions of ego or others. This role of emotion is quite unusual.
We often find emotions as the outcome of emotions. Here, for example,
putuih aso/putus asa produce moderate amounts of emotion (their
emotion-genic scores are 19%, 15%). But *nekaik/nekad* does not produce
emotions; rather, emotions are named as antecedents at this unusually
high rate: 41%, 26%.

Not only is *nekaik/nekad* often the result of negative emotions, there is a degree of positive action outcome (19%, 30%) that is almost totally lacking with *putuih aso/putus asa* (4% in each).

However, the element of sadness that is generally so important in depression seems lacking here (see, for example, Kleinman and Good 1985). The maps and scenarios give only the slightest hints of a sad connection.

In the Boucher analysis of Indonesian emotion words, clusters were formed through a rather different methodology than that used here. They report (Brandt and Boucher 1986) on a "Depression" cluster, but it does not correspond to any of these clusters. Of their 13 words, 10 did not appear in either of these Indonesian maps and one of the 10 seems to be Javanese (it is absent from the Indonesian dictionaries, present in the Javanese dictionary). Three words do appear in the maps – *hina* in the "Mocking" cluster, and *putus asa* and *putus harapan* in this *kecewa* area. That is, in Minangkabau Indonesian *putus asa* is on a twig next to *kecewa*, and in Javanese Indonesian *putus asa* and *putus harapan* are on an isolate branch. Brandt and Boucher note that some languages, including Malaysian, have "depression"-type words but no actual "Depression" cluster. The data presented here, from Minangkabau and from Yogyakarta Javanese, look much more like the Boucher Malaysian results than like the generalized Indonesian results they gathered from a mixture of ethnic groups in Indonesia.

There seems every reason to assume that the Indonesian archipelago includes cultures with quite a wide range of emotion patterns. The systematic differences revealed by the comparisons here of Minangkabau and Javanese support this assumption. Thus, the Boucher group's lumping of Indonesian cultures, as well as their different methodology, make it difficult to compare their results with results in this book.

"SHAME" AREA (see Figs. 35.1–35.3)

The four clusters and branch, all interconnected in Minangkabau Indonesian, correspond in Minangkabau to three clusters and two branches, none of which are interconnected, and in Javanese Indonesian to three clusters and a branch, all interconnected, plus one isolated twig. Taking the cue from the Minangkabau Indonesian map, the units of this area can be described as follows:

35.   "Mocking/Disapproval" clusters (*ejek*)
36.   "Outraged" clusters (*sindir*)

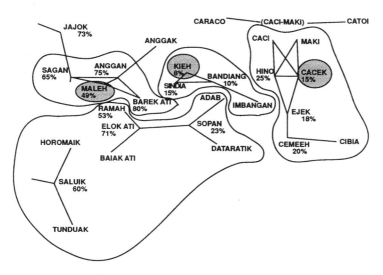

Figure 35.1. "Shame" area BM

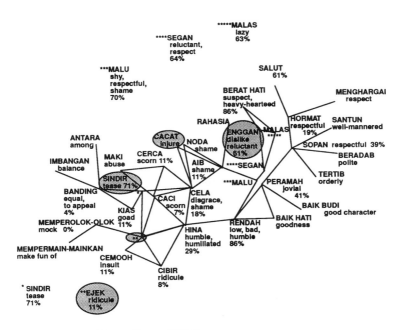

Figure 35.2. "Shame" area BI(M)

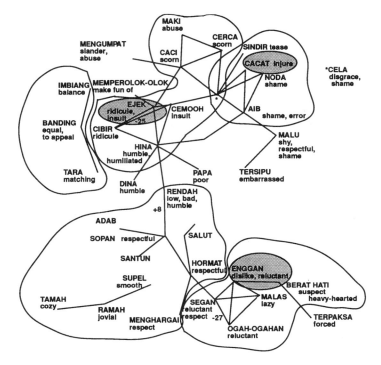

Figure 35.3. "Shame" area BI(J)

37.   "Shame" clusters (*cacat*)
38.   "Lazy" clusters (*enggan*)
39.   "Respectful" clusters (*sopan*)

35. The "Mocking/Disapproval" clusters *(ejek)*

This appears as a cluster in each map. In Minangkabau it is an isolated
cluster, while in the two Indonesian maps it is linked to other clusters
of the "Shame" area.

A. Defining the clusters (see Figs. 35.1, 35.2)

BM (Fig. 35.1): an isolated 5-word cluster with three twigs, and
cacek as the key word.

BI(M) (Fig. 35.2): a 9-word cluster with one twig, and *ejek* as the
key word. External connections: *Cela* is a hinge word with the
"Shame" cluster, *sindir* is a hinge word with the "Teased" clus-

ter; *hina* has a bridge to the "Respectful" branch and, via *keji*, to the "dirty" cluster.

BI(J) (Fig. 35.3): an 8-word cluster with three twigs and *ejek* as the key word. External connections: *Cela* is a hinge word with the "Shame" cluster, *hina* has bridges to the "Shame" cluster via *nista*, and to the "Respectful" branch.

B. Key words

The key words are as follows:

BM	*cacek*
BI(M)	*ejek*
BI(J)	*ejek*

Antecedent and outcome tasks were done:

BM	*cacek–ejek–cemeeh*
BI(M)	*ejek–cemooh*

(*Sindia/sindir*, which in Minangkabau Indonesian is a hinge word with the "outraged" cluster [#36], is part of a set with other words in that cluster and is analyzed below.)

C. English glosses (see Figs. 35.2, 35.3)

D. Membership in the realm of emotion: prototypicality ratings

In Minangkabau, the 4 words have an average prototypicality ratings of 18%.

In Minangkabau Indonesian the 9 words, even including the abberrant 71% of *sindir*, average only 19%.

These are surprisingly low prototypicality ratings. But because the words in both languages, rated by different groups of subjects, are so similar, and because in other clusters these prototypicality ratings seem to reflect the membership in the emotion realm, it is difficult to explain these particular ratings.

E. Translation equivalents

From BM to BI(M)
    the key word *(ejek)* gets none
    hina gets 3
    cemooh gets 2
    cognates get 1

From BI(M) to BM
> the key word *(cacek)* gets 3
> cognates get 3

From BI(J) to Javanese
> cognates get 1
> for one word, blanks are the mode
> others:
>> *cela* > *cacat*
>> *hina* 1/2 > *asor*
>> *ejek, cemooh* > *ngenyek*
>> *cibir* > *menjeb*
>> *caci* > *ngonekakg*

F. Antecedent/outcome sentence completion tasks

Minangkabau: *cameeh – ejek – cacek*

BM *cameeh* antecedents from 26 subjects
> 15   another acts badly
> 2   another has more
> 5   ego's emotion (*takut* fear; *maleh* lazy; *banci* hate; *iri* jealousy; *ati busuak*) E–G: 19%

BM *cameeh* outcomes from 26 subjects
> 7   sneered at other
> 8   ego's emotion (*hina*; *iri* jealousy; *barabo* anger; *gadang ati* content; 2 *banci* hate; *bimbang* confused; not *sanang* not happy) E–G score: 33%
> 1   other's emotion (*berang* anger)

BM *ejek* antecedents from 26 subjects
> 5   other acts badly
> 1   other has more
> 6   ego's emotion (*sakik ati* 3; *iri* jealousy; *jajok; sanang* happy)
> 4   other's emotion (*sombong*; 2 not *disenangi* not pleased; *angkuah*)

BM *ejek* outcomes from 26 subjects

5	ego sneered at other
6	ego's emotion (2 *menghina; banci* hate; *mamaki; memperolok–olok;* not *sanang* not happy)
4	other's emotion (2 *marah* anger; not *disanangi* not happy; laughed at)

BM *mancacek* antecedents from 26 subjects

11	other acts badly
3	ego acts badly
2	other has more
2	other has physical defect

BM *mancacek* outcomes from 26 subjects

6	ego hurts, takes revenge on other
2	ego got punished, hurt
6	ego's emotion (*hina; singgung; pembusuk; jajok; iri ati;* not *sanang* not happy)
4	other's emotion (*maki; marahi; sadiah; benci* hate)

BI(M) *cemooh* antecedents from 27 subjects

12	other acts badly, including 4 specifically in violation of custom *(adat)*
4	ego's emotion (3 *sombong;* not *senang* not happy)
3	other's emotion (2 *angkuh; marah* anger)

BI(M) *cemooh* outcomes from 27 subjects

4	ego scorned/rejected by other
3	ego sneered at other
4	ego's emotion (*gembira* happy; *puas* content; *malas* lazy; not *senang* not happy)
5	other's emotion (*dicemoohkan; naik pitam* anger; laughed at 2; not *disenangi* not happy at)

BI(M) *ejek* antecedents from 27 subjects
    9   other acts badly
    5   other has physical defect
    5   ego's emotion (2 *sakit hati; benci; angkuh;* not *senang* not happy)
    4   other's emotion (2 *sombong; benci* hate; *sakit hati*)

BI(M) *ejek* outcomes from 27 subjects
    3   mocked crippled other
    3   was rejected by other
    5   ego's emotion (*bersalah* guilty; *senang* happy; 2 *benci* hate; *hina*)
    5   other's emotion (3 *marah* anger; *benci* hate; *sombong*)

In summary:

BM *cameeh:* other acts badly, negative emotion 19%
Outcome: emotion 35%, rejected by, sneered at other.

ejek caused by negative emotion (38%).
Outcome: emotion (38%) sneered at other.

cacek: other acts badly, ego acts badly, other has physical defect.
Outcome: takes revenge on other, emotion (38%)

BI(M) *cemooh:* other acts badly, negative emotion 22%
Outcome: emotion 33%, sneered at other.

ejek: other acts badly, has physical defect, negative emotion (33%).
Outcome: emotion (37%) mocked cripple, was rejected.

G. Ethnography of "Mocking/Disapproval"

Although the prototypicality ratings of these words are low, the antecedent/outcome scenarios show a high degree of emotion involvement in both antecedents and outcomes.

36. "Outraged" clusters (sindir)

A. *Defining the clusters (see Figs. 35.1 – 35.3)*

BM: an isolate 3-word triangle cluster with *kieh* as the key word; one twig.

BI(M): a 3-word triangle cluster with *sindir* as the key word; two twigs. External connections: *Sindir* is a hinge word with the "Contempt" cluster.

BI(J): an isolate chain.

B. *Key words (see Figs. 35.1–35.3)*

BM	*kieh*
BI(M)	*sindir*

Antecedent and outcome tasks were done:

BM	*sindia–kieh–bandiang*
BI(M)	*sindir – kias*

C. *English glosses (see Figs. 35.1–35.3)*

D. *Membership in the realm of emotion: prototypicality ratings*

For the 3 words of the Minangkabau triangle, the average prototypicality rating is 11%

For the three words of the Minangkabau Indonesian triangle, even with *sindir* at 71%, the average is only 29%

E. *Translation equivalents*

From BM to BI(M)
   to key word *sindir* 2
   to cognate 1

From BI(M) to BM
   to *sindia* 2
   to cognate 1

From BI(J) to Javanese
   to cognate 2
   for *kias* as starter, no consensus, but 72% give nothing

For the Javanese *kias*, the result is remarkable. Generally, people have been quite willing to give a translation equivalent for each word on the list, usually choosing the key word in the other language or a cognate.

The subjects have been very cooperative, and few ever leave blanks. But here, 72% of the responses were blank. Is it possible that *kias*, but not the other words in the cluster, is unknown in Javanese Indonesian, or that it has no equivalent in Javanese?

F. Antecedent/outcome sentence completion tasks

Minangkabau: *sindia–kieh–bandiang:*

BM *sindia* antecedents from 26 subjects

8	other's behavior is lacking, not proper
7	emotion (5 *sakik ati; ongeh; paneh ati*)
3	ego doesn't (dare) speak directly to other
2	something is not compatible (*sesuai*)
2	other's behavior is bad

BM *sindia* outcomes from 26 subjects

11	emotions (2 *berang* anger; *bangih* anger; *birunguik* sullen; *takut* fear; not *disanangi* not happy; *tenang* calm; *sanang* happy; *mancaraco*; not *sanang* not happy; laughed); emotion-genic: 42%
4	ego scolded, advised
3	ego or other understand
1	ego was quiet
1	physical reaction (felt ears hot)

BM *kieh* antecedents from 26 subjects

8	emotion (2 *berang* anger; *banci* hate; *gadang ati; sakik ati;* not *suko* doesn't like; not *sanang* not happy; *pongah*); emotion-genic: 31%
4	other's behavior lacking
3	lack of understanding
2	other's behavior bad

     2   in reference to Minangkabau
            custom
     1   not compatible (*sesuai*)

BM *kieh* outcomes from 26 subjects

     9   emotions (2 *malu; maleh* lazy;
            *tersinggung; aib; sakik ati;
            sanang ati; pueh; naiak darah*);
            emotion-genic: 35%
     6   does know/understand
     3   does not know/understand
     4   spoke in a certain way
     2   made comparisons

BM *bandiang* antecedents from 26 subjects

     11   comparisons, inequalities
     3   something not compatible (*ses-
            uai*)
     5   emotion (*manecek–ecek; banci;
            sakik ati; takut; murah ati*)

BM *bandiang* outcomes from 26 subjects

     6   emotion (2 *berang* anger; *mar-
            abo* anger; *pueh* satisfied;
            manyasa; ibo ati)
     5   dissatisfied, wants something
            else
     3   understands
     2   withdrawal

   Minangkabau Indonesian: *sindir–kias*

BI(M) *sindir* antecedents from 27 subjects

     13   emotion (5 not *senang* not
            happy; 5 *sakit hati; disepelkan*
            was ridiculed; *marah* anger;
            iri jealous); E–G score: 48%
     6   other's behavior lacking, not
            proper
     5   other's behavior bad
     4   something not compatible (*ses-
            uai*)
     1   doesn't speak directly

BI(M) *sindir* outcomes from 27 subjects

11	emotion (2 not liked; 2 *senang* happy; *marah* anger; *dimarahi* other angry at; *puas* satisfied; *benci* hate; *sakit hati*; *dibenci* hated; *ejek*); E–G score: 41%
4	fight
2	scolded, advised
1	clarifies, explains
1	rejected

BI(M) *kias* antecedents from 27 subjects

10	emotion (*benci* hate; 2 not *senang* not happy; not *suka* dislike; not *puas* unsatisfied; *sombong*; 2 *marah* anger; *suka* like; *sakit hati*)
3	understands
2	other's behavior is bad
2	other's behavior is lacking
2	not compatible (*sesuai*)
2	re: Minangkabau custom
1	doesn't speak directly

BI(M) *kias* outcomes from 27 subjects

8	emotion (3 *puas* satisfied; 2 not *disenangi* not happy; not *senang* not happy; *suka* happy; *lega*)
3	spoke
3	opposed
2	ego hit other
1	makes comparison
1	doesn't understand

In summary:

Sindia/sindir. Other's behavior is inadequate, defective, inappropriate, not compatible, and in Minangkabau Indonesian there is more outright bad behavior; much negative emotion in Minangkabau (27%), and more in Minangkabau Indonesian (48%).

The outcome is negative emotion: The emotion-genic score for Minangkabau is 42%, for Minangkabau Indonesian, 41%. In Minangkabau there is more scolding, withdrawal, and understanding, whereas in Minangkabau Indonesian there is more fighting.

Kieh/Kias. Again, but less strongly, other's behavior is not quite right, not compatible, and there is much negative emotion (31%, 37%).

The outcome is negative emotion (35%, 30%) and there is more understanding in Minangkabau, more conflict in Minangkabau Indonesian.

BM Bandiang. This is the result of making comparisons between nonequals, and here the negative emotion is relatively low (19%).

The outcome is dissatisfaction, desire for something else; and there is some negative emotion (23%).

These are reactions to inappropriate behavior. The word *sesuai* – fitting – recurs, and more, these words are secondary emotions in the sense that they are emotions caused by, and resulting from, emotions. As we have seen elsewhere, the low prototypicality rating of the words in this cluster is accompanied by a high incidence of other emotions in both antecedent and outcome parts of the scenarios.

37. "Shame" clusters *(cacat)*

A. Defining the clusters (see Figs. 35.1–35.3)

> BM: doesn't appear in this map (Fig. 35.1)
> BI(M) (Fig. 35.2): a 4-word cluster with *cacat* as the key word, and one twig. External connections: *Cela* is a hinge word with the "Contempt" cluster; there is a bridge from *aib* to *malu*, of the "Lazy" cluster.
> BI(J) (Fig. 35.3): a 4-word cluster with *cacat* as the key word, including a twig with *malu* on it. External connections: *Aib* has a link via *nista* to the "Contempt" cluster, *cela* is a hinge word with the "Contempt" cluster.

B. Key words (see Figs. 35.2, 35.3)

The key word in both BI(M) and BI(J) is *cacat*.

C. English glosses (see Figs. 35.2, 35.3)

D. Membership in the realm of emotion: prototypicality ratings (Figs. 35.1, 35.2)

For the only 2 starter words in BI(M), the average is 14.5%.

E. Translation equivalents

From BI(M) to BM, *cela* chooses *cacek*, a member of the "Contempt" cluster, while *aib* chooses *malu*, on a twig from the "Lazy" cluster. In BI(J) to Javanese, both choices go to *cacat*, which is presumably the Javanese key word.

F. Antecedent/outcome sentence completion tasks

None were done.

G. The ethnography of "Shame"

Although the English glosses suggest this is an important "Shame" cluster, there are not enough data on enough words to do anything with it.

38. "Lazy" clusters (*enggan*)

Although the key word, *enggan* (lazy), identifies this cluster, also present peripherally are the important "Shame" words *malu* and *segan*.

A. Defining the clusters (see Figs. 35.1–35.3)

> BM (Fig. 35.1): a 4-word cluster with *maleh* as the key word, and with two twigs. External connections: a bridge via *jajok* to *banci*, and a bridge to *ragu* in the "Confusion" cluster.
> BI(M) (Fig. 35.2): a 4-word cluster with *enggan* as the key word, and *malu* on a twig. External connections: via *malu* to *aib* in the "Shame" cluster, and *rendah* in the "Respectful" words.
> BI(J) (Fig. 35.3): a 4-word cluster with *enggan* as the key word, and a twig with *berat hati*. *Malu*, on a twig from the "Shame" cluster,

is included here on the authority of the BI(M) map. External connections: a bridge to the "Respectful" words.

B. Key words

BM	maleh
BI(M)	enggan
BI(J)	enggan

Antecedent and outcome scenarios were elicited for:

BM	sagan–malu
BI(M)	segan–malu
BM	maleh–anggan
BI(M)	malas–enggan

and for the between-language set:

BM *sagan*/BI(M) *malu*

C. English glosses (see Figs. 35.2, 35.3)

D. Membership in the realm of emotion: prototypicality ratings

In Minangkabau the prototypicality ratings for the 4 words plus *malu* average 68%.

In Minangkabau Indonesian for the 4 words plus *malu* the average is 69%.

In both languages, *barek ati/berat hati* has the highest rating (80%, 86%) and *malu*, which certainly seems to be one of the most strongly emotional of all Indonesian words, is only 70% in each language.

E. Translation equivalents

From BM to BI(M)
    the key word gets 0
    malas gets 2
    segan gets 2
    cognates get 3

From BI(M) to BM
    the key word gets only its cognate
    other cognates get 3
    anggan gets 2
    sagan gets 2

From BI(J) to Javanese
   wegah gets 2
   kesed gets 1
   isin gets 1
   [k]abot[an] gets 1

It is noteworthy that between the two Minangkabau lists none choose *malu* as the first choice. Again, this violates the prior expectations that *malu* would be an extraordinarily important word in the landscapes of emotion in Indonesia.

Also, the Javanese choose various non-cognates as translation equivalents. According to Horne, there are no cognates in Javanese for 4 of these words (she does list *berat* [heavy] as a Javanese word). This is very unusual and may be the only cluster with no Javanese cognates. *Isin* is an important Javanese word for "shame," but unfortunately it lies beyond the scope of this study. (However, see H. Geertz 1959:232; Keeler 1987:66.)

F. *Antecedent/outcome sentence completion tasks*

Minangkabau: *anggan–maleh:*

BM *anggan* antecedents from 27 subjects

8	work is difficult, unsatisfactory
7	emotion (2 *maleh*; *malu*; *ragu*; *bosan*; dislike 2)
4	ego isn't up to doing something
4	ego was ordered to do something
1	other acted badly

BM *anggan* outcomes from 27 subjects

12	withdrawal/avoidance
3	doesn't do it, not enthusiastic
3	emotion: *curiga*; *bingung*; *maleh* (11%)

BM *maleh* antecedents from 27 subjects

10	ego is tired, sleepy
6	ego is ordered to do something he doesn't want to

    2   the work is difficult
    1   emotion (*berang* anger) (4%)

BM *maleh* outcomes from 27 subjects
    11   withdrawal/avoidance
    7   doesn't want to
    1   tired
    0   emotion

Minangkabau Indonesian: *enggan–malas:*

BI(M) *enggan* antecedents from 28 subjects
    8   ego is not up to doing some-
                thing
    4   work is difficult, dissatisfied
    2   was ordered to do something
    2   emotion (*segan; ganjal*) (7%)

BI(M) *enggan* outcomes from 28 subjects
    10   doesn't do it, avoids it, loafs
    11   withdrawal
    2   emotion (*marah* anger; *jengkel*)
                (8%)

BI(M) *malas* antecedents from 28 subjects
    8   work is difficult
    8   ego is tired
    3   emotion (*bosan; diejek; kesuli-*
                tan) (11%)

BI(M) *malas* outcomes from 28 subjects
    10   withdrawal/avoidance
    7   ego doesn't want to be forced
                to
    2   emotion (*segan; marah* anger)
                (7%)

    In summary:

Anggan/enggan. This is caused by difficult, unpleasant work forced on ego, and in Minangkabau by negative emotions (26%) but much less by negative emotions in Minangkabau Indonesian (7%).

    The outcome is passive, avoidance, and a very low amount of emotion (11%, 8%).

    So here it is Minangkabau that has more emotionality, but also Minangkabau where *anggan* was higher in the prototypicality rating than Minangkabau Indonesian (75% vs. 61%).

Maleh/malas. In Minangkabau, this is caused by tiredness, and ordered to do something the ego does not want to; in Minangkabau Indonesian, it is "tired" also, but work is difficult and unrewarding.

The outcome is withdrawal, or ego doesn't want to do it.

Thus, both of these are passive avoidance of unpleasant tasks or demands, not far from the dictionary glosses "lazy, reluctant, dislike."

Minangkabau: *malu–sagan:*

BM *malu* antecedents from 27 subjects

12	ego did wrong including 3 unpaid debt
5	has a stigma, physical or poor clothes
3	ego's problem is publicized
1	other is superior
2	emotion (*takuik; maleh*)

BM *malu* outcomes from 27 subjects

16	withdrawal/avoidance/silence
3	acts to improve, change
2	physiological reaction (red face, chew thumb)
1	emotion (*maleh*) (4%)

BM *sagan* antecedents from 27 subjects

6	emotion (*dihormati; kasiah–sayang; 2 maleh; takuik* fear; *randah diri*)
4	meets someone for the first time; stranger
4	helped by other
3	must face other
3	ego did wrong; ego's fault
2	other is superior

BM *sagan* outcomes from 27 subjects

10	withdrawal/avoidance
6	obeys other/doesn't oppose other

5	emotion (2 *horomaik;* 2 *maleh; malu*) (19%)
3	ego acts decently
1	ego helps

Minangkabau Indonesian: *malu–segan*

BI(M) *malu* antecedents from 27 subjects

11	publicized wrong or stigma
8	ego did wrong, including not paying debt
5	stigma: physical, poor clothing
2	emotion (2 *dimarahi*)

BI(M) *malu* outcomes from 27 subjects

23	withdrawal/avoidance/silence
1	physical act (bowed head)
1	ego acts to improve situation
1	emotion (*tersipu* embarrassed) (4%)

BI(M) *segan* antecedents from 27 subjects

6	ego did wrong
4	other is superior
3	helped by other
2	emotion (not *suka* dislike; *simpati*)
1	meets for the first time
1	must face other

BI(M) *segan* outcomes from 27 subjects

13	ego acts decently
9	ego withdraws/avoids
4	emotion (4 *menghormati* respects) (15%)
1	obeys other
1	helps other

Between-language set: BM *sagan*/BI(M) *malu*

BM *sagan* antecedents from 60 subjects

11	presence of other is problem
7	emotion (*dicaci; disayangi; malu; sombong; dihormati; menghormati; randah diri*)

10	ego is inadequate
4	helped by other
4	meets other for the first time
2	ego did wrong

BM *sagan* outcomes from 60 subjects

28	withdrawal/avoidance
15	ego acts decently
6	ego obeys/doesn't oppose
3	emotion (*enggan; maleh; malu*)

BI(M) *malu* antecedents from 60 subjects

12	stigma: physical, poor clothing
9	ego's problem is publicized
8	newly met stranger
6	ego did wrong
5	emotion (3 *rendah diri; menaruh hati; dihina*)
5	debt to other not paid
3	ego failed

BI(M) *malu* outcomes from 60 subjects

44	withdrawal/avoidance/silence
5	physical acts (head bowed, turned, hidden)
2	emotion (*rendah diri; takut*)
1	ego acts to improve situation

In summary:

Malu. This is caused when ego does wrong, or has some stigma of poverty or a physical nature. In Minangkabau Indonesian public knowledge of ego's shortcoming is much more important than in Minangkabau (41%–11%).

The outcome is withdrawal/avoidance, especially in BI(M), where it is 85%. The Emotion-genic score is very low – 4% in each language.

Sagan/segan. This is when ego is put at a disadvantage by another who is a stranger, is superior, has aided ego, or when ego did wrong. Emotion figures in Minangkabau are 22%, in Minangkabau Indonesian, only 7%.

The outcome is withdrawal/avoidance, and even more frequent is positive obeyance, decent actions, and help to others. Again, the emotion-genic score is low (19%, 15%).

In the between-language responses:

BI(M) *malu* is similar to the above, but different order: stigma, debt, doing wrong, failing, and publicity is less important (15%.) The emotion-score is 8%.
Outcome is withdrawal.
Emotion-genic score is 3%.

BM *sagan*, as above, but put at disadvantage by another, and ego is inadequate. Emotion-genic score is 12%.
Outcome is withdrawal, obeyance, decent action.
Emotion-genic score 5%.

39. "Respectful" clusters *(sopan)*

A. *Defining the clusters (see Figs. 35.1–35.3)*

BM: On the authority of the BI(M) map, one isolate branch and one branch from the "Surprise" Cluster.

BI(M): This 6-word string, between the other "Shame" units and the "Surprise" cluster, includes one triangle cluster and five twigs.

BI(J): Here, 3 words are strung out between the "Contempt" and the "Lazy" clusters; there are four twigs and one isolate twig. External connections: one, a link via *salut* to the "Surprise" cluster.

B. *Key words*

Not applicable to these strings of words.

C. *English glosses (see Figs. 35.2, 35.3)*

D. *Membership in the realm of emotion: prototypicality ratings (Figs. 35.1, 35.2)*

In BM the 4 words average 52% prototypicality

In BI(M) the 5 words average 49%.

It is noteworthy that *hormat*, which Poerwardaminta in his dictionary lists as an examplary emotion word, here gets a prototypicality rating of only 19%, the lowest in the set.

E. Translation equivalents

From BM to BI(M)
   sopan chooses *tertib*
   elok and *ramah* choose *baik hati*

From BI(M) to BM
   hormat chooses *sopan*
   sopan chooses *bataratik*
   rendah and *ramah* choose *elok ati*

From BI(J) to Javanese
   cognates 2
   ramah chooses *gapyak/grapyak*

F. Antecedent/outcome sentence completion tasks

Minangkabau: *sopan–horomaik:*

BM *sopan* antecedents from 28 subjects:
   20   ego is well brought up, edu-
           cated in etiquette
   4   other is good/decent to ego
   3   other is superior to ego

BM *sopan* outcomes from 28 subjects
   17   ego behaved properly
   9   emotion (4 *disyangi;* 2 *disen-
           angi; dicintai; sanang; dihor-
           mati*) (32%)
   1   ego is treated well

BM *horomaik* antecedents from 28 subjects
   18   other is superior/older/more
           experienced
   3   other does good to ego
   2   emotion *(sagan; menghargai–
           hargai)*

BM *horomaik* outcomes from 28 subjects
   19   ego behaved properly
   7   emotion *(dimuliakan;* 2 *disagani;
           dipuji; sagan; disayangi; dis-
           anangi)*

Minangkabau Indonesian: *sopan–hormat:*

BI(M) *sopan* antecedents from 28 subjects
17	ego is well brought up, educated in etiquette
6	other is superior to ego
5	emotion (2 *menghormati; menghargai; disenangi; rendah hati*)

BI(M) *sopan* outcomes from 28 subjects
19	emotion (8 *disenangi;* 6 *dihargai;* 2 *disukai;* 2 *disegani; dihormati*)
6	ego behaved properly

BI(M) *hormat* antecedents from 28 subjects
18	other is older/superior to ego
5	ego acts well
3	emotion *(segan; takut; simpati)*
2	other does good to ego

BI(M) *hormat* outcomes from 28 subjects
20	emotion (8 *disegani* respected; 7 *disayangi;* 2 *disenangi; diperhatikan; takut; dihargai*)
7	ego behaved properly
1	ego has lots of friends

In summary:

Horomaik/hormat. This is reaction to a superior/older other.

As the outcomes, ego is the recipient of much positive emotion and praise and ego behaves properly. There is a difference between languages (Table 39.1).

So there are very similar antecedents, but Minangkabau Indonesian is much more likely to have an emotion outcome, while in Minangkabau ego acts properly and gets less emotional response.

Sopan. This is caused by ego's good upbringing and knowledge of proper behavior, especially customary Minangkabau *adat.* No emotion in Minangkabau, but slight (18%) in Minangkabau Indonesian. The outcomes show a pattern like that of *horomaik/hormat* (Table 39.2).

In Javanese there is a cognate, *urmat,* that Hildred Geertz has ana-

Table 39.1

	Emotion		Behaves properly
BI(M)	20	71%	7
BM	7	25%	19

Table 39.2

	Emotion		Behaves properly
BI(M)	19	68%	6
BM	9	32%	17

lyzed in some detail, saying that it is "peculiarly Javanese" (1959:232). She says it is closely associated with three other emotions (*wedi, isin,* and *sungkan*), which cover a "Fear"/"Shame"/"Guilt" area. This relationship does not show up in these Minangkabau data, but without comparable Javanese data it is hard to conclude much. However, Javanese society is much more concerned with status and rank than is Minangkabau. "Respect" is an acknowledgment of rank. Thus, one might suspect that Javanese would invest "respect" with more risk than do the often aggressively egalitarian Minangkabau.

In his description of Australian Aborigine Pintupi emotion patterns, Fred Myers has described how "kunta as 'shame' and kunta as 'respect' are two sides of the same coin, in that showing 'respect' for someone by consulting that person's wishes, by not overstepping one's bounds, or by 'shyness' in stating claims, avoids embarrassment" (1979:365).

This is essentially the same association that accounts for the proximity of "respect" and "shame" in these Indonesian maps.

40. "Arrogance" clusters (sombong)

These clusters are each closely knit, isolate, and unusually similar.

A. Defining the clusters (see Figs. 40.1–40.3)

> BM: A 9-word isolate cluster with *sombong* as the key word and with one twig.

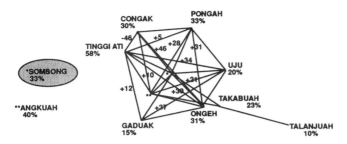

Figure 40.1. "Arrogance" cluster BM

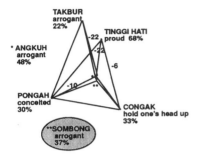

Figure 40.2. "Arrogance" cluster BI(M)

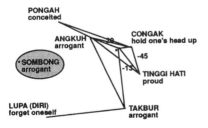

Figure 40.3. "Arrogance" cluster BI(J)

BI(M): A 6-word isolate cluster with *sombong* as the key word.
BI(J): A 6-word cluster with *sombong* as the key word and with one
   twig.
Note that this is the only set of clusters in the entire study in which
the Minangkabau cluster has more words than the Indonesian clusters.

B. Key words

In each map the key word is *sombong*.
  Antecedents and outcomes were elicited for:
      BM   *sombong–angkuah*
      BI(M)   *sombong–angkuh*
and for the between-language set: BM *angkuah*/BI(M) *sombong*

C. English glosses (see Figs. 40.2, 40.3)

D. Membership in the realm of emotion: prototypicality ratings (see Figs. 40.1, 40.2)

The average prototypicality rating for the 9 words in BM is 31%; for the six words in BI(M) it is 39%.
  In neither language does the key word, *sombong*, have the highest prototypicality rating.

E. Translation equivalents

From BM to BI(M)
      the key word (*sombong*) gets all 9 first choices
From BI(M) to BM
      the key word (*sombong*) gets 3 first choices
      angkuah gets 2
      another cognate gets 1
From BI(J) to Javanese
      umuk (to boast) gets 5
      anggak (boastful) gets 1

   There is an unusually high consensus on the key word *sombong* with both Minangkabau sets, especially from Minangkabau into Minangkabau Indonesian. And the Javanese are nearly unanimous in choosing *umuk*, which is presumably the key word in the Javanese cluster. Here it is noteworthy that cognates were available in Javanese. In fact, the unanimous second choice into Javanese was the cognate *angkuh*, and some tertiary choices went to the Javanese cognates *sombong* and *takabur*. (Horne agrees that these cognates – *angkuh*, *sombong*, and *takabur* – are legitimate Javanese words.) So the question is: Why do Javanese prefer as translation equivalents the non-cognate words *unuk* and *anggak* when cognates, presumably strongly suggestive for translation answers, do exist? And further, why does this pattern occur in a cluster like this, where the key word, *sombong*, is so unusually strong in its own right?

F. Antecedent/outcome sentence completion tasks

Minangkabau: *sombong–angkuah:*

BM *sombong* antecedents from 27 subjects
- 16   ego is rich/richer
- 8   ego is good/better
- 3   ego achieved something

BM *sombong* outcomes from 27 subjects
- 8   ego shunned others
- 6   ego acts superior
- 5   others shunned ego
- 1   ego is isolated

BM *angkuah* antecedents from 27 subjects
- 15   ego was better than others
- 5   ego was rich
- 4   ego achieved something

BM *angkuah* outcomes from 27 subjects
- 7   ego shunned others
- 5   others shunned ego
- 4   ego acts superior

BI(M) *sombong* antecedents from 28 subjects
- 14   ego is rich/richer
- 8   ego felt he was better than oth-
       ers
- 5   ego achieved something

BI(M) *sombong* outcomes from 28 subjects
- 14   others shunned ego
- 8   ego shunned others
- 4   ego acts superior
- 1   ego is isolated

BI(M) *angkuh* antecedents from 28 subjects
- 16   ego was better than others, in-
       cluding

	8	ego felt that he was better
7		ego was rich/richer
5		ego achieved something

BI(M) *angkuh* outcomes from 28 subjects

12	others shunned ego
10	ego shunned others
3	ego acts superior
3	ego is isolated

The between-language set: BI(M) *sombong*/BM *angkuah:*

BI(M) *sombong* antecedents from 60 subjects

29	ego is rich
16	ego feels better than others
6	ego achieved something

BI(M) *sombong* outcomes from 60 subjects

26	ego shunned others
16	others shunned ego
13	ego acts superior

BM *angkuah* antecedents from 60 subjects

28	ego was better than others
22	ego was rich
4	ego achieved something

BM *angkuah* outcomes from 60 subjects

21	others shunned ego
18	ego shunned others
13	ego acts superior

To summarize:

Sombong. This is caused by ego being, feeling, achieving more than others, and especially by being richer than others.

The outcome is social isolation:

In BM, it is more often that ego does the shunning;

In BI(M), it is more often that others shun ego.

Angkuah/angkuh. This is very similar to *sombong*, but being rich is less important than many other things in making ego better.

The outcome, also, is similar: social isolation.

In BM, ego does slightly more of the shunning;

In BI(M), others more often shun ego.

In the between-language comparison, this shunning pattern does not hold. There, BI(M) *sombong* is caused by ego being richer, and other sorts of superiority.

The outcome is social isolation, especially ego shunning others and acting superior.

BM. *angkuah* is caused by ego being better than others in many ways, wealth being quite important.

The outcome is social isolation, ego shunning others slightly more than others shun ego, and ego acting superior in other ways.

In the composite picture of the scenarios for this cluster, several things stand out. The antecedents are mainly actual superiority, unlike conceit in English, for which the superiority may be only in the mind of the conceited. The importance of material wealth runs through all the response sets. And the outcomes are overwhelmingly social isolation, initiated from both sides. It is not that the rich, *sombong* person associates now only with other rich *sombong* people, but rather that being *sombong* just results in breaking all social ties.

G. The ethnography of "Arrogance" (see Section 6.40).

"CALM" AREA (*TENANG*)

This is a large complex branch in Minangkabau, a triple isolate cluster and a linked cluster in Minangkabau Indonesian, and two isolate clusters in Javanese Indonesian. Although the two Indonesian maps each show two separate units, in Minangkabau they are linked. Thus, the whole will be considered here as the (loosely defined) "Calm" area with four clusters.

A. Defining the clusters (see Figs. 41.1–41.3)

> BM: a complex branch, a chain of small clusters linked to *sakik ati* of the "Anger" area.
>
> BI(M): a 3-word triangle cluster with *sabar* as the key word, connected to the "Surrender" cluster by the hinge word *tawakkal*, plus an isolate of three clusters.

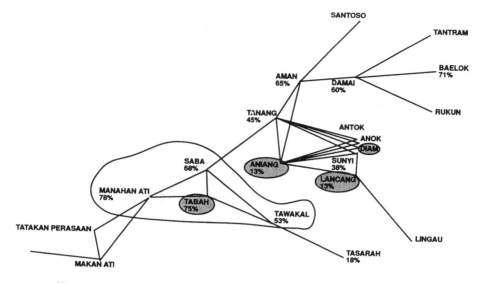

Figure 41.1. "Calm" area BM

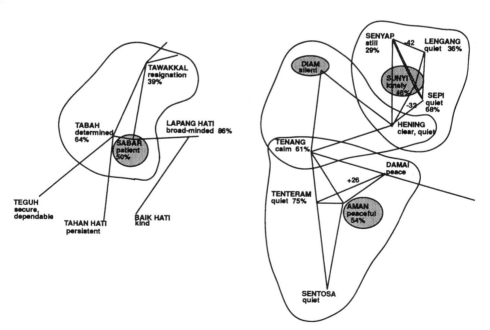

Figure 41.2. "Calm" area BI(M)

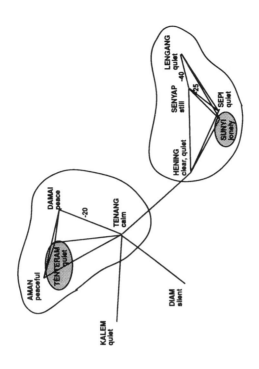

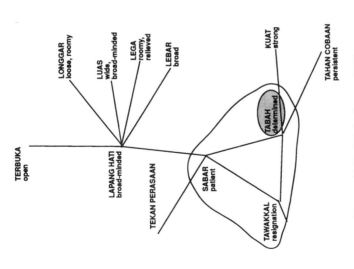

Figure 41.3. "Calm" area BI(J)

Table 41.1

BM		BI(M)		BI(J)
MAKAN ATI	85%			
41. "Patient" cluster:				
TABAH	27%	SABAR	51%	TABAH
42. "Calm" cluster:				
ANIANG	27%	AMAN	63%	TENTERAM
43. "Quiet" cluster:				
DIAM	41%	DIAM	36%	—
44. "Lonely" cluster:				
LANCANG	41%	SUNYI	38%	SUNYI

BI(J): an isolate 3-word triangle cluster plus two isolate linked clusters.

B. Key words and prototypicality ratings

The correspondence of the various clusters in the three maps are shown
by their key words in Table 41.1. Also, the average prototypicality ratings are included for the two Minangkabau sets.

C. English glosses (see Figs. 41.2, 41.3)

G. Ethnography of "Calm"

On the basis of their prototypicality ratings, these clusters are clearly
within the *perasaan hati* realm. They do show great range in the strength
of the prototypicality ratings. Unfortunately not enough data were gathered to make more sense of this part of the fringe area.

Bibliography

Abu-Lughod, Lila
    1985   Honor and Sentiments of Loss in a Bedouin Society. *American Ethnologist* 12.2:245–61.

Anwar, Khaidir
    1980a   *Indonesian: The Development and Use of a National Language.* Yogyakarta: Gadjah Mada University Press.
    1980b   Language Use in Minangkabau Society. *Indonesian Circle* 22:55–63.

Aveling, Harry
    1969   The Thorny Rose: The Avoidance of Passion in Modern Indonesian Literature. *Indonesia* 7:67–76.
    1974   A Thematic History of Indonesian Poetry: 1920 to 1974. Special Report No. 9. Center for Southeast Asian Studies. DeKalb, Illinois: Northern Illinois University.

Bagchi, Amalendu
    1983   Feelings and Emotions in Indian Psychology. *Indian Journal of Psychology* 28:87–102.

Benedict, Ruth
    1934   *Patterns of Culture.* Boston: Houghton Mifflin.
    1946   *The Chrysanthemum and the Sword. Patterns of Japanese Culture.* Boston: Houghton Mifflin.

Boas, Franz
    1911   Handbook of American Indian Languages. *Bulletin of the Bureau of American Ethnology.* No. 40, Part 1. Washington, D.C.

Boucher, Jerry D.
    1981   Antecedents to Emotions Across Cultures. Paper presented to the NATO Human Factors Panel: Human Assessment and Cultural Factors International Conference, Queen's University, Kingston, Ontario, August 18, 1981.
    1983   Antecedents to Emotions Across Cultures. In S. H. Irvine and John W. Berry (Eds.), *Human Assessment and Cultural Factors,* pp. 407–20. New York: Plenum (condensation of 1981 version).

Boucher, Jerry D., and Mary E. Brandt
    1981   Judgment of Emotion. American and Malay Antecedents. *Journal of Cross-Cultural Psychology* 12.3:272–83.

Boucher, Jerry D., and Gary E. Carlson
    1980   Recognition of Facial Expression in Three Cultures. *Journal of Cross-Cultural Psychology* 11.3:263–80.

Brandt, M. E., and J. D. Boucher
  1986   Concepts of Depression in Emotion Lexicons of Eight Cultures. *International Journal of Intercultural Relations* 10:321–46.
Briggs, Jean
  1970   *Never in Anger*. Cambridge, Mass.: Harvard University Press.
Brown, Raymond E.
  1966   Appendix I: Johannine Vocabulary. In *The Anchor Bible: The Gospel According to John (i–xii)*, pp. 497–518. Garden City, N.Y.: Doubleday.
Carucci, Laurence Marshall, Michael Brown, and Lynne Pettler
  1989   Shared Spaces. *Contexts of Interaction in Chicago's Ethnic Communities*. New York: AMS Press.
Casagrande, J.
  1954   The Ends of Translation. *International Journal of American Linguistics* 20:335–40.
Casson, Ronald W.
  1983   Schemata in Cognitive Anthropology. *Annual Review of Anthropology* 12:429–62.
Clore, G. L., A. Ortony, and M. A. Foss
  1987   The Psychological Foundations of the Affective Lexicon. *Journal of Personality and Social Psychology* 53:751–66.
Collins, Alan M. and Elizabeth F. Loftus
  1975   A Spreading-Activation Theory of Semantic Processing. *Psychological Review* 82.6:407–28.
D'Andrade, Roy
  1987   A Folk Model of the Mind. In Dorothy Holland and Naomi Quinn (Eds.), *Cultural Models in Language and Thought*, pp. 112–48. Cambridge: Cambridge University Press.
Davitz, Joel R.
  1969   *The Language of Emotion*. New York: Academic Press.
de Rivera, Joseph, and Carmen Grinkis
  1986   Emotions as Social Relationships. *Motivation and Emotion* 10.4:351–69.
Derocquigny, Jules
  1931   *Autres mots anglais perfides*. Paris: Librairie Vuibert.
Deutsch, Eliot
  1975   Studies in Comparative Aesthetics. Monograph No. 2, Society for Asian and Comparative Philology. Honolulu: University of Hawaii Press.
Dobbin, Christine
  1983   *Islamic Revivalism in a Changing Peasant Economy. Central Sumatra, 1784–1847*. London: Curzon Press.
Echols, John M., and Hassan Shadily
  1963   *An Indonesian-English Dictionary*. 2nd ed. Ithaca, N.Y.: Cornell University Press.
Ekman, Paul
  1977   Biological and Cultural Contributions to Body and Facial Movement. In John Blacking (Ed.), A.S.A. Monograph 15. *The Anthropology of the Body*, pp. 39–84. London: Academic Press.
  1985   *Telling Lies*. New York: Norton.
Ekman, Paul, and Wallace V. Friesen

1969   The Repertoire of Nonverbal Behavior: Categories, Origins, Usage, and Coding. *Semiotica* 1.1:48–98.

1975   *Unmasking the Face.* Englewood Cliffs, N.J.: Prentice-Hall.

Ekman, Paul, Wallace V. Friesen, and Maureen O'Sullivan

1988   Smiles When Lying. *Journal of Personality and Social Psychology* 54.3:414–20.

Ekman, Paul, Wallace V. Friesen, Maureen O'Sullivan, Anthony Chan, Irene Diacoyanni-Tarlatzis, Karl Heider, Rainer Krause, William Ayhan LeCompte, Tom Pitcairn, Pio E. Ricci-Bitti, Klaus Scherer, Masatoshi Tomita, Athanase Tzavaras

1987   Universals and Cultural Differences in the Judgments of Facial Expressions of Emotion. *Journal of Personality and Social Psychology* 53.4:712–17.

Ekman, Paul, and Karl G. Heider

1988   The Universality of a Contempt Expression: A Replication. *Motivation and Emotion* 12.3:303–8.

Ekman, Paul, Robert Levenson, and Wallace V. Friesen

1983   Autonomic Nervous System Activity Distinguishes Among Emotions. *Science* 221.4616:1208–10.

Errington, Frederick K.

1984   *Manners and Meaning in West Sumatra. The Social Context of Consciousness.* New Haven, Conn.: Yale University Press.

Errington, Joseph

1985   *Language and Social Change in Java: Linguistic Reflexes of Modernization in a Traditional Royal Polity.* Southeast Asia Series Number 65. Athens: Ohio University.

Fehr, Beverley, and James A. Russell

1984   Concept of Emotion Viewed From a Prototype Perspective. *Journal of Experimental Psychology: General* 113.3:464–86

Flores-Meiser, Enya P.

1986   Sociophobic Data and the Cross-Cultural Perspective. In David L. Scruton (Ed.), *Sociophobics. The Anthropology of Fear*, pp. 60–72. Boulder Colo.: Westview Press.

Geertz, Clifford

1960   *The Religion of Java.* Glencoe, Ill.: Free Press.

Geertz, Hildred

1959   The Vocabulary of Emotion. A Study of Javanese Socialization Processes. *Psychiatry* 22:225–37.

1961   *The Javanese Family.* Glencoe, Ill: Free Press.

Gerber, Eleanor Ruth

1985   Rage and Obligation: Samoan Emotion in Conflict. In Geoffrey M. White and John Kirkpatrick (Eds.), *Person, Self, and Experience. Exploring Pacific Ethnopsychologies*, pp. 121–67. Berkeley: University of California Press.

Griffith, Belver C., Henry G. Small, Judith A. Stonehill, and Sandra Dey

1974   The Structure of Scientific Literatures. II: Toward a Macro- and Microstructure for Science. *Social Studies* 4:339–65.

Hall, Edward T.

1959   *The Silent Language.* Garden City, N.Y.: Doubleday, Anchor.

Heelas, Paul

1986   Emotion Talk Across Cultures. In Rom Harre (Ed.), *The Social*

Construction of Emotions, pp. 234–66. Oxford: Basil Blackwell.
Heelas, Paul, and A. Lock
1981   *Indigenous Psychologies*. London: Academic Press.
Heider, Karl G.
1969   Sweet Potato Notes and Lexical Queries. *Kroeber Anthropological Society Papers* 44:78–86.
1976   Dani Sexuality. A Low Energy System. *MAN* 11:188–201
1979   *Grand Valley Dani. Peaceful Warriors*. New York: Holt, Rinehart & Winston.
n.d.   Dani Patterns: Ethos, Cognition, and Sexuality in the New Guinea Highlands (manuscript)
1984   Emotion: Inner State versus Interaction. Unpublished paper delivered at the American Anthropological Association Meetings, November 15, 1984, Denver.
1987   Emotion in Indonesian Cinema. Paper presented at American Anthropological Association Meetings, November 21, 1987.
1991   *Indonesian Cinema. National Culture on Screen*. Honolulu: University of Hawaii Press.
Hiatt, L. R.
1978   Classification of the Emotions. In L. R. Hiatt (Ed.), *Australian Aboriginal Concepts*, pp. 182–7. Atlantic Highlands, N.J.: The Humanities Press.
Hollan, Douglas
1988   Staying "Cool" in Toraja: Informal Strategies for the Management of Anger and Hostility in a Nonviolent Society. *Ethos* 16.1:52–72.
Hood, Mantle
1963   The Enduring Tradition: Music and Theater in Java and Bali. In Ruth T. McVey (Ed.), *Indonesia*, pp. 438–71. New Haven, Conn.: HRAF Press.
Horne, Elinor Clark
1974   *Javanese-English Dictionary*. New Haven, Conn.: Yale University Press.
Humboldt, Wilhelm von
1816   Introduction to Aeschylus' Agamemnon, translated by WvH. In Andre Lefevere, *Translating Literature: The German Tradition*, pp. 40–5. Amsterdam: Van Gorcum, Assen, 1977.
Izard, Carroll, and S. Buechler
1980   Aspects of Consciousness and Personality in Terms of Differential Emotions Theory. In Robert Plutchik and Henry Kellerman (Eds.), *Emotion: Theory, Research, and Experience*. Vol. 1: *Theories of Emotions*, pp. 165–87. New York: Academic Press.
Kahn, Joel S.
1981   *Minangkabau Social Formation: Indonesian Peasants and the World Economy*. Cambridge: Cambridge University Press.
Kato, Tsuyoshi
1982   *Matriliny and Migration. Evolving Minangkabau Traditions in Indonesia*. Ithaca, N.Y.: Cornell University Press.
Keeler, Ward
1983   Shame and Stage Fright in Java. *Ethos* 11.3:152–65.
1987   *Javanese Shadow Plays, Javanese Selves*. Princeton, N.J.: Princeton University Press.

Kleinman, Arthur, and Byron Good (Eds.)
    1985   *Culture and Depression*. Berkeley: University of California Press.
Klineberg, Otto
    1935   *Race Differences*. New York: Harper.
Knoke, David, and James H. Kuklinski
    1982   *Network Analysis*. Beverly Hills, Calif.: Sage.
Koentjaraningrat
    1985   *Javanese Culture*. Singapore: Oxford University Press.
Kroeber, A. L.
    1909   Classificatory Systems of Relationship. *Journal of the Royal Anthropological Institute* 39:77–84.
Lakoff, George
    1987   *Women, Fire, and Dangerous Things. What Categories Reveal About the Mind*. Chicago: University of Chicago Press.
Levy, Robert
    1973   *Tahitians. Mind and Experience in the Society Islands*. Chicago: University of Chicago Press.
Lutz, Catherine A.
    1982   The Domain of Emotion Words on Ifaluk. *American Ethnologist* 9:113–28
    1988   *Unnatural Emotions. Everyday Sentiments on a Micronesian Atoll and Their Challenge to Western Theory*. Chicago: University of Chicago Press.
Mitchell, Istutiah Gunawan
    1969   The Socio-Cultural Environment and Mental Disturbance: Three Minangkabau Case Histories. *Indonesia* 7:123–36.
Myers, Fred R.
    1979   Emotions and the Self: A Theory of Personhood and Political Order Among Pintupi Aborigines. *Ethos* 7.4: 343–70.
Naim, Mochtar
    1979   *Merantau. Pola Migrasi Suku Minangkabau*. Yogyakarta: Gadjah Mada University Press.
    1983   Minangkabau Dalam Dialektika Kedbudayaan Nusantara. In A. A. Navis (Ed.), *Dialektika Minangkabau Dalam Kemelut Sosial dan Politik*, pp. 56–67. Padang: Genta Singgalang Press.
Navis, A. A.
    1984   *Alam Terkembang Jadi Guru. Adat dan Kebudayaan Minangkabau*. Jakarta: Grafitipers.
Neisser, Ulric
    1987   *Concepts and Conceptual Development: Ecological and Intellectual Factors in Categorization*. Cambridge: Cambridge University Press.
Nida, Eugene A.
    1964   *Toward a Science of Translating*. Leiden: E. J. Brill.
Obeyesekere, Gananath
    1981   *Medusa's Hair. An Essay on Personal Symbols and Religious Experience*. Chicago: University of Chicago Press.
Ortony, A., G. L. Clore, and M. A. Foss
    1987   The Referential Structure of the Affective Lexicon. *Cognitive Science* 11:341–64.
Ortony, Andrew, Gerald L. Clore, and Allan Foss
    1988   *The Cognitive Structure of Emotions*. Cambridge: Cambridge University Press.

Osgood, Charles E., William H. May, and Murray S. Miron
  1975   *Cross-Cultural Universals of Affective Meaning.* Urbana: University of Illinois Press.
Pamoentjak, M. Thaib gl. St.
  1935   *Kamoes Bahasa Minangkabau – Bahasa Melajoe-Riau.* Batavia: Balai Poestaka.
Peacock, James L.
  1979   Dahlan and Rasul: Indonesian Muslim Reformers. In A. L. Becker and Aram A. Yengoyan (Eds.), *The Imagination of Reality: Essays in Southeast Asian Coherence Systems*, pp. 245–68. Norwood, N.J.: Ablex.
Phillips, H.
  1959   Problems of Translation. *Human Organization* 18.4:184–92.
Poerwadarminta, W.J.S.
  1982   *Kamus Umum Bahasa Indonesia.* Jakarta: PN Balai Pustaka.
Quinn, Naomi, and Dorothy Holland (Eds.)
  1987   *Cultural Models in Language and Thought.* Cambridge: Cambridge University Press.
Rice, G. Elizabeth
  1980   On Cultural Schemata. *American Ethnologist* 7.1:152–71.
Rosaldo, Michelle Z.
  1980   *Knowledge and Passion: Ilongot Notions of Self and Social Life.* Cambridge: Cambridge University Press.
Rosaldo, Renato
  1984   Grief and a Headhunter's Rage: On the Cultural Force of Emotions. In Edward Bruner (Ed.), *Text, Play, and Story*, pp. 178–95. American Ethnological Society Proceedings. Washington, D.C.
Rosch, Eleanor, and B. B. Lloyd (Eds.)
  1978   *Cognition and Categorization.* Hillsdale, N.J.: Erlbaum.
Rosch Heider, Eleanor
  1972   Probabilities, Sampling, and Ethnographic Method: The Case of Dani Colour Names. *MAN* 7.3:448–66.
Russell, James A.
  1983   Pancultural Aspects of the Human Conceptual Organization of Emotions. *Journal of Personality and Social Psychology* 45.6:1281–8.
Scherer, Klaus R. (Ed.)
  1988   *Facets of Emotion. Recent Research.* Hillsdale, N.J.: Erlbaum.
Scherer, Klaus R., Harald G. Wallbott, David Matsumoto, and Tsutomu Kudoh
  1988   Emotional Experience in Cultural Context: A Comparison Between Europe, Japan, and the United States. In Scherer (Ed.), *Facets of Emotion* (1988), pp. 5–30.
Scherer, Klaus R., Harald G. Wallbott, and Angela B. Summerfield
  1986   *Experiencing Emotion. A Cross-cultural study.* Cambridge: Cambridge University Press.
Schmidgall-Tellings, A. E., and Alan M. Stevens
  1981   *Contemporary Indonesian English Dictionary.* Athens: Ohio University Press.
Seward, Robert D.
  1947   *Dictionary of French Cognates.* New York: S. F. Vanni.
Shaver, Philip, Judith Schwartz, Donald Kirson, and Cary O'Connor
  1987   Emotion Knowledge: Further Exploration of a Prototype Approach. *Journal of Personality and Social Psychology* 52.6:1061–86.

Shimanoff, Susan B.
    1984   Commonly Named Emotions in Everyday Conversations. *Perceptual and Motor Skills* 58:514.
Siegel, James
    1966   Prayer and Play in Atjeh: A Comment on Two Photographs. *Indonesia* 1:1–21.
    1983   Images and Odors in Javanese Practices Surrounding Death. *Indonesia* 36:1–14.
    1986   *Solo in the New Order. Language and Hierarchy in an Indonesian City.* Princeton, N.J.: Princeton University Press.
Simons, Ronald C., and Charles C. Hughes (Eds.)
    1985   *The Culture-Bound Syndromes. Folk Illnesses of Psychiatric and Anthropological Interest.* Dordrecht: D. Reidel.
Small, Henry
    1980   Co-citation Context Analysis and the Structure of Paradigms. *Journal of Documentation* 36.3:183–96.
Spores, John C.
    1988   *Running Amok. An Historical Inquiry.* Southeast Asia Series Number 82. Athens: Ohio University Center for International Studies.
Stange, Paul
    1984   The Logic of RASA in Java. *Indonesia* 38:113–34.
Steiner, George
    1975   *After Babel. Aspects of Language and Translation.* New York: Oxford University Press.
Swartz, Marc J.
    1988   Shame, Culture, and Status Among the Swahili of Mombasa. *Ethos* 16.1:21–51.
Tavris, Carol
    1982   *Anger. The Misunderstood Emotion.* New York: Simon & Schuster.
Thomas, Lynn L., and Franz von Benda-Beckmann (Eds.)
    1985   *Change and Continuity in Minangkabau. Local, Regional, and Historical Perspectives on West Sumatra.* Monographs in International Studies, Southeast Asia Series, No. 71. Athens, Ohio: Ohio University.
van der Toorn, J. L.
    1891   *Minangkabausch-Maleisch-Nederlandsch Woordenboek.* The Hague: Martinus Nijhoff.
Wandruszka, Mario
    1978   Die "falschen Freunde" des Uebersetzers. In Lillebill Graehs, Gustav Karlen, and Bertil Malmberg (Eds.), *Theory and Practice of Translation,* pp. 213–34. Bern: Peter Lang.
Watson, O. Michael
    1970   *Proxemic Behavior. A Cross-Cultural Study.* The Hague: Mouton.
Wellenkamp, Jane
    1988a   Order and Disorder in Toraja Thought and Social Ritual. *Ethnology* 27.3:311–26.
    1988b   Notions of Grief and Catharsis Among the Toraja. *American Ethnologist* 15.3:486–500.
White, Geoffrey M.
    1980   Conceptual Universals in Interpersonal Language. *American Anthropologist* 82.4:759–81.

White, Howard D.
    1983   A Cocitation Map of the Social Indicators Movement. *Journal of the American Society for Information Sciences* 34.5:307–12.
White, Howard D., and Belver C. Griffith
    1981   Author Cocitation: A Literature Measure of Intellectual Structure. *Journal of the American Society for Information Sciences* 32:163–71.
    1982   Authors as Makers of Intellectual Space: Co-citation in Studies of Science, Technology, and Society. *Journal of Documentation* 38.4:255–71.
Wierzbicka, Anna
    1986   Human Emotions: Universal or Culture-Specific? *American Anthropologist* 88.3:584–94.
Wikan, Unni
    1989   Managing the Heart to Brighten Face and Soul: Emotions in Balinese Morality and Health Care. *American Ethnologist* 16.2:294–312.
Wolff, John U., and Soepomo Poedjosoedarmo
    1982   Communicative Codes in Central Java. Data Paper 116. Southeast Asia Program. Ithaca, N.Y.: Cornell University.

Author index

Subject index

For specific emotions, refer to Contents